The Road M.A.P. of My Life

Martha A. Pierie - 2021

The Road
M.A.P.
of My Life

Martha A. Pierce

Charleston, SC
www.PalmettoPublishing.com

The Road M.A.P. of My Life

Paperback ISBN: 978-1-64990-556-7

To my beloved late husband, Jon Wesley (Wes) Pierce, who was looking forward to reading this book but passed away shortly before it was published.

AND

To my children and their spouses:
Kim Kelsey Rinke and husband, Mike
Ron Kelsey and wife, Jan

AND

To my grandchildren:
Lindsey Rinke Binninger and husband, Bryan
Michelle Rinke
Chase Muschong

AND

To my twin great-grandchildren:
Charley Rinke Binninger
Blakely Brynn Binninger

Table of Contents

Preface

I've always said I would someday write a book about my life. Not that I'm so important that I want others to know about me, but mainly so my children and grandchildren can know about my life growing up, and about my parents, whom they never knew. I'm now eighty-two years old, and if I'm ever going to write the book, I'd better do it now. Especially since we're going through unprecedented times in the world right now, and I have more time than usual.

To explain what I'm talking about, the world is in the middle of a pandemic—something I never thought would happen. The coronavirus (known as COVID-19) is rampant as of July 4, 2020, when I'm starting to write this book. We are supposed to stay at home as much as possible, and we're required to wear masks if we go out in public. This virus has been going around since at least March, and it's getting worse right now. The economy is hurting, because restaurants, beauty salons, bars, churches, and department stores were all shut down for two months. In June they were allowed to reopen; however, there was a spike in the number of cases and deaths, so now the bars and gyms have been shut down again. Some of the people at the bars, as well as people involved in protests, didn't think they had to wear masks or stay six feet apart, so this may have caused an increase in cases. Our church, Arizona Community Church in Tempe, has been livestreaming services on their website every Sunday morning. In June they started allowing a limited number of worshippers to call, make reservations, and come on Sunday mornings with social distancing (staying six feet apart). I haven't been attending on Sunday mornings, as I'm enjoying watching the service on the computer in my pajamas!

As I finish this book, I'll give an update on the pandemic. The Lord is in control, so as Christians, we don't have to worry, although we do need to be cautious.

I'm living by myself right now, as my husband, Wes, is at Hawthorn Court at Ahwatukee, a memory care and assisted living facility. It's 1.7 miles from my house and takes me five minutes to drive there. You'll learn more about Wes and his health in upcoming chapters.

I had three possible titles for this book: (1) *All About M.E.*, by Martha Endicott Pierce, because that was the title I used in my high school English class in 1955 for the essay about my life; (2) *My Road M.A.P. of Life*; or similarly, (3) *The Road M.A.P. of My Life*. After debating back and forth and asking others their opinions, I chose the title *The Road M.A.P. of My Life*, by Martha A. Pierce. M.A.P. are my initials, and my son-in-law, Mike, often calls me MAP.

I hope as you read this book you will laugh, cry, learn something new, and enjoy reading about my life. There may be some chapters that are too detailed and boring, so you have my permission to skim or skip them. The chapter on travel might not be interesting to you unless you happened to travel with us. I tried to give some interesting statistics or things not well known about the trips.

Before I sent the final manuscript in to the publishing company for printing, the Lord took Wes to his heavenly home on January 1, 2021. He died from the coronavirus, pneumonia, and a bacterial infection. I will talk more about his passing in a later chapter.

CHAPTER 1

My Beginnings

1938: Martha, three months old

On a cold, windy day, February 11, 1938, a sandy-haired, blue-eyed baby girl was born to Vena Ethel (Lewis) and Harley LeRoy Endicott. That baby girl was me—Martha Ann Endicott. I weighed in at eight pounds, two ounces, and I was twenty-one inches long. I was born at St. Joseph Hospital in Mishawaka, Indiana, at 3:50 p.m. I was named after my maternal grandmother, Martha Frances Lewis, and my paternal grandmother, Ann Fenton Endicott. I was the last of five children born to my parents, so there's not much in my baby book. It doesn't even say how old I was when I took my first steps. I said "mama" and "dada" at six months.

I was a "change of life" baby, as my mother was forty-three years old when I was born. My oldest sister, Winifred (we called her Sis), was pregnant, and Mom thought she was just going through menopause. Wrong! She was pregnant with me at the same time her oldest daughter was also pregnant. Sis gave birth to Barbara Ethel Stayton on December 18, 1937, eight weeks prior to my birth. I was already an aunt when I was born! Barbara never called me Aunt Martha Ann, thank goodness. My family has always called me Martha Ann, which is what Mom wanted.

1939: Martha's first birthday with Barbara on the right

You'll never see very many pictures of me by myself, as Sis was the photographer and always took pictures of both Barbara and me together. We were pretty inseparable. For my first birthday, Sis made me a cake with animal crackers around the edge and a pink candle in the middle with pink ribbons tied to it, going out to the animal crackers. I had on a pink dress Mom made for me, which I talk about in a later chapter. As Sis and her husband, Johnny, did not have a car, they went with us almost everywhere and quite often were at our house.

Our home was at 115 Miami Club Drive in Mishawaka, Indiana. Dad never wanted to own a house, so we rented our home for twenty-five dollars a month for over fifteen years. The family moved from Elkhart, Indiana, in 1933, to this two-story home prior to my birth. Sis and Johnny got married in the house in January 1937. Mom was a housewife. Dad was a freight agent for the New York Central Railroad. I remember going with him several times to inspect and make reports on various train wrecks in the area. One of our neighbors was trying to stop at a railroad crossing. It was icy, and he couldn't stop. The car slid into the side of the moving train, killing the baby in the car and cutting off the mother's feet. To this day, I stop way back from railroad crossings! Thankfully I did not go with him on that inspection.

The pink dress Mom made for Martha's first birthday

Summer of 1938: Front row: Martha and Barbara; Second row: Nancy, Tippy, and Jack; Back row: Sis, Lewie, and Johnny

I had four older siblings. Sis was almost twenty-two years older than I. I remember reading in her life story about her being very sickly when she was very small. One time she was so sick that the family thought she was in a coma. Grandma Lewis knelt beside her crib and prayed for her recovery. While she was praying, Sis opened her eyes and smiled at Grandma. Sis recovered, but Grandma said to Mom, "You'll never raise that child; she's too puny." Sis proved her wrong and lived to be over one hundred years old.

Lewie came next and was fifteen years older than I. I remember one day my sister Nancy and I were doing the dishes together. We were arguing over who was going to wash and who was going to dry the dishes. We both wanted to wash. Lewie settled the argument by choosing me to wash, and I promptly said, "Ha, ha. I won!" Lewie said, "Okay. Nancy gets to wash now," and she replied, "Ha ha." He switched us again, and I was smart enough to keep quiet! Lewie got married when I was five years old to Alene Zion. They moved into a small house on the next street, and I often walked there and played with Alene's jewelry. She made up a small jewelry box with a few pieces of costume jewelry in it just for me. I specifically remember a three-inch gold spider pin or brooch with a bright pink stone in the middle.

Next in line came my brother Jack, who was nine years older than I. He was the ornery one in the family and very humorous. He was babysitting with me one evening when his friend called and wanted Jack to come to his house. Jack called Sis and got permission to take me to her house. He sat me in the basket of his bicycle and pedaled me there. There was a shortcut at the end of our street. It was a vacant lot with a bicycle path that had five or six small hills that were each about two feet high. We called it the bumps. That's the way Jack went to Sis's. However, since I was a little bit too heavy for his basket, we tipped over on the shortcut, and I ended up with skinned elbows and knees. He got into big trouble for that!

Closest to me in age was my sister Nancy, who was six years old when I was born. We shared a bedroom with twin beds. I loved the story she told of me getting lost at the Brookfield Zoo in Chicago when I was three years old. Later in life, Nancy wrote an article about the event. Here are snippets from her story:

My Sister's Lost!
by Nancy Nelson

Recurring nightmares plagued me. Cold sweat poured from my body as I relived the scene night after night. I recalled running frantically through a crowded area, searching for my little sister. "Martha Ann, Martha Ann!" I called. But no answer came. Panic stricken, I awoke and looked across to the twin bed where my sister slept. What a relief to see her curled up with her stuffed animals, sleeping peacefully.

The nightmares began after my mom, dad, sister and I visited Brookfield Zoo in Chicago. I was nine years old at the time; my sister was three. We all enjoyed the animal exhibits and stayed together to view each group until we came to the monkeys. My parents watched along with

Martha Ann and me for fifteen minutes, when they decided it was time to move on. Fascinated with the monkeys' antics, I resisted leaving. "Let me stay here for a few minutes more, then I'll catch up with you," I pleaded. They agreed that it was okay, but then Martha Ann piped up, "I want to stay too." This exasperated me. Now I wouldn't be able to concentrate on the monkeys—I'd have to watch my sister as well. What a bother baby sisters can be!

Just as I suspected, my sister soon missed our parents and wanted to join them. I told Martha Ann that Mom and Dad were right over at the next exhibit with the bears. She left, and I glanced around to make sure she headed in the right direction. About ten minutes later, I left my post and sought the family. I spotted Mom and Dad by the bear cage, but horror of horrors, there was no Martha Ann! I took off frantically looking for her.

I asked several people if they had seen a little blond girl with banana curls, wearing a red cape. No one recalled seeing her. Fear struck like lightning. Dashing through the grounds, I continued to call her name. After five minutes of terror, I spotted her. To me, she had never looked so beautiful, even though dirt streaked across her face from crying. "You little monkey!" I exclaimed. "I'm even happier to see you than all those monkeys I loved so much back there." My thoughts were no longer about what a bother little sisters were but what a blessing they were!

For years, my sister loved hearing this story re-told, as she delighted in hearing how loved and valuable she was (and still is) to me.

Nancy was a good writer. I'm not sure this article she wrote was ever published, but I think it should have been. She went on to compare my being lost to our many "lost" friends and loved ones who do not know Jesus as their savior. When they find him, we can rejoice and celebrate!

1944: Dad, Martha, Barbara, Mom, and Nancy at the acres..

My parents owned two acres of vacant land in an unde-veloped area in the southern part of Mishawaka. They often talked about building a home there sometime in the future. At an earlier time, Dad had dug the foundation of the house. I can remember Barbara and I playing house in that dug-out area. A little later, Mom and Dad planted a strawberry patch on the acreage. We went there quite often in the summer months to pick strawberries. Mom made delicious strawberry shortcake for our family, generally for supper on Sunday evening. I still have the platter she used to serve it in.

For my second birthday, Sis wrote the following poem about me:

Martha Ann
by Winifred Stayton
February 1940

Just two years old today!

Now, that's the time to be happy and gay,

But you're always feeling that way

And full of mischief the livelong day.

You arise in the morning with
a song on your lips

And sing "Oh Johnny" and that and this,

And love to tease the kids
and make them mad,

But they know you're really not bad.

You make Mama and Daddy angry with you,

And they give you scoldings
and spankings too,

But they love you just the same

And will always bless the day you came.

Your big blue eyes look up so innocently

When you've done something
that wasn't right,

And your blond curls encircle your head

Like a halo in the night.

You're a real chubby little thing,

And a mighty cute one too,

And we hope you'll always be happy

And your troubles few.

So here's "Happy Birthday,"
Martha Ann,

Martha, two or
three years old.

And may you grow up to be
a fine young woman,

As sweet and as happy as you are today,

And always travel along the Christian way.

Barbara and I were almost four years old when Pearl Harbor took place on December 7, 1941. I remember it well. I can still picture Mom, Dad, Sis, and Johnny huddled around the large RCA floor radio in the living room, listening intently to the news. Barbara and I knew something bad was taking place, so we climbed under our huge dining room table for protection, as we felt safe and secure there. As a side note, December 7 was also Nancy's tenth birthday.

Our dog Tippy, a toy collie, was a year old when I was born. Since we actually grew up together, Tippy went everywhere I went. Mom had given me strict instructions not to cross the street. As I thought she would never know, I crossed the street anyway and went to play in my friend's backyard, out of Mom's sight. However, Tippy was standing in the driveway, watching me, so Mom knew exactly where I was. I happened to be playing at the time with a wooden paddle and ball. Mom used the paddle to spank me. Thanks, Tippy! I also remember when we drove to our acres in the country. When we turned off the paved highway and onto Ireland Road, which was dirt, Tippy would start to whine. Dad, knowing what Tippy wanted, stopped the car, opened the car door, and Tippy jumped out and raced us to the acres.

When I was five years old, my brother Jack was showing off his new BB gun to the neighbor boys. I was curious too, so I was standing nearby when he shot the gun. In fact, I was too nearby. A BB grazed my stomach! Of course, all of the boys were very concerned. I remember being extremely embarrassed when Jack lifted up my dress to see what damage the BB had caused. Mom just put a bandage on it, so it must not have been too serious!

One other time, I was in the kitchen, watching Jack and Nancy mop the floor with Spic and Span. Somehow the chemical got into my eyes! Jack and Nancy called Mom and Dad for help. Dad arrived on the scene first, and he was so nervous everyone thought he was going to have a nervous breakdown. He was no help at all! Mom finally came and washed out my eyes with a lot of water, which seemed to take care of it. (There was no urgent care back then).

I used to play Sunday school with Donnie Colver, the little neighbor boy who lived across the alley. I sat on a box in the backyard; he sat cross-legged on the ground in front of me while I read Bible stories to him. I was probably six years old. He enjoyed hearing what I had to say until I told him there was no Santa Claus! Then he  really revolted. Nothing I said convinced him, and I'm glad it didn't, since he was only three years old. Donnie's parents owned Colver's Drug Store, located next to their home. I loved to walk there and order a ten-cent cherry soda at the soda fountain. For some reason, the cherry soda was cheaper than the chocolate soda, which was fifteen cents.

The following are some of the things I can remember from my childhood, although I don't know my age at the time.

My favorite doll was a bride doll. My mom had made the wedding dress for her. I can remember vividly the time Dad told me he couldn't lift me anymore. He said I was too big and needed to walk on my own. My dad made a dollhouse for me. It was pretty big—about three feet high and five feet wide. He didn't think I played with it enough, so he gave it to Barbara, my niece. Then I *really* wanted to play with it! Dad also made me a miniature dresser and cupboard, just my size. I kept them for years and gave them to my daughter, Kim, when she was little. They were left by mistake in the attic in one of our houses when we moved.

Dad gave me twenty-five cents for a weekly allowance. I immediately went to Colver's Drug Store and bought two Wonder Woman comic books for ten cents each and a Payday candy bar for a nickel. One day Dad said, "You've been doing your chores well; I think you need an increase in your allowance." He increased it to a dollar every week! I did try to save some of it. I made little boxes marked ten cents for church, ten cents for savings, and the rest for spending. That didn't last long, and soon it all went into the spending box!

Mom used to iron the bedsheets on a large mangle ironer. One time, a catalpa worm from the catalpa tree in our backyard, unbeknownst to Mom, fell on one of the sheets that was hanging on the clothesline. She ironed the worm along with the sheet and created quite a mess!

My favorite food Mom prepared was creamed chicken over homemade biscuits. I've tried to make it, but it never turns out the same. Strawberry shortcake was another favorite. Mom quite often made a dessert called Holland Rusk. I have that recipe and make it once in a while. The food I didn't like was mushroom soup and stewed tomatoes. I remember I was still in the high chair, and because I hadn't eaten all my food, Mom made me stay there until I finished the stewed tomatoes on my plate. Jack came by and started killing flies near my food, and I protested. To this day, I do not like stewed tomatoes, nor will I let anyone near food with a flyswatter. I really liked peanut butter and mayo mixed together and ate it as a sandwich spread. I still like peanut butter and mayo on a BLT.

I remember Sis reading the Sunday comics to Barbara and me before we learned how to read; I remember all the box-elder bugs that always seemed to be on our front porch. We had a wooden swing on the porch, but we seldom sat on it because of the many bugs. I remember having chicken pox. I had a scab on the tip of my nose, and it seemed to last forever. In fact, I still have a small scar on the end of my nose. Some of my friends from school visited me through our sun parlor window in the front of the house.

I remember Nancy and I often made fudge in the evenings. We took turns beating it, as it had to be just right before pouring it into a dish to harden. We also popped popcorn many times. One day I wanted to bake a cake, but no one had time to help me. I said, "I can do this myself!" (This was before cake mixes.) I did okay until I decided to use bacon grease instead of shortening. The cake tasted terrible, and Mom had to throw it away!

In 1943, the All-American Girls Professional Baseball League was formed, since most of the men had been called to fight in the war. It was created by the owner of the Chicago

Cubs. South Bend (the twin city of Mishawaka) had a team called the South Bend Blue Sox. Nancy used to take me with her on the bus to the games, which were held at Playland Park in South Bend. My favorite player was Bonnie Baker, the catcher. We became quite avid baseball fans! In 1992, a movie called *A League of Their Own* was filmed and became very popular. The Blue Sox were known as "A Team of Their Own." Recently one of the retired Blue Sox players, Betsy Jochum, was interviewed. She related that the rules to play on the team were very strict. They could not drink, smoke, or use foul language, were chaperoned on dates, and were required to attend charm school. Their uniforms were very short skirts with shorts underneath. They played until 1954.

Speaking of baseball, Nancy was a die-hard Cubs fan. Dad was a fan also, but not the die-hard type. When Nancy wanted to know whether the Cubs had won or lost a game, she paid me a quarter to call WSBT, the local radio station, and ask them if there was a final score on the game. If the game wasn't over, she gave me another quarter to call again. (It was an easy way to make money.)

During World War II, the kids in our neighborhood formed a victory club. There were about twenty of us. I remember collecting newspapers in Jack's little red wagon for the war effort. Half the time I rode in the wagon while someone else pulled it. At five years old, I might have been one of the youngest in the club. I still have some of the war ration books and tokens that were given to each person, even young children like me.

Barbara and I enjoyed playing together. We loved playing with dolls, the dollhouse, and paper dolls. We cut out pictures of furniture from magazines and set them up for the paper dolls. By the time we had everything set up, it was generally time to quit. We enjoyed roller-skating on the sidewalk or in the basement in bad weather. As we got a little older, we pretended to be teachers, as I had a school desk in my bedroom. We also liked to design houses. I guess one of us should have been an architect. I liked to ride a bike. My parents first bought me a small two-wheeler with training wheels. I can still remember when Dad took off the training wheels but was holding onto the seat of the bicycle while I was riding it. I soon looked back, and Dad was not there. I was riding all by myself! As I got older, I often rode a bicycle to town instead of paying to ride the bus.

Speaking of roller-skating, I remember once Barbara and I were skating in the basement, as it was almost dark outside. Sis came to the top of the stairs and told us the Colvers' house (our neighbor across the alley) was on fire. We didn't hear the word "Colvers," and we both thought *our* house was on fire. We were hurriedly trying to take off our skates. I was so nervous I was shaking all over. When we climbed to the top of the stairs, we realized it wasn't our house after all. Both of my brothers, Jack and Lewie, helped put the fire out. They also carried one of the boys from the burning house. Later in life, both Jack and Lewie were volunteer firemen for the rural fire department. They both also served as fire chiefs.

We attended First Christian Church, which was near downtown Mishawaka. Sis, Johnny, and Barbara attended there also. In fact, that's where Sis and Johnny met. Sis was a Sunday school teacher and taught kindergarten-age children. She had a lot of flannelgraph stories that she told, and Barbara and I loved to pretend we were teachers, using the flannelgraph pieces to tell the stories. I remember going to

Bible school in the summer months. At one of the lunches with the entire group of children, the pastor asked me to say grace without asking me first. I remember mumbling something incoherent; I was really embarrassed!

Our pastor, Reverend Hayes, and my dad loved limburger cheese. Mom and Dad occasionally invited the Hayes family to our home for dinner. After dinner, all the kids went into the living room while the adults talked at the dining room table (and ate limburger cheese, which smelled terrible). Jack had gotten out the playing cards and was teaching the Hayes kids how to play gin rummy. (Reverend Hayes and his wife did not believe in playing cards.) In a few minutes, Dad came in to check on us. When Dad saw the cards, he was really upset and told Jack to "put those cards away right now!"

Uncle Orla, my mother's brother, was a Gospel artist. He generally came to our church once a year and held nightly services for a week. He painted, sang, and preached. Each night he gave the painting to whomever brought the most guests. He was an excellent artist but not such a great singer! On Easter Sunday, when Barbara and I were seven years

old, we went forward to acknowledge we had accepted Jesus as our Savior. We were baptized the following Sunday evening. When Barbara and I were eight or nine years old, Reverend Hayes asked us several times at the Sunday evening service to come up in front of the congregation to sing and do the motions to the song "Behold," a children's song.

Due to some of the strictness of the church, we left when Barbara and I were in the eighth grade and started attending Immanuel Baptist Church, where we later became members.

In April 1947, when Barbara and I were nine, Sis and Johnny hosted Mrs. George Moore, a missionary to the Navajo Indians in Gallup, New Mexico. Mrs. Moore also brought an Indian girl, Lola, with her. They both stayed with Sis and Johnny for several days. At that time, Sis was the secretary of the Navajo Indian Gospel Crusade. Mrs. Moore gave a presentation at Sis and Johnny's home and at church. She gave Sis a beautiful Navajo rug, which Sis later gave to me. I have since passed it on to Sis's grandson, Mike Armstead, who lives in El Paso.

Barbara and I went to church camp at Winona Lake in Indiana, twice that I can remember. I just ran across a letter and a postcard that Barbara wrote to her mother in 1947. We were nine years old. In the letter, Barbara asked for her mom (my sister) to bring or mail us some cookies. If I remember correctly, Sis baked and brought cookies to the camp. Then Barbara did not want Sis to leave and cried for Sis to take us home. Barbara says it was the other way around, and it was me who cried to go home. We stayed at the camp for the remainder of the two-week period.

Winona Lake is where the Billy Sunday Tabernacle was at that time. In case you don't know who Billy Sunday was, Billy was born in Iowa in 1862 and died in Chicago in 1935. He was an American athlete who, after being a popular outfielder in the National Baseball League, became a most influential American evangelist during the first two decades of the twentieth century. He was famous for his one-liner "Going to church doesn't make you a Christian any more than going to a garage makes you an automobile." I laughed when I read this other quote from Billy Sunday: "I'm against sin. I'll kick it as long as I have a foot. I'll fight it as long as I have a fist. I'll butt it as long as I have a head. I'll bite it as long as I've got a tooth. And when I'm old and fistless and footless and toothless, I'll gum it till I go home to glory and it goes home to perdition." (Perdition means eternal damnation.) When Barbara and I were twelve years old, we attended a revival at the tabernacle. A young new evangelist by the name of Billy Graham was speaking there that day. I vividly remember how old we were, as he asked for all the teenagers thirteen and older to stand. Barbara and I couldn't stand because we were only twelve. Billy Sunday was only surpassed by Billy Graham in leading people to Christ.

Sis and family went on many vacations with us. Almost every summer, Mom and Dad rented a cabin at Shavehead Lake in Michigan, about an hour's drive away. I remember Mom waking me up at 3:00 a.m. and Dad carrying me to the car, letting me sleep on the way. One time our car's brakes failed, and Dad had to drive through several red lights, hoping no other cars were coming. A pedestrian policeman tried to stop us, and Dad yelled out the window, "No brakes!" The policeman quickly jumped out of the way!

My parents and Sis and Johnny loved to fish. I decided to go out on the boat with Mom and Dad and learn how for myself. However, I didn't want to touch the worm to put it on the hook, much less take the fish off when I caught one. Dad said I couldn't fish anymore (that was okay with me), and he motioned for Sis and Johnny, who were in a nearby boat, to take me back to the cottage. I've never yet caught a fish, so I do not enjoy fishing! The others caught a lot of bluegills, which Mom fried for our suppers. Mom always warned us about the bones

Mom showing off the fish that she caught

in the fish. To this day I do not like to eat any fish that have bones, as I'm afraid a bone might get caught in my throat. My sisters felt the same way. One thing I remember buying at the country store at Shavehead Lake was Orange Crush served in a dark brown bottle. I know we can buy Orange Crush today, but it doesn't quite taste the same in a clear bottle!

We also went to Turkey Run in Indiana one summer when I was seven or eight years old. We rented a cabin, spent several nights, and did some hiking on the trails. It was a beautiful area.

In 1946, when I was eight years old, a six-year-old girl in Chicago was kidnapped from her second-story bedroom. A ladder had been put up to her window, and she was later found dead and dismembered. I used to lie in bed at night, scared that someone might kidnap me. Since I generally went to bed earlier than the rest of the family, I usually sat on the top step of the staircase and waited there until I heard someone start to come up the stairs. Then I ran (quietly) and got into my bed. My dad was usually the first one to go to bed after me. Sometimes he went to bed the same time I did, which always made me happy.

We didn't have air-conditioning in our house, and during July and August, it was very hot in the upstairs bedrooms, especially at night. Our house had a porch on the second floor outside Mom and Dad's bedroom where we often slept when it was so hot. After a few years, Dad said it wasn't very stable anymore, so we were no longer allowed to go out on the porch. After that, I quite often took my pillow and light blanket downstairs and slept on the floor in the living room, where it was a little bit cooler. Sometimes others in the family were already there.

I had a severe toothache when I was eight or nine. I remember that it was infected, and I was running a fever. I stayed home from school and was actually in bed because it hurt so bad. I got up to go to the bathroom, and when I tried to return to the bed, I passed out, hitting my head on the bed frame. Mom was frantic and put a washcloth on my forehead and was able to get me onto the bed. She later took me to the dentist, and since the tooth was infected, he pulled it without any deadener. (I had wondered why he asked my mother to hold down my legs!) I screamed so loudly that the people in the waiting room wondered what was going on. Their eyes were as big as saucers when we came out! We never went back to that dentist. Mom found a new dentist that we liked and went to for years.

In 1948, when I was ten years old, our family went on a driving trip to Northern Michigan. We went to Traverse City, Sault Ste. Marie, Mackinac Island, and Ontario, Canada. We also rented a cottage for a week at Bear Lake. Lewie and his family joined us, along with Sis and family. Jack and Phyllis were dating then, and Jack brought her along. It was a wonderful trip, and the last one

Martha and Barbara on Mackinac Island

Mom and Dad ever went on with the family, as they both died the following year.

Mom was a very good seamstress. She had an old pedal sewing machine, and she made not only most of my clothes but Barbara's also. For our first birthdays, she crocheted a pink dress for me and a blue dress for Barbara. We still have those dresses, and the grandchildren and great-grandchildren have worn them. One Christmas, when we were nine years old, she made identical dresses for Barbara, me, and a friend, Barbie Shields. The dresses were red velvet on the top and striped taffeta on the bottom. She also made coats for us. The ability to sew like this did not get passed down to me, nor to my sisters Nancy or Sis. It seems to have skipped a generation, as Barbara is a very good seamstress.

Speaking of Barbie Shields, I was invited to her house to spend the night when I was ten years old. For breakfast, her dad, Bill, made waffles for everyone. The waffles were quite rich, so I only ate one. I turned down a second waffle, but Bill insisted that I eat another one. I did, and it made me sick. They never knew it, but when I walked home, I threw up all over the sidewalk. I still to this day will not eat waffles for breakfast.

Barbie's family owned a very nice cottage on Diamond Lake in Michigan, about an hour's drive from home. They often invited Barbara, another friend named Sharon Wiekamp, and me to spend a week at the cottage. We generally did this every summer. There were several boys our age who lived nearby, so that made it more interesting! I learned to water-ski behind the Shields's speedboat. As I didn't like to go underwater, I tried my best to stay upright on the skis!

In 1954, when I was sixteen, the four of us girls were on the lake in a rowboat, and we were dared by the boys to try to maneuver through the channel that curved around and emptied back into the lake. There was a thick patch of lily pads in the shallow channel, and we got stuck. We were stuck for three and a half hours; it was beginning to get dark, and we were being eaten by mosquitoes. The boys who'd dared us in the first place tried to help us, and their boat also got stuck. Barbie's parents found out where we were and came to get us in their speedboat. There were four other speedboats there to help also. People in the area turned on their car lights to help the rescue in the growing darkness. We got into trouble but nearly tried it again the next day!

I can remember Mom playing the piano beautifully, and I said that someday I wanted to play like she did. When I was five years old, I sat down at the piano and composed a song, not by plunking it out with one finger but by using both hands. Mom thought I might have some musical talent. Nancy was already taking lessons, so I joined her. I recently found a program from a piano recital that was held at our church, First Christian Church, on May 28, 1945. I would have been seven years old. I played "On the Bright Blue Sea," which I don't remember at all. Dr. Summers was our piano teacher for years. Instead of having us count our own timing, he would say, "One-y-and-a-two-y," which we thought was really funny. I still have trouble today with my timing, as I don't feel we were taught properly. When I was thirteen years old, I played in another recital under the direction of Irene Granger, who had been a classmate of Sis's. I played "Glow Worm" as a duet with Barbie Shields and "Pomp and Circumstance" as a piano solo. The recital was held at the South Bend Conservatory of Music.

Barbie Shields and I played that same piano duet later that year near Christmastime at a school for blind children. Two of the girls who were blind sang a duet, "Silver Bells." I always think of them when I hear that song. It was an awesome experience, and I'll never forget it. It made me so thankful for my sight, which we so often take for granted.

Mom played two songs that I loved: "Edelweiss Glide Waltz" and "The Fireman's Dream." The sheet music for these two songs was in tatters and was almost unreadable. However, I was able to make out enough of the notes to play and memorize the music. When I got married and moved to Michigan, all of my music was wrapped up in newspaper and put in the basement at Sis and Johnny's house. Since I didn't have a piano, I had no need for the music until later. Johnny thought the pile of music was just a pile of old newspapers, and he threw them all away. Later I was able to buy "Edelweiss Glide Waltz," but I could not find "The Fireman's Dream." I looked for it for over twenty years. I finally found it in 1987 while vacationing in Washington, DC. A clerk working at the Library of Congress looked it up at the patent office and made a copy for me. I had earlier learned to play both of these songs by memory (but not completely accurately). Now I could play them correctly. I had purchased a spinet piano for $300 from a coworker at the bank when I was in my midtwenties. It was nice to be able to play the piano again.

CHAPTER 2

More About My Family

Circa 1910: Mom about 15 years old. This is a photograph of a picture.

Mom, Vena Ethel Lewis, was born in Lincoln, Nebraska, on May 19, 1895, in a covered wagon. Her father, Charles Albert Lewis, and mother, Martha Frances Johnston Lewis, had gone west to settle in a new land in Nebraska. Martha, my grandmother, became very homesick and insisted they return to Illinois. She was pregnant, and Mom was born on the return trip. Mom had two older brothers at the time, Clyde and Orla. Mom went by her middle name, Ethel. Mom was a very loving person, and she loved to talk on the telephone with her many friends.

Sis gave me some of Mom's diaries, which I've enjoyed reading (probably the main reason I started writing in a diary). In her 1913 diary, I laughed at the number of boys she dated.

Mom was seventeen years old at the time and turned eighteen on May 19. Here's a summary of her dating experiences:

- March 22 and 23—two dates with George Perry
- March 23—Roy (Endicott) broke our date
- March 24 to 27—three dates with George Perry
- March 27 to May 3—Roy back in the picture
- June 26 and June 27—Joe Ichus
- July 4 to July 6—Otto Porter
- July 12 to July 31—Roy
- August 2, 23, and 24—Joe Hamm
- August 3 to August 17—Roy
- August 23 and 24—Joe Hamm
- August 24-26—Roy
- August 28—Roy and Otto on the same day
- August 31 to October 19—Roy
- October 20—Quarreled and Roy quit. He said he would never come back.
- October 27—Roy came into the store and invited me to a party. He wanted to come back all the time. I let him come.

1915: Mom, 20 years old

- December 24—Roy gave me a diamond ring. (I, Martha, have this ring.)

Unfortunately I do not have Mom's diary for 1914, the following year. I know Mom and Dad (Roy) were married on June 22, 1915. I wonder how many times they broke up (or "quit") before then. Mom must have been quite popular and had many friends. She mentioned many times about riding a horse and buggy home from church or going other places. Many of her dates were to the movies, church, and parks, and she mentioned "confectionary" many times, which was where they ate ice cream or drank hot chocolate. She worked at Lewis Electric Supply for four months. She started working for Lewis Bros. and was there for two months. She worked for

1915 Mom and Dad shortly after their marriage.

Lewis Electric Co. from March 1914 until June 1915, when she and Dad were married. Since her last name was Lewis, I expect these places might have been owned by family members, possibly uncles or cousins.

Dad, Harley LeRoy Endicott, was born in Champaign, Illinois, on June 8, 1892. He was the youngest of ten children born to John Thomas Endicott and Ann Fenton Marsh Endicott. Dad and Mom were married on June 22, 1915, in Champaign. He preferred to be called Roy. He worked for the New York Central Railroad for thirty-seven years. Dad was a very nervous person. Sis told me that prior to my birth, he'd had a nervous breakdown and was almost a different person after that.

I talked a little about my brothers and sisters in the previous chapter, but I want to tell you more details about each one. I loved my brothers and sisters very much. They meant a lot to me. I'm the only one living as I write this, and I really miss them.

Information on the Five Children of Roy and Ethel Endicott

I.   Winifred (Sis) Josephine Endicott, was born in Champaign, Illinois, on October 25, 1916.

She married John Stayton and had one child, Barbara. Sis worked at First National Bank of Mishawaka for twenty-two years.

Johnny worked at the I & M (Indiana and Michigan Electric Co.) for over forty years.

Johnny died in 1990.

Sis married Kenny Rea, who owned and retired from Tribe-O-Rea Drugs.

Kenny died in 1995.

Sis died in 2017 at the age of one hundred.

1984: Front row: Sis and Johnny; Back row: The Armsteads: Pam, Doug, Barbara, Mike, and Jim

B. Barbara Ethel Stayton married James (Jim) Armstead in 1957.

They had three children: Pamela, Michael, and Douglas.

Barbara drove a school bus for nineteen years for special education children in Michigan.

Jim was a supervisor in the highway construction industry.

Jim died in 1998 from myelofibrosis, a cancer of the bone marrow.

Barbara married Paul Kerekes, a retired farmer and car-pattern maker, in 2004.

2007: Barbara and Paul Kerekes

Paul died in 2016. Barbara lives in Eaton Rapids, Michigan, and Florida in the winter.

1. Pamela Kay Armstead married Kenneth Finegood.

They had three children: Eric, Kevin, and Sarah.

Pam was a special education teacher in Michigan for thirty-three years before recently retiring.

Ken is currently a personal injury and civil rights attorney. They live in Huntington Woods, Michigan.

2011 The Finegood family: Kevin, Pam, Sarah, Ken, and Eric

1994: Mike Armstead holding Elijah and Elyshia

a. Eric Daniel Finegood has his doctorate in psychology and is currently working at Northwestern University in Illinois in the research department.

b. Kevin Jonathon Finegood lives in Connecticut and is an aquarium specialist, working with exotic fish. He recently married Eva Eleuteri on November 1, 2020.

c. Sarah Ruth Finegood recently graduated from Michigan State University with a degree in ecology and agriculture.

2. Michael Edwin Armstead married Elizabeth Reyes and later divorced. They had two children: Elijah and Elyshia.

Mike was in the army for twenty years and has since worked for seventeen years in civil service at Fort Bliss.

a. Elijah James Armstead is a professional dance instructor and dancer and is engaged to Deenie Tusalem.

b. Elyshia Seberina Armstead lives in Las Vegas, where she is a manager and voice instructor.

Michael Armstead married Selina Saenz, who has two boys from a previous marriage. Selina is a part-time physical therapist. She and Mike live in El Paso.

a. Steven Ray Saenz and his wife, Maria, have three children and live in El Paso.

1. Erin Elia Saenz, age seven

2. Steven Bear Saenz, age four
3. Jason Ray Saenz, three months old
b. Shane Saenz and his wife, Angela, have one daughter.
1. Samantha Lee Saenz, age seven
3. Douglas LeRoy Armstead married Keith Morris. They live in Lansing, Michigan.

Doug was a choral music teacher for twenty-six years in Michigan. He is now a hotel night manager.

Doug is an excellent musician as soloist, choir director, and pianist.

2011: Doug, Pam, and Mike

Keith is the lead attorney for Elder Law of Michigan, Inc.

1998: Lewis Endicott's Family left to right: Katie, Phillip, Jill, Emily, Ed, Lewie, Diana, Larry, and Al in back

II. Lewis (Lewie) Edward Endicott was born on December 10, 1922, in Marion, Indiana.

Lewie married Alene Zion on April 30, 1943, in Mishawaka. They had two children: Diana and Ed.

Lewie worked for Standard Oil of Indiana for many years prior to moving to California.

Alene died in 1987 from cancer. Lewie died in 1999 from influenza complications.

    A. Diana Lou Endicott married Al Hagerstrand, who had a daughter from a previous marriage: Melissa (Missy)

1990: Missy, Al and Diana

Diana was an eighth-grade history and English teacher in San Jose, California, for thirty-seven years.

Diana retired in 2004. She died in 2011 from colon cancer.

Al has remarried and lives in Hawaii.

      1.   Melissa (Missy) Hagerstrand, daughter of Al Hagerstrand, raises French bulldogs.

          Missy owns Devil Mountain Design and lives in Lubbock, Texas.

    B. Edward Lee Endicott married Jill McKinnon. They have three children: Katie, Emily and Phillip.

2011: Jill and Ed Endicott

Ed and Jill live in Martinez, California.

      1.   Mary Katherine (Katie) Endicott married Randall Harris. They have three children: Hanna, Maura, and London

          Katie is an assistant professor at Penn State World Campus, working out of Logan, Utah.

a. Hanna Skye Harris, age thirteen
b. Maura Kate Harris, age ten
c. London Rose Harris, age nine

2020: The Harris Family

2. Emily married Ian McGee. They have two children.
    a. Campbell (Cami) Rose McGee, age fifteen
    b. Theodore (Teddy) John McGee, age eleven

2012: The McGee Family

3. Phillip Endicott and his wife, Jennifer Muller, have one child.

    a. Eleanor Leigh Endicott, age four (no photo available).

III. Jack Albert Endicott was born on June 25, 1929, in Elkhart, Indiana.

Jack married Phyllis Hartstein in 1949 in Mishawaka. They had three children: Larry, Gary, and Jack Duane (Jackie).

1964: Jack Endicott's family: Jackie in front; Jack and Phyllis; Back row: Gary and Larry

Jack was a salesman in the meat industry for many years.

Phyllis worked as a medical receptionist until the boys were born.

Phyllis died in 1991 from a heart attack.

Jack died in 1997 from esophageal cancer.

    A. Larry Alan Endicott had brain damage at birth, causing mental retardation. He worked at Logan Industries for years and lived in group homes after Jack died. Larry died from Parkinson's disease in 2020

2008: Gary Endicott's family: Jeffrey, Cam, Christine, and Gary at Christine's graduation.

B. Gary Lynn Endicott married Cam Van Thi Vo, originally from Saigon, Vietnam. They have two children: Christine and Jeffrey.
Gary retired from IBM in Vermont and works part-time for People's United Bank in Florida.
Cam retired from IBM in Vermont. They winter in Florida.

1. Christine Elizabeth Endicott married James Warren. They have two children: Abby and Rory.
Christine has a PhD in chemical and biomolecular engineering from the University of Connecticut.
Christine just accepted a job with Alexion as of January 2021.
James is currently a manager for the Travelers.

a. Abigail (Abby) Kate Warren is in kindergarten, age five.

    b. Rory James Warren, age two and a half, goes to daycare.

2020: Rory and Abigail Warren

2. Jeffrey Alexander Endicott married Kameron (Kami) Escajeda; they have one child. (no picture available)

    a. Remy Garrison Endicott is six months old.

C. Jack Duane (Jackie) Endicott married Patricia Dale and later divorced. They had two children: Casey and Tim.

Jackie has worked for Burnips Equipment Co. as a farm mechanic for forty-one years.

1. Casey Marie Endicott married Paul Grove and later divorced. They had two boys.

    a. Kevin Emmanuel Grove, age seventeen

    b. Preston Eli Grove, age thirteen

Casey married Will Groves; they have two girls: Aniston and Olivia.

Casey is a sixth-grade teacher at Walkerton Elementary School.

Will is an assistant principal at LaVille Elementary School.

    c.   Aniston Kate Groves, age seven

    d.   Olivia Charlotte Groves, age five

2020: Tim Endicott's family: Rory in front; Tim holding Nolan; Blair holding Brynn

    2.   Timothy Robert Endicott married Blair Decker; they have three children: Rory, Brynn, and Nolan.

Tim is an account manager at Press Ganey Associates LLC.

Blair is a speech language pathologist at LaVille Elementary and Jr./Sr. High School.

    a.   Rory Addison Endicott, age eight

    b.   Brynn Harper Endicott, age six

    c.   Nolan Robert Endicott, age four

1990: Jack, Phyllis, Cindy, Jackie, and Larry

Jackie Endicott married Cynthia (Cindy) Stevens; they have two children: Elizabeth and Matthew.

Cindy has worked in home daycare for twenty-three years. Elizabeth Marie Endicott is a second-grade teacher at Jimtown Elementary School.

2013: Casey, Matthew, Elizabeth, and Tim

3. Matthew Harold Endicott is a salesman for Hilti Tools in Indianapolis, Indiana.

IV. Nancy Louise Endicott was born on December 7, 1932, in Elkhart, Indiana.

1965: Nancy holding Tim with Debbie and Dirk looking on

Nancy married Dirk Nelson in Chicago in 1961; they had three children: Debbie, Tim, and Rebecca.

Nancy was a nurse for many of her early years and a secretary in later years.

Dirk was a pastor at various churches. They were both missionaries in Korea.

Nancy died in 2007 from cancer.

Dirk married Deborah Sistrunk, whom he met on Eharmony, and they lived in Apple Valley, California.

Dirk died in 2017 from dementia and other health issues.

A. Deborah (Debbie) Jean Nelson married Mike Padgett and had one child, Manda.

1. Manda Rose Padgett has two children with Michael Shearer.

    a.   Cohen Michael Shearer, age eleven

    b.   Harper Shearer, age seven

Debbie married Martin Hayes; they had two children.

    2.   Glenna Hayes, age thirty-two

    3.   Alison Hayes, age twenty-nine

1998: Glenna age 10, Debbie, Dirk, Nancy, and Alison, age 7

    B.   Timothy Nelson married Kathryn (Kathy) Edin; they have two adopted children: Kaitlin and Marissa.

Tim and Kathy were previously Harvard professors and Bostonians when offers came their way to teach at John Hopkins University. They are currently employed at Princeton University and reside in Baltimore, Maryland.

    1.   Kaitlin Nelson, age twenty-eight

    2.   Marissa Nelson, age twenty-six

C. Rebecca Nelson married Sung Kim and later divorced; Rebecca has two children: Miya and Haley.

Rebecca was born in Korea. Her name was originally Insook. Nancy and Dirk adopted her when she was five years old. As she grew older, she chose the name Becky, which later became Rebecca. After obtaining her bachelor's, master's, and doctoral degrees, she is currently a clinical child and adolescent psychologist.

1. Miya Nelson Kim is twenty-two years old and has been dancing for twenty years. She recently obtained her certification as a physical trainer.

Merrier THAN EVER

HAPPY HOLIDAYS from Rebecca, Miya & Haley | 2020

2. Haley Nelson Kim, age seventeen, is a high school senior. She plays the violin and viola. They live in the Chicago area

V. Martha Ann Endicott (that's me!) married Bill Kelsey in 1956 and divorced in 1969. They had two children: Kim and Ron.

Martha married Murry Ginis in 1972 and divorced in 1975 (no children).

Martha married Jon Wesley (Wes) Pierce in 1978 (no children).

2008: Martha's family: Mike, Michelle, Jan,
Ron, Kim, Lindsey, Martha, and Wes

A. Kim Jeanine Kelsey married Pat Harris and later divorced (no children).

Kim married Mike Rinke; they have two children: Lindsey and Michelle.

Kim retired from Bank of America in July 2020 after forty-two years.

Mike retired from owning a Mission Foods tortilla delivery route.

2017: Front row: Blakely, Michelle, Charley; Back row: Mike, Bryan, Lindsey, and Kim

1. Lindsey Nicole Rinke married Bryan Binninger; they have twin girls: Charley and Blakely born in 2017.

   Lindsey is a CPA, currently working for Tyvak as their corporate controller.

   Bryan works for S. L. Fusco, Inc. as a purchasing agent. They live in Costa Mesa, California.

   a. Charley Rinke Binninger, age three and a half

   b. Blakely Brynn Binninger, age three and a half

2. Michelle Rinke is unmarried, age thirty-one. Michelle lives at home with Mike and Kim. Michelle has Down syndrome and attends One Step Beyond in Peoria.

1996: Ron, Jan, and Chase

B.   Ronald David Kelsey married Jan Muschong. Jan has a son, Chase, from a previous marriage.

Ron owns his own semi and generally hauls pipe from Phoenix to California.

Jan has worked at Phoenix Children's Hospital since 1983 in the ICU as a health unit coordinator.

1.   Chason (Chase) Jared Muschong
       Chase lives in Peoria, Arizona, and works in Tempe with computers, his specialty.

CHAPTER 3

Beiger School (Kindergarten to Eighth Grade)

1944: Martha's first-grade class at Beiger (in the second row, fifth from the left); Barbara is in the back row, first on the left.

My kindergarten days are not very vivid, but I will always remember the first grade. My teacher was Miss Persinger. I had completed the daily written lesson and was doodling on my paper, drawing dots on the points of my letters. The teacher looked at my paper and slapped me. I was so embarrassed that I just put my head down on the desk. I'm not sure I even told my mom.

From kindergarten through fourth grade, we stayed in the same classroom with the same teacher all day. My favorite teacher was Miss Betts in the second grade. When we went into the fifth grade, we had a homeroom teacher but moved from room to room for each different subject. Our reading teacher was Miss Chadwick. She often asked students to read orally to the class. After I read, she corrected the way I pronounced "recipe." I pronounced it as "recype." We also had a spelling bee in her class. I was in the finals but misspelled "calendar" as "calender."

My brother Jack and sister Nancy previously had many of the same teachers I did. Jack always mimicked Miss Blind, our English teacher, as she walked around the room beating the rhythm of a poem on her hand with a pencil, saying, "Hickety Pickety, my fat hen. She lays eggs for gentlemen." Miss Duncan taught geography. One time she dyed her hair, and it came out purple. Mr. Gould was our eighth-grade Indiana history and science teacher. He sat on a stool behind a tall desk. One morning the stool broke, and he fell on the floor behind the desk. We all sat there, trying our best not to laugh! When he got up and we saw that he was okay, we all burst out laughing. He was very embarrassed, and his face was beet red. Our math teacher was Miss Porter. If someone did something wrong (usually one of the boys), she asked him to hold out his hand, whereupon she slapped his hand with a ruler. (She wouldn't get away with that today!)

I was not a morning person, even as a child. I often got up in the morning and told Mom I couldn't go to school because I did not have any clean socks or underwear. So she told me to go back to bed. After she did some laundry, I went to school in the afternoon. This must have happened quite often, as one day I was called into the principal's office to discuss why I was missing so many mornings. After that, it didn't happen again!

Barbara and I went to Beiger School together from first grade through eighth grade. We were in the same class, and the teachers enjoyed telling others that they had an aunt and a niece in class, and the aunt was the younger one! I loved school and generally earned straight A's. In the sixth grade, I joined the knitting club. I didn't know how to knit, so the teacher asked me to practice making a gold-colored, six-inch square with yarn that my mom gave me. Mom and I were on the train, and I decided to take my knitting with me. The ball of yarn dropped off my lap and traveled down the entire length of the train car, underneath all the seats. I had to walk down to the other end of the car, asking each person to roll the yarn back. I was so embarrassed! It took me all year to knit this one square, and the teacher put it in the middle of the afghan, since it was the only gold-colored square. I did not do any knitting after that, as the teacher asked me not to join the knitting club again.

Many of us girls had "boyfriends," basically in name only. From first grade through part of the eighth grade until he moved to Texas, my boyfriend was Tim Doll. I remember in the fourth or fifth grade at Christmastime, he gave me a very pretty bracelet with blue hearts on it. We also had a gift exchange, and I traded names with others until I got his name. He had only gotten the one gift from me, which was part of the gift exchange. I remember him saying, "How come you got two gifts and I only got one?" I guess it wasn't such a good idea to get his name in the exchange and not give him an additional gift. I lost track of Tim after he moved, and a few years ago, a fellow Beiger classmate, Richard Klotz, tracked him down and gave me his email address at our next class reunion. After contacting Tim and catching up on our lives, Wes and I visited Tim and his lovely wife, Linda, and family, several times. Barbara's boyfriend was Danny Snyder, and Marilyn Vance's boyfriend was Bob Bush. Marilyn was my best friend all through grade school and high school. Some of my other good friends in grade school, in addition to my niece Barbara Stayton, were Barbara Hahn, Barbie Shields, Carolyn Chapman, Susie Jones, and Sharon Wiekamp. (Lots of Barbaras!)

At the beginning of sixth grade, in September of 1949, my mother died of colon cancer. Less than four months later, in January, my dad died of liver cancer. More details regarding their deaths are in the next chapter.

I was in the seventh grade when I told Sis I couldn't read the words on the blackboard at school. She took me to an eye doctor, Dr. Kuhn, who checked my eyes and said I was *very* nearsighted. He fitted me with glasses, but my eyes kept getting worse. Every six months, he needed to change the prescription for my glasses. He had some tests run to see if I had something seriously wrong. The word circulated at school that I might have a brain tumor and could die. One girl cried, as she said she didn't want me to die. When all the tests came back negative, I gave the good news to my friends. Dr. Kuhn never charged me for any of my glasses or office calls, as he knew about the situation with my parents.

Shortly after I started wearing glasses, I began a bad habit of wrinkling my nose, evidently trying to keep my glasses in place. I wasn't even aware of what I was doing, so Sis and Johnny started tapping me on the nose. I finally stopped, but it took a while. In the meantime, some of my friends gave me the nickname Bunny.

Eighth grade was a busy time for me. I wrote for the school paper; I was on the winning team in intramural basketball; I played bells in the band; and I was chosen to play the lead in the drama club's play, to be performed for the entire school. However, it was getting too close to class day for our graduation from eighth grade, so the play was canceled. That's the closest I've ever gotten in having a big part in a play. On class day, Barbara and I sang a duet, and I also played a piano solo.

The DAR award was given every year to an outstanding student graduating from the eighth grade. It was awarded to a boy and a girl. When my name was called, I could barely walk up to the front of the auditorium to accept the medal. My legs were shaking so much I'm surprised I didn't fall. The DAR award represents honor—honesty, high principles, trustworthiness, loyalty, truthfulness, punctuality, moral strength and stability, cleanliness in mind and body; service—cooperation, kindliness, unselfishness, and true Americanism; courage—mental and physical, and determination to overcome obstacles; leadership—personality, ability to lead others, good sportsmanship, and responsibility; and scholarship—effort and application. My friends Marilyn Vance and Barbara Hahn received honorable mentions. Bob Bush received the award for the boys, and John Meengs received honorable mention.

CHAPTER 4
The Death of My Parents (1949 and 1950)

1949: Martha, Sis, Nancy, Jack, and Lewie (not in age order).

I was eleven years old when my mom died. I still remember every detail. She died September 6, 1949. In February of that same year, she discovered a lump in her stomach area. Surgery was immediately scheduled. She hugged me tightly, and we both cried as she left for the hospital. Her long brown fur coat was so warm and fuzzy as she held me in her arms. Neither of us wanted to let go! I was unaware of the seriousness of the operation. Because of my young age, my dad and older siblings all decided that I was too young to handle any bad news. However, I heard bits and pieces from conversations: "cut her open and sewed her back up...cancer...roots entwined around her heart...six months to live!" None of this was explained to me at the time. One day Nancy and I were sitting on the front lawn, and she said, "If I were to die, what would you do?" I said that I would cry! She asked this same question about others in the family, and I responded the same. Then she said, "What if Mom were to die?" I said, "I would cry and cry and cry." She never said anymore.

All of our family got together for Easter at Sis and Johnny's house. Pictures were taken of the entire family, of Mom and Dad, and the five siblings.

Mom got sicker and sicker. Sis, Johnny, and Barbara moved in with us, and Sis took care of Mom. She was moved from her upstairs bedroom to the downstairs guest bedroom to take better care of her. This was in 1949, and there was no chemo or radiation given to people with cancer. No one was telling me anything, but I heard snippets of conversations from people. They looked at me and said, "You poor thing." In June of that same year, 1949, my dad became sick and went to the hospital for surgery. I heard, "He has the same thing." (My mom had colon cancer, and my dad had liver cancer). When our next-door neighbor asked me how the surgery had gone for my dad, I said, "He has the same thing as Mom." She

Spring of 1949: The last picture of Mom and Dad before they died.

said, "Oh, no!" I knew then it was serious! Mom lost a lot of weight during her illness. She weighed fifty pounds when she died. I don't remember my dad losing weight. He was already pretty thin.

During this time, I wondered what was going to happen to me if my parents passed away. I heard some people tell Sis that they wanted to adopt me. Since none of my family told me anything, this was a worry for me.

When the time came, Sis and Johnny took me in and raised me. My brother Lewie wanted me to stay with them also, which I did one summer. I also went on vacation with Lewie and Alene to the Wisconsin Dells. I didn't have to worry after all about who was going to take care of me.

Previous to their passing, everyone was praying diligently for my parents. Sis sent Barbara and me to church camp in Shipshewana, Indiana, and all the girls were praying for Mom and Dad. I really felt God was going to heal them. Barbara and I also were taken to Champaign, Illinois, where we stayed a week or more with Uncle Clyde and Aunt Mable. Sis then sent me to Alene's sister Irene's farm in Niles, Michigan, so I wouldn't be at home when Mom died. I was doing some ironing for Irene when she received a phone call and said, "Oh, I'm sorry." It was my brother Lewie, and he told her he'd be there shortly to tell me about Mom and take me home. When Lewie arrived, he sat down with me and told me what I already knew, that Mom had died. I rode home in silence, but I didn't cry. The entire family was lined up at the back door like a reception committee to greet me when we walked into the house. They each hugged me, and when I got to my sister Nancy, I lightly punched her in the stomach and started crying.

The next few days were a blur—receiving friends, spending time at the funeral home, greeting callers, and seeing out-of-state relatives. I remember Uncle Orla, Mom's brother, being at the funeral home. I was wearing a two-piece red suit, and he criticized me for wearing something so bright and cheerful. He also told me he didn't believe we would recognize each other in heaven. Even though he was a pastor, I didn't agree with him.

Mom's funeral was held at First Christian Church in Mishawaka. The funeral was very sad for me. My mother was very loved, so there were a lot of people who attended. I remember sitting in the front pew with Sis next to me and Barbara on her other side. Our pastor had a beautiful voice, and he sang one of Mom's favorite songs, "My Father Watches Over Me." I love that song to this day and will have it sung at my funeral. Reverend Hayes read many Bible scriptures and talked about Mom's deep faith. He also mentioned that she was an excellent leader but also a good follower. He then read the words from the song "Trust and Obey." Over five hundred people attended Mom's funeral. The hardest part for me was when they lowered the casket into the open grave at the cemetery and filled it with dirt. Everything was so final!

I'd like to quote what the church paper, *The Behold*, said about Mom: "We are deeply grieved over our loss of Mrs. Ethel Endicott, but we rejoice in knowing that she is now home with the Lord. Mrs. Endicott served her Lord conscientiously and well, never failing to respond to a call of service for her church. We shall remember her pleasing personality and winning smile. Her simple trust and undying faith in the Lord Jesus, through the days of her illness, was a testimony to the glory of God." Beautiful words! (I don't remember this, but I found this copy in Sis's scrapbook.)

Mom died on September 6, 1949, the day before school started. Barbara and I had new dresses for the first day of school, so we went ahead and went to school, since it was a half day and a get-acquainted day. We were in the sixth grade. When we went home from school that day, we didn't go back to my house. We went to Sis and Johnny's house. Everything of mine and Nancy's and Jack's had been moved over. I really missed my house. I would lie in bed at night and walk through the house room by room in my mind, remembering every light switch, heat register, et cetera. Then I would cry myself to sleep. No one ever knew that. Sis often tried to console me and would put her arms around me for comfort. I withdrew from her and told her I did not like that. I grew very cold and standoffish. Years later, I finally learned to be more affectionate with my family.

Jack was twenty years old and had planned on getting married to Phyllis Hartstein on October 29, which was shortly after Mom died. They felt that Mom would have wanted them to go ahead and have the wedding as planned. They were married at Coalbush Evangelical United Brethren Church in Mishawaka. Phyllis's dad owned many acres of farmland with a small two-bedroom home on the property on Ireland Trail in Mishawaka. Jack and Phyllis moved into this home where they raised their three sons. I remember one winter day when I spent several days with Jack and Phyllis. Phyllis and I walked through the forest between their house and her father's farmhouse after a huge snowfall. Seeing the untouched snow glisten on the trees was one of the most beautiful winter scenes I have ever seen.

Prior to Mom's death, Sis and Johnny had their two-bedroom home remodeled in order to accommodate us. They had the roof raised and a second story added with four more bedrooms and a bathroom. Nancy, Jack, Barbara, and I would all have our own bedrooms. Dad would stay downstairs. The upstairs addition wasn't quite finished, and there was no heat yet, when I started living there. I can remember getting dressed for school in bed under the covers!

Prior to Dad's death on January 10, 1950, he called all of us into his bedroom and said good-bye to us. He said, "Ethel is calling me. It's time to go." Nancy was supposed to be the installing officer for Rainbow Girls that night, so she, Barbara, and I went to the Rainbow installation. When we arrived home, Dad had died, and his body had been taken away. His funeral was also held at First Christian Church and burial at St. Joseph Valley Memorial Park. His favorite song, "The Old Rugged Cross," was sung. He was honored for belonging to the Masonic Lodge, Scottish Rite, White Shrine; the South Bend Transportation Club; and the New York Central System Square Club. There were 350 people who attended, and thirty-one baskets or sprays of flowers were given.

For years, I've said that the first thing I'm going to inquire of God is for what purpose he took Mom and Dad when I was so young, and Mom was only fifty-four years old and Dad was fifty-seven. However, their deaths did not hinder my faith at the time. I knew without a shadow of a doubt that they were in heaven with the Lord. I did miss them terribly and cried myself to sleep many nights. As I've matured, both in age and spirituality, I've stopped asking why and have been content to claim the promise of Romans 6:28: "And we know that in all things God works for the good of those who love him, who have been called according to his purpose" (NIV). I feel that I am a stronger person and a stronger Christian from this experience. I can counsel and help others going through a similar situation.

I don't know if Mom and Dad had a last will and testament or not, but it was up to Sis to take care of everything. I was given Mom's gold engagement ring with a solitary diamond. Sis later gave me Mom's wedding band. I put both rings on a gold chain and wear them as a necklace. I also eventually received Mom's wedding dress, which I have displayed on a mannequin (size extra petite) in our bedroom. About a year or two prior to her death, Mom ordered a complete set of red-and-white dishes. I thought they were beautiful, and I said I someday wanted a set just like them. After I was married, I got my wish, and Mom's dishes were given to me. I also have her china and some other antique dishes.

That next fall, Nancy left for William Jennings Bryan University in Dayton, Tennessee. Several of her friends from church were also attending there. She graduated from this school in 1954 and then entered nurse's training at Swedish American Hospital's School of Nursing in Rockford, Illinois.

That summer, 1950, Barbara and I boarded a Greyhound bus, and we traveled to Indianapolis to visit Mrs. Gladys McColgin. Her husband was the previous pastor at First Christian Church in Mishawaka. We stayed with her one or two weeks, and she took us various places, including the James Whitcomb Riley home and the Benjamin Harrison Home, both in Greenfield, Indiana. This may be why I like to visit old homes. They were quite interesting. Gladys had a neighbor girl, Ellen Bowers, who was a few years younger than we were. We had a good time playing with her. She had a storybook doll collection that I really liked. To this day, I like dolls and have a collection of them, although they're not storybook dolls. Gladys's cat had kittens, and we loved playing with them. I remember playing hide-and-seek with Ellen and Barbara. Barbara was "it," and Ellen and I hid in her coalbin in the basement. We ended up being filthy from the coal dust. Ellen's mom was not very happy with us!

Either that summer or the next, Sis and Johnny took Barbara and me on vacation to Niagara Falls in New York and Canada. The falls were beautiful. I remember wearing yellow raincoats as we walked under the falls. We had a motel nearby, and that night, I kept yelling that Barbara was pinching me. This kept up until Sis got out of bed to see what was going on. Barbara said that she wasn't pinching me, but something certainly was. Sis found a cricket in my pajama bottoms, which was doing all of the biting!

CHAPTER 5

My Teen Years

When Barbara and I were thirteen years old, we joined Rainbow Girls, a Masonic youth service organization that teaches leadership training through community service. My parents and Sis and Johnny were very involved in the Order of the Eastern Star and the Masonic lodge. In fact, Mom was the worthy high priestess of the White Shrine the year before she died, and Sis was an officer. (In order to join Rainbow Girls, one of your parents had to be in the Eastern Star or the Masonic lodge.) I held various stations within Rainbow Girls, and when I was sixteen, I was elected worthy advisor. I still have a mustard seed necklace that was given to me as a gift at my installation in 1954. That summer I attended the fourteenth annual Grand Assembly of the International Order of the Rainbow for Girls at Purdue University in West Lafayette, Indiana. I prepared and gave a report regarding our local chapter.

I was also in Blue Birds, then Camp Fire Girls, and then Horizon Club. Mrs. Smith, our Camp Fire leader, was having a chili cookout one Saturday, which I didn't sign up for because I didn't like kidney beans. When she found that out, she promised me she would make a small amount without the beans. I attended the cookout and enjoyed it. But I still do not like kidney beans!

Barbara and I were thirteen when Johnny finally consented to buy our first television set. Prior to having our own, we were all invited to Kenny and Phyllis Rea's home on Sunday evenings to watch *What's My Line*. We all sat in a dark room and watched the snowy picture. We held our breath, hoping we could read the person's line of work, as the picture was so poor. The closest TV station at that time was in Chicago, ninety miles away, and the reception was pretty bad. A year or so later, South Bend got their first TV station, and Sis and Johnny bought our first TV set. We could only get one channel, and at midnight the programs went off the air and the test pattern came on.

When Barbara and I were fifteen, Sis and Johnny went away for two or three nights, and we said we were old enough to stay by ourselves. We were of course given a lot of instructions as to what to do and not do. It was in the winter, and I remember Johnny telling us not to leave the front door open too long, as it could cause the furnace door in the basement to come open and possibly start a fire. Well, we took that to heart. When we went out the front door, we opened it just wide enough to squeeze through, as we didn't want to start a fire! (I don't think that's what he meant.) We were really scared one night, and we sat awake in our bed, afraid to go to sleep in case someone was in the house. We were glad when Sis and Johnny arrived back home. Maybe we weren't so brave after all!

At Christmastime, our entire family generally got together in the afternoon or evening on Christmas Day. I loved it when we were able to be together.

1954: Sis, Lewie, Jack, Nancy, and Martha

One summer, when Barbara and I were seventeen years old, Jack and Phyllis asked us to stay at their house and baby-sit my nephews, Larry and Gary. Larry was three years old, and Gary had just turned one. Jack and Phyllis were driving to Florida for two weeks with another couple. Phyllis's dad, Paw-Paw, stayed at night so we wouldn't be afraid. One morning Larry was in his high chair, and I went into another room for just an instant. I came back, and Larry had put his cereal bowl upside down on top of his head. Milk and cereal were running all down his face and body. That would teach me to walk away, if only for an instant!

Barbara and I were very lonely during those two weeks, as Jack and Phyllis lived in the country, and we didn't have a car to go anywhere. We listened to the record player quite a bit. I loved two of their records, "The Old Lamplighter" and "The Girl That I Marry," by Eddy Howard. I always dreamed of being "that girl." Our friend Marilyn came to visit one afternoon, and we brought one of Jack's baby lambs into the house so that Larry could pet it! (I don't know why we did that.)

We were anxious for Jack and Phyllis to come home. (Our excitement for the day was to walk across the road to the mailbox and pick up the mail.) We soon received a call from Jack, saying they had been in a terrible head-on collision in Florida, and Phyllis had a compound fracture of her right leg. She would have to stay in the hospital for a while. So we stayed with Larry and Gary a little longer until Jack and Phyllis arrived home a few weeks later. Phyllis had a huge cast on her right leg and was carried into the house on a stretcher. Gary cried, as he didn't recognize her and was afraid of the cast. Barbara and I stayed a little longer in order to help Phyllis.

Barbara and I loved the Chicago White Sox! Johnny used to take us to the games in Chicago. He had an aunt and uncle who lived in East Chicago, Indiana, and Uncle Arne often went with us to the games. Barbara and I knew all of the baseball statistics of our favorite players. My favorite players were Sherman Lollar, Billie Pierce, and Jim Riviera. Barbara's were Chico Carrasquel and Minnie Minosa. Sometimes Barbara and I stayed with Uncle Arne and Aunt Pauline for a week or so. Aunt Pauline taught us how to crochet. I remember Uncle Arne quizzing us about the state capitals. Whichever one of us got the correct answer first received a penny.

CHAPTER 6
High School Years— MHS (1952-1956)

We had many fads during our high school years. The girls wore poodle skirts, saddle shoes, and rolled socks. We were not allowed to wear slacks or shorts to school. Under the poodle skirts were crinoline slips. Hayrides were popular for dating, and we generally wore blue jeans with the pant legs rolled up. One year duck shoes were popular. We also wore small colored scarves tied around our necks.

During my high school years at Mishawaka High School (MHS), I kept very busy. I was second scholastically in my class of four hundred students all through high school. All my average grades at the end of the semester were A's. In one class, the teacher, Mr. Hill, didn't believe in giving an A for the first semester, so he gave everyone a C. I knew this might be a problem for my average grade. The next grading period, I got a B. He gave a final exam and said that this grade would mean a lot. He gave a hint that he might just ask for an outline of the entire book. So I memorized all of the chapter names in order, and when he asked us to outline the book for the test, I was able to do it. He gave me an A+, which brought my average to an A. I was the only one who had listened to his little hint about the test.

During my freshman year, my English teacher was Miss Ward. When I introduced myself in class, as everyone did, she said, "I've had all of your brothers and sisters in this class. I don't know what to expect from you, as the girls were very smart and the boys were very ornery!" (Lewie didn't graduate, and Jack passed his last class with a D- with a circle around it. That meant he almost didn't graduate!)

I was involved in book club, Spanish club and commercial club. When I was a freshman in the book club, we chartered a bus and drove to Chicago to see the play *The King and I*. That was a nice experience. During my junior year, I was news editor and feature editor of the school newspaper, the *Alltold*. The *Alltold* received its eighth consecutive All-American rating that year. During my senior year, I became the editor of the newspaper. Every year on April 1, we put out a paper called *The Can't Tell*, where we wrote crazy articles about escalators and elevators being built, or that spring break was canceled. Speaking of elevators, when I was a freshman, Jack told me I had to buy elevator tickets from the seniors. I kept looking for the elevator but never found it. I'm glad I didn't buy any tickets for it! I was inducted into the National Honor Society and Quill and Scroll honor society for journalism. We put on a play, *Little Dog Laughed*, in our junior year and *Charley's Aunt* in our senior year. I was cochair of the properties committee.

When Barbara and I turned sixteen, we wanted to learn how to drive and get our learner's permit. Johnny did not want to teach us, as he said it made him too nervous. I signed up for driver's education class in high school, but it was full until the next year. By the time I got my driver's license, I was seventeen. I think Barbara was also. Once in a great while, we were allowed to drive Johnny's 1952 Chevrolet. I remember one evening driving home from a Rainbow Girls meeting downtown, I thought I was so grown up! As I was leaving the brightness of the downtown area, I wondered why it was getting so dark. I had forgotten to turn on the headlights! That took me down a peg or two!

In my junior year, in 1955, MHS had a very good basketball team. You've probably heard of "Hoosier hysteria" or "Hoosier madness." We were on top in our division in the regular season. We beat Riley in the sectional game. We beat Nappanee for the regional title. We thought we were going all the way to state. We played two games in the semifinals in Elkhart. MHS beat Hartford City in the first game but lost to Fort Wayne North in the second game. We were only one game away from going to state! The next day the *South Bend Tribune* said, "MHS won like champions and lost like champions." We had not gone this far since 1939, sixteen years earlier. Earlier, after winning the sectional game, the team of ten young men went to one of the local churches and knelt down, and each one thanked God for their blessings. I liked that about our team! Our mascot was the caveman, and our colors were maroon and white.

The following poem was in the *Mishawaka Enterprise* newspaper and was written by James Tansey from Beiger Junior High School:

The Finest Team

Watch, dear fans, and you will see

The Cavemen perform on your TV;

They're the finest team we've ever seen

And we hope they're the winner
of the Sweet Sixteen.

On the twelfth day of March in '55,

Hardly a booster is alive

Who'll forget that famous day and year

And the maroon-clad team
for whom we cheer.

Leroy, Pat, George, and Gene,

Bruce and Carl form quite a team;

Then there are Acrey, Ankney, and Skip,

And "Moose" Lechlitner is
there to prevent a slip.

If that's not enough to make us tough,

There are thousands of fans to call the bluff

Of Hartford City and North Side Fort Wayne,

And cheer our Cavemen on to fame.

*1956: Martha and Bill
prior to the prom*

I was faculty editor of the school year-book, the *Miskodeed*, and I took pictures of all of the faculty for the book. I finished my section early, so I helped the editor with her job. The word "Miskodeed" is an Indian word meaning spring blossom, and it is mentioned in Longfellow's poem "Song of Hiawatha." One day I was called out of one of my classes by the journalism teacher. I was told that I was a winner of the South Bend Press Club's contest for high school journalists. I had written an editorial for the newsletter about our rivalry with Central High School in South Bend. I was given a nice leather briefcase (still have it today). I was also in the band all four years of high school. I played the bells and especially enjoyed being in the marching band for all of the football games. We also had several band concerts during the year. I attended the senior prom with Bill Kelsey. In my senior year, I was voted the girl most likely to succeed.

I mentioned earlier in the book that Sis and Johnny had added four bedrooms and a bath onto their house. Since Jack had gotten married and no longer lived there, and Nancy had gone to college in Tennessee, we only needed one bedroom for Barbara and me. Sis and Johnny converted two of the bedrooms into a living room and kitchen and rented out the one-bedroom apartment. We had some very nice tenants rent the apartment through the years. Eventually it was mainly rented to schoolteachers from the high school, since we lived only two blocks away. That was a nice perk for Barbara and me, as we had an "in" with the teachers.

1956: Martha and Barbara on graduation day

Upon graduation from high school in 1956, I was named salutatorian of the class of nearly four hundred students. I gave a speech on class night, and I was scared to death! I asked if I could have a podium so I could hang onto it, and they said no, I could only have a microphone on a stand. I made it through the speech, but I'm sure my knees and legs were shaking! Our theme song was "Moments to Remember." My speech was about our many memories during our four years at MHS. I interspersed the names of some of the current popular songs within my speech. At class night, I was also awarded the typing award for being the fastest typist—120 words per minute. I can still type pretty fast today. Playing the piano helped keep my fingers nimble.

I was awarded a four-year scholarship to Ball State University in Indiana. However, I gave up the scholarship to get married instead. I've since regretted not going to college, but I ended up doing well in my banking career without the degree.

During the summer months between my junior and senior year, Sis helped me get a job at the First National Bank of Mishawaka, where she worked. I was in the bookkeeping department and really enjoyed it. I also worked after school during my senior year. This banking experience helped me a lot in later life.

Starting in 1954, when I was sixteen, I played the organ every other Sunday for the morning worship service at our church, Immanuel Baptist Church. I also directed the Christmas program for the youth group in 1955. During Youth Sunday, I was asked to give the sermon. The previous week, I'd overheard two women talking in the church lobby about a lady who had cancer and was dying. One of them said they needed to pour on the prayers for the sick lady. The second lady replied that she was too far gone for even God to heal her! That's when I decided to speak on faith. I'm sure I directed my sermon to them! I wish I had kept the sermon, but I cannot find it. (I usually keep everything!) I would have liked to read it today. I was in the adult church choir, and I was asked to sing a solo part in the choir's anthem one Sunday morning. I sang the solo, but I was shaking so much that I said I would never sing a solo again, and I never have!

That same year, my sister Nancy was working in Chicago for a publishing company. She asked me if I wanted to come there during my Christmas break and stay with her. I took the South Shore train, and she picked me up in Chicago. I went to work with her, and I earned a little money by helping out with their mailings. I was sixteen years old.

When I was seventeen years old, my best friend, Marilyn Vance, introduced me to Bill Kelsey, her cousin from Michigan. In fact, we went on a double date together. Marilyn knew I did not like to kiss a boy on the first date, but in spite of that, Marilyn and her boyfriend, Ken, drove to a nice parking spot for "making out." I honestly can't remember if I let Bill kiss me or not on that first date, but we ended up liking each other and wrote letters back and forth. Bill enlisted in the US Air Force and visited me whenever he could. He always hitchhiked from his base to Mishawaka and stayed with his grandma Vance in South Bend.

Bill had a large extended family in Mishawaka, South Bend, Bremen, and Fort Wayne, Indiana. I enjoyed his family, which included three uncles, two aunts, and many cousins. Grandma Vance, whose husband had died many years ago, always seemed to have enough food on hand to feed any of the family who dropped in to visit. I remember her cooking fried chicken and all the trimmings. Before retiring, she was a cook at Robertson's Department Store in South Bend, so she prepared wonderful-tasting meals.

Bill and I became engaged in my senior year of high school. Bill wanted to get married in secret before I graduated, as he would receive extra money from the Air Force for his spouse. He said we could save the extra money for later. We had the necessary blood tests and marriage license and were in the car on our way to Michigan, where the minimum marriage age was eighteen. As I just didn't feel right about it, I told Bill I couldn't go through with it! I'm not sure anyone else ever knew about it except Marilyn and Ken, who were driving us to Michigan.

CHAPTER 7
Marriage and Babies

I graduated from high school in June 1956, and Bill and I were married on October 13, 1956. We were married at Immanuel Baptist Church in Mishawaka. My sister-in-law, Phyllis, helped me pick out my wedding dress. It was a powder blue (my favorite color) cotton lace street-length dress over satin with back panels and a slim skirt. I wore a blue crescent-shaped half hat with shoulder-length veil. I carried Mom's white Bible with sweetheart roses on top. My oldest brother, Lewie, walked me down the aisle and gave me away. Barbara was my maid of honor, and Sharon Wiekamp sang. A reception was held in Fellowship Hall after the wedding.

My brother Lewie helped Bill and me purchase a 1949 Chevrolet, which we drove to Michigan a few days later. Bill was stationed at Kinross Air Force Base in Sault Ste. Marie, Michigan, where we rented a one-bedroom furnished apartment for sixty-five dollars a month. Lewie and Alene had given us a small portable television set for our apartment. The nearest TV station was Sault Ste. Marie in Canada, so we watched Canadian TV while we were there.

I remember some funny things that happened during our first year of marriage, although they weren't so funny at the time. I was a new bride and not very accomplished in cleaning, cooking, or doing laundry. The only meal that I knew how to cook was ham steak. There was only one problem—Bill did not like ham! He liked deep-fried shrimp, and I was cooking the shrimp in hot oil when the oil caught on fire. I yelled for Bill to come, and he carried the flaming pan out through the house and threw it outside the front door into the snow. I remember his eyebrows were singed, but nothing caught on fire along the way. The pan got pretty bent up!

I was trying to do the laundry one morning. The washing machine was an old one, with a wringer, and I did not realize I had to lock down the wringer. The clothes kept coming out really wet. Hanging out the sopping-wet sheets in the wind and snow was not a fun thing to do!

We soon started looking for a different apartment, as the landlord wanted to raise our rent. We found a very nice apartment for fifty dollars a month, so we moved. We were really hurting for money, so I got a job at the local dime store, working in the notions department. I made sixty-seven cents an hour. I worked at Christmastime, and I told my boss I would only work through the end of the year. He must not have remembered or didn't pay attention, as the end of the year came, and when I reminded him that it was my last day, he looked so surprised! I had been helping with the inventory the last week or so, and he asked if I could stay until it was done. I agreed but told him that would be all.

I made an appointment for an interview at First National Bank. It was twenty-five degrees below zero that morning, and our car wouldn't start. I had to walk to the bank for my interview, crossing a bridge on the way. Everything was covered up on me except my eyes! The bank manager didn't like to hire wives of servicemen, as the husbands so often were transferred out. Because I had experience, though, I was hired as a bookkeeper.

Shortly after I started working at the bank, I became pregnant. I didn't want my boss to find out, since I had just started the job. As I filed checks in the drawers located in a stuffy vault, I made many trips to the restroom because of morning sickness. Actually I was sick all day, not just in the morning.

After working at the bank for several months, Bill was transferred to Chanute AFB in Rantoul, Illinois. I wasn't allowed to go with him as it was a temporary assignment. I quit my job at the bank and returned to Mishawaka, staying with Sis and Johnny (in my old bedroom).

My doctor at the base had told me I could gain as much weight as I wanted, since I was so thin. I had already gained forty-five pounds by the time I went to the new doctor in Mishawaka. She said my maximum weight gain should be no more than fifty pounds, so I had to watch what I ate during the last few months. When I was three weeks away from my due date, I took the bus to the doctor for my checkup. I was having some pains, but the doctor said it was just false labor and not to worry about it. I took the bus back home, having complete faith in the doctor. My friend Marilyn had a baby shower for me at her house that evening. I was still having the pains, but I played the games and took part with everyone else. After the party, I went home and went to bed. At midnight my water broke, and I called Sis to come and help me. She called the doctor (who was very surprised), and Sis and Johnny took me to South Bend Orthopedic Hospital. Kim Jeanine Kelsey was born at 4:00 a.m. on September 25, 1957, three weeks early.

About noon that same day, I started feeling strange. The nurse brought me my lunch, and in order to eat it, I had to actually "tell" my hand to pick up the food and put it in my mouth. Nothing was automatic like it should have been. I also had a bad headache. Suddenly I felt my head, body, and neck jerk to the right so hard that I fell out of bed. I did not remember anything after that, but I had just experienced a grand mal seizure! In fact, I had two seizures. I foamed at the mouth and screamed and thrashed around. When I awakened, my sister-in-law Phyllis had come to visit. She asked me what was going on. I didn't know what had happened, but I was completely exhausted! I had shaken up the entire hospital. Bill surprised me and arrived that afternoon.

After Kim and I were discharged from the hospital, we stayed with Lewie and Alene. When Bill returned to Chanute AFB, Kim and I stayed with Sis and Johnny. Sis and Bill did not get along very well, so she preferred we stay elsewhere when he was home.

Kim was a beautiful baby. In fact, when we were still in the hospital, the nurses called her the "baby doll" of the nursery! She was a good baby also. When she was six weeks old, Bill was sent back to Kinross AFB in Sault Ste. Marie, Michigan. We packed up our things and all of the baby items and drove up to Northern Michigan. A scary thing happened on the way. It was nighttime, and I was driving in order to let Bill sleep. I hit a patch of ice on the narrow road, and I panicked and hit the brakes, exactly what I shouldn't have done! The car skidded off of the highway, narrowly missing several trees. I was screaming and praying. The screaming woke Bill up, and the praying worked! As I couldn't quit shaking, Bill drove the rest of the way. God was really watching over us that evening!

1958: Kim, 7 months old

We found a nice apartment where the landlady lived on the first floor and we lived on the second floor. She was like a grandmother to Kim and gave me some much-needed advice. Kim had her days and nights mixed up. Everyone told us not to ever give her a pacifier, but out of desperation, we did, and it took care of her sleeping through the night. When Kim was three months old, I had laid her on our big bed, in the middle so she wouldn't fall off. She hadn't even rolled over yet. I stepped out of the room for a few minutes and then heard a thump and a loud wail! She had rolled over several times and fallen on the floor. I was very shaken up and called our doctor right away. He asked me some questions and said it sounded as if she was okay, but I needed to settle down and take it easy! I was already in tears.

That following March we drove to Arizona to visit Bill's parents, who had recently moved to Phoenix from Michigan. Bill's parents told us to go through Flagstaff and Oak Creek Canyon. We looked at the map and thought it would be faster and shorter to go another way. Wrong! At midnight, we were driving through snow in Salt River Canyon. We hoped we were through with the narrow, twisting road but discovered that we were at the bottom and had to climb up out of the canyon. It was pitch black and still snowing! We arrived at Bill's parents in the middle of the night. Bill's mom said, "I told you to come through Flagstaff! Now you know why!"

They lived in a nice mobile home near Twenty-Seventh Avenue and Northern. The weather was wonderful, and one

1958: Kim, ten months old

afternoon we sat Kim on a blanket on the front lawn and enjoyed the sunshine. They took us to visit many places, and we fell in love with Arizona. I remember them taking us on the Apache Trail in the East Valley, a narrow, winding dirt road in the mountains. Bill's mom pointed out every car that had ever plunged over the side. We even stopped, got out of the car, and looked at the wreckage below! In spite of that, we still enjoyed Arizona.

I soon found out I was pregnant again. Bill was transferred to another base, so Kim and I went back to Mishawaka. It was August and time for the baby to be born. Bill took a month's leave, and this time we stayed with Jack and Phyllis. Since Kim had come three weeks early, Bill came home a month before my due date. Ron took his time and came only one week early. Bill and I had a difficult time agreeing on a name. I wanted Kevin Keith Kelsey, but he reminded me that the initials KKK wouldn't be very appropriate. We both agreed on Robert, but Bill's mother reminded us that her ex-husband's name was Robert. At the last minute, we agreed on Ronald.

1958: Ron, two months old

Ronald David Kelsey was born on August 26, 1958, at the same hospital where Kim was born. The doctors and nurses remembered me from my previous seizures! This time the doctor gave me medicine to prevent another seizure, and I didn't have any problems. Kim was only eleven months old and didn't understand about this new baby in the house. The first time she saw him, she slapped him in the face! After that first encounter, she was pretty good with him. Now we had two babies, both in diapers, both in high chairs, and both in baby cribs. It was like having twins. Ron was always hungry (just like today). He would drink eight ounces of milk and want more. Then he'd spit up most of it!

Bill was soon discharged from the Air Force, and we moved to South Bend, the twin city of Mishawaka. Bill got a job at a Standard Oil service station on the Indiana Toll Road, thanks to my brother Lewie, who worked for Standard Oil. We rented a home on Maple Lane in South Bend, not too far from Bill's job.

An incident I remember too well happened when I was at Sis and Johnny's house and had borrowed Barbara and Jim's red-and-white Chevrolet. I was just starting to back out of Sis and Johnny's driveway when I saw Johnny coming home. I tried to back out of the driveway so he could get in, but in the meantime, he stopped for some reason. I backed into the side of his car! Thank goodness Johnny was not hurt, but I felt terrible! I had just messed up two cars that belonged to other people. Fortunately the only thing that needed to be replaced on Jim's car was a broken taillight. Johnny's insurance covered the damage to his car.

We were still attending Immanuel Baptist Church in Mishawaka. Kim was dedicated to the Lord on July 20, 1958, by Reverand Edward Finley. I taught Bible school the summer of 1959, so I took both Kim and Ron with me. I put Ron in the nursery, and Kim went to one of the classes, as she was older and very well behaved. They had planned to give her an award for being the youngest participant, but she got the measles the last day and could no longer attend. We also dedicated Ron at church in a ceremony officiated by Reverend Finley.

Barbara and Jim were building a home on the outskirts of Mishawaka and were living in the garage until the rest of the house was built. The kids and I were visiting them when Ron, about nine months old, pulled over onto himself a gallon-sized pan of used cooking oil. Fortunately it was not hot, but he and the cement floor were a greasy mess!

CHAPTER 8

Arizona, Here We Come!

Bill lost his job at the service station in December of 1959, and we thought it was a good time to relocate to Arizona. We gave our notice to the landlord and sold our appliances and furniture. Since it was close to Christmas, Sis and Johnny had us over and gave Christmas gifts to Kim and Ron. Sis was not happy to see us go.

As a side note, Kim and Ron were called Kimmy and Ronnie for years. However, it's difficult for me to refer to them now as Kimmy and Ronnie!

We had an old Plymouth at the time; we packed it up, and with $150 in our pockets, we started out for Phoenix. This was before car seats and seat belts, so the kids had free rein in the back seat (on top of tons of clothing and household items). Kim was two years old and Ron was one. This time we went through Oak Creek Canyon instead of Salt River Canyon! It was much easier, faster, and safer! We arrived at Bill's parents' home a couple days before Christmas.

We hadn't purchased any Christmas gifts for the kids, so on Christmas Eve, Bill and I went to Walgreens and bought a doll and rocking chair for Kim and a red windup car and wagon for Ron. On Christmas Day, the little boy next door came over and sat on Ron's car and broke it. (It wasn't meant to be sat on, as it was only about eighteen inches long.) So much for his Christmas gift!

Bill's parents, Ralph and Edna Kelsey, were retired and now lived in a home at Thirteenth Avenue and Indian School in Phoenix. The kids called them Grandma and Baba. They told us we could stay with them until Bill found a job. He looked and looked and was having trouble finding anything suitable. I decided to job hunt too, since I had banking experience.

I began by applying for a job at Valley National Bank. They didn't want to hire me until Bill got a job, as they were concerned we might return to Indiana. I told them that was why I wanted a job—so we didn't have to go back! I then applied at The Arizona Bank. I was too honest and told them since I had two small children, I just wanted to work for a short time. Doug Reutter, who interviewed me, said they would not hire me because I didn't want to work very long. I was just getting up from the chair when I said, "Do you have anything on a part-time or temporary basis?" He said, "Sit back down. We do have something that might interest you." He called A. W. Cornelsen, the manager at the Stockyards branch, and he said I could start there and probably work for six weeks until they hired someone permanently.

I started working at the Stockyards branch at 5001 East Washington in Phoenix in February 1960 in the bookkeeping department. I ended up staying there for eleven years! The manager hired me on a permanent basis in April of that same year, 1960. I've always kidded my original interviewer, Doug Reutter, asking him if I stayed long enough on the job!

In the meantime, Bill got a job working for Dydee Service, which was great, as we were furnished with free, clean diapers each week. With two babies in diapers, that was a real bonus! Ironically, the day I started working at The Arizona Bank, Valley National Bank called and wanted to hire me.

We were still living with Bill's parents, but there were some problems between us. When I first met Baba, he kept kidding me, and we got along great. One day Bill had punished Ron for doing something wrong, and Bill told him he had to sit on the couch for fifteen minutes. Baba soon told Ron he could get down. Bill got mad and told him Martha didn't like that! (I hadn't said a word.) After that, Baba would not speak to me or even look at me. Bill's mother said Ralph had some emotional problems. However, after he threatened us, we moved into a furnished rental home on Garfield Street in an old part of Phoenix. My sister Nancy had surprised us and moved to Arizona from Chicago to work in a nearby hospital. She moved in with us and watched the kids during the day and worked at the hospital at night. She slept when the kids took their naps. Prior to her coming, Bill's mother had watched the kids while we went to work. Both Kim and Ron had beautiful curly hair.

When Ron was two years old and still had the curls, many people mistook him for a girl. Bill's mother said, "It's time to get his hair cut!" Bill took him to the barbershop for his first haircut.

Things got a little better between us and Baba, as he and Bill's mother asked us if we would manage a set of five furnished rental apartments that they owned on Fifth Avenue. We said

1960: Kim 3 years old and Ron 2 years old

we would, and we moved into one of the two-bedroom apartments. We lived there for a year and met some nice neighbors. There was a nice grassy area in the front where Kim and Ron could play outside. Ron fell one day and came screaming into the house, blood pouring down his face. I panicked and didn't know what to do. Our neighbor Irene Clark, who had two older boys, just took over and knew exactly how to handle it. Irene and I became good friends after that.

In September of 1961, we purchased a three-bedroom home at 325 East Fillmore Street in Tempe. It was in North Tempe, just a couple blocks south of the Scottsdale border. We paid $11,000 for it, and our monthly payment was ninety-six dollars per month. Kim was four at the time, and Ron was three. We had to buy furniture for the entire house, including beds for all of us. Little by little we settled in.

I loved going to carnivals and going on the rides. A local carnival came to a nearby shopping center, and I took the kids. As we rode the Tilt-A-Whirl, Ron screamed so loudly that the operator stopped the ride to let us off. One of the vendors gave Kim a large stuffed pink teddy bear. I tried my best (and also used up all my grocery money) trying to win a bear for Ron. I was unable to win one for him. I'm sure the vendor knew when he gave Kim the bear that a "compassionate" mother would spend money to get the second child a stuffed animal. It worked for him, as he got all my money!

When Kim and Ron were finally out of diapers, the three of us took a train from Phoenix to Chicago, where Sis and Johnny were planning to pick us up. We had a choice of traveling two nights and one day or two days and one night. I decided to get on the train at night, as the kids would be tired and fall asleep. Wrong! They were so excited when we boarded the train at midnight that they stayed awake most of the night! I kept trying to keep them quiet, as others were sleeping. When we arrived in Chicago, I was trying to juggle an overnight train case and a large paper shopping bag full of toys and extra clothes while holding onto Kim and Ron's hands. Then, horror of horrors, the paper bag broke, and everything spilled out! I had given Kim (four years old) the train case to carry, and she was visibly struggling with it. Two wonderful people helped me: one man carried the train case, and a lady gave me an extra bag to put the spilled items in. As I was walking about a mile to the depot, I spotted Johnny coming toward me. He had talked the people in charge at the train depot into letting him come and help me. Believe me, the trip was quite an ordeal!

1959: Ron the Cowboy   *1960: Ron the Sailor 2 years old*

1961: Ron the Fireman 3 years old

*1962: Ron the Fisherman
4 years old*

CHAPTER 9
Kim and Ron's Early Years

Kim was now five years old and soon started kindergarten at Supai Elementary School, which was actually in Scottsdale, although we lived in Tempe. Sis and Johnny had just come to visit from Indiana. I took Kim to school before I went to work, and Johnny met her and walked her home after school. He said it was a good thing he was there, as she had started walking the opposite way. Ron started kindergarten the following year, and Kim was able to help him. She was very protective of her little brother, even though he was the same size as she was and maybe even a little bigger. Many people thought they were twins. One day I picked up Ron's metal lunch box to clean it out, and there was a dead bird inside! He had found it on his way home from school and thought it would be cool to keep it.

There was a small church, Parkway Baptist Church, about two blocks away, and I started attending there, along with my neighbor Sandra Timmons. Neither of our husbands wanted to go with us, so we took the kids, and Sandra and I sat together. I soon started teaching first grade in Sunday school, joined the choir, and later played the piano and/or organ for congregational singing. One Sunday morning, at the end of the service, I tried to quietly walk to the piano during the closing prayer. My foot had gone to sleep and was like rubber. I could not walk on it at all. When the pastor finished his prayer, he looked at me as if to say, "Why aren't you coming to play the piano for the closing song?" I kept rubbing my ankle so that he could see that I couldn't walk.

Sandra started babysitting Kim and Ron after school. She did this for several years. Sandra and Carl had three children at the time: Jennifer, Stacy, and Steve. They later had twins, Todd and Amy. We all became very good friends, even after they moved to South Tempe. We're still best of friends today.

After working at Dydee Service, Bill got a job with Coca-Cola, where he worked for several years. We were able to get all of the soda pop that we wanted at a discount. Then he started working at Salt River Project. I was still working at The Arizona Bank, Stockyards branch.

We became good friends with some of Bill's coworkers and their wives, and we all went camping a lot at a nice spot north of Payson. We had a pickup truck with a camper shell on the back, and we had an icebox and a stove built in the back. Our family could all sleep in the back plus have a few conveniences. The other couples had children also, so Kim and Ron had a great time camping. Dean and Clara Holderman had five children, and they became very good friends of ours. We spent a lot of time together and all went on vacation one summer to Yellowstone National Park. We also camped one night at Jackson Hole, Wyoming. I got eaten up by mosquitoes! I must have had sixty bites on my legs and arms. I was an itchy mess!

Kim belonged to the Girl Scouts along with her best friend, Babette, whose mother was the Girl Scout leader. The girls often went up north camping. I generally went along and hauled some of the equipment in our pickup truck. One time Bill and Ron went also. I volunteered to be the "cookie mom" during the Girl Scout cookie sales campaign. We had boxes of cookies stacked all over the living room.

Dean and Clara's dog had puppies, and we decided to get one of them for Kim and Ron as a surprise for Christmas. The puppy was a German shepherd and collie mix and was so cuddly and cute. We left the puppy overnight with our neighbors Carl and Sandra Timmons. We put a note on the Christmas tree that Santa had a surprise for Kim and Ron at Carl and Sandra's. On Christmas morning, we took Kim and Ron across the street, and they found the puppy. We named her Princess.

Kim asked me to make a dress for her when she was seven or eight years old. She informed me that all the other girls had mothers who made their clothes. We went to the fabric store, and Kim picked out a pattern and pink-and-white-checked fabric. (As you may remember, I didn't get my mother's talent for sewing!) It took me so long to make the dress that when I tried it on her, she had already outgrown it! She didn't ask me after that to sew anything else for her.

A few years later, Kim, Ron, and I had taken the train back to Indiana to visit family. When we returned, the kids were so anxious to see our dog, Princess. Bill picked us up in Flagstaff at the train station, and we were eating lunch at a restaurant when Bill informed us that he had given Princess to the dog pound. You could have heard a pin drop! We couldn't believe it, and the kids cried. The next day I called the pound and was told that Princess had been adopted out. We were all so disappointed. Bill said that Princess was missing us so much she kept trying to get out of the backyard. He was afraid she might hurt herself, and he didn't have time to take care of her, as he had meetings to attend at work.

It may have been on that same trip to Indiana that Barbara, Nancy, and I, along with our children, all stayed at Sis and Johnny's house in Mishawaka while they went on vacation. It was summertime, and the apartment was vacant, so several of us slept in the apartment. We had such a great time together. There were six children, as Barbara's third child, Doug, hadn't been born yet. The kids all had fun playing in the apartment as if it were their house. Sis had left all sorts of notes for us, both informational and also things to do while they were gone. One note we could not figure out. A note on top of a stack of paper plates said, "Savings is in the refrigerator." We looked high and low in the fridge, hoping to find some money, which we never did. When they returned, the first thing we asked Sis was what that note meant. She laughed and said that was a note for the employees in the savings department at the bank to look in the refrigerator for their snacks that day! We could have used some savings, as the plumbing got clogged while they were gone, and we had to call Roto-Rooter. Tree roots had completely clogged the toilet, and with nine people there at the time, that was disastrous! None of us had enough money to pay the plumber, but he said he could wait until Sis and Johnny got home.

We had several dogs at different times. One was a beagle named Duke. He loved to dig, and he would quite often dig under our block fence in the backyard and run away. One time we couldn't find him for weeks. Kim was at school on the playground when someone pointed at a dirty, mangy dog. When he came up to Kim, she realized that it was Duke! She didn't claim him, but when I arrived home from work, Kim told me about it. We drove down to the school and found him. We brought him home and decided to give him to a good home where he had room to run around. I told Kim and Ron, "No more dogs!"

When Ron was nine years old, he brought home a tiny little dog that was about as big as a rat, holding it in the palm of his hand. He said, "Mom, can I keep her? I'll take care of her." The neighbor boy's dog had just had puppies six weeks earlier in May 1967, and he was trying to find good homes for the pups. I reluctantly told Ron that he could keep her. We named her Peanuts. She was part dachshund and part terrier and had a shiny black coat. She later had puppies, and we kept one of them and named him Snoopy. He was ornery and kept running away, taking Peanuts with him. We finally gave him away to a good home. After Ron and Kim were on their own, Peanuts became my dog.

Ron and Martin, his friend next door, wanted twenty-gauge shotguns in order to hunt doves with Martin's dad. Many of our neighbors helped by paying them to mow their lawns and do odds and ends. After Ron and Martin earned

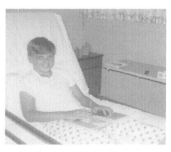

1970: Ron in the hospital

enough money, they purchased the guns. They had both gone hunting in the area with Gene, Martin's dad, when I received a call saying that Ron had been shot accidentally by Martin, who was aiming at a rabbit. Sis and Johnny were visiting and saw my face turn white. Gene said that Ron was at St.

Luke's Hospital but would be okay. We immediately dropped everything and went to the hospital. He was in the hospital for several days. The doctor removed some of the buckshot, but Ron still had several pieces in his body. One had grazed the side of his face, narrowly missing his eye. Another was in his chest and couldn't be removed. The neighbors felt bad, as they had helped the boys earn money to buy the guns. Ron was twelve years old at the time.

Kim and Ron were eight and nine years old when we bought our first color RCA television set. A salesman came to our house from a referral. He said if we would be able to refer others to him and they purchased a color TV, we would earn fifty dollars from each sale. We purchased the set for $800, if I remember correctly. The next day I tried to get some of my fellow workers to listen to the presentation when the assistant bank manager said it was illegal and they shouldn't get involved. Wow! That certainly shot me down! We ended up paying for the TV without any referral help, but it was worth it, as we really enjoyed watching the programs in color!

Bill and I bought a new car, a beautiful 1967 Chrysler, and I drove it to work the first morning. I was not used to power steering, and as I was turning right, I hit a sign, scraping the right side of the car. I was just sick (and scared to tell Bill). It was a Friday, and we generally visited our friends Norm and Irene Clark on Friday evenings. I waited to tell Bill about the scraping incident until we were showing Norm and Irene the new car. Bill was not happy!

CHAPTER 10
Marriage Problems and Divorce

Unfortunately Bill and I were having some marriage problems. We seemed to be drifting apart. Bill went out on Saturday nights, telling me he was playing poker with the guys. I never knew where he was going, and I told him one time that I really should know where he was in the event that I needed to get in touch with him for an emergency. (This was before cell phones.) He told me that he always picked up a friend, and the friend would tell him where they were going. Therefore he couldn't give me a phone number. I started feeling suspicious. He wasn't treating me very well, either, and was always saying he wanted a divorce, especially if I didn't go along with whatever he wanted. One evening he told me he didn't love me anymore. I cried most of the night, and in the morning before he went to work, I asked him if what he told me was true or if he was just joking. He said it was true. On Mother's Day, he informed me he was leaving to get an apartment somewhere (he wouldn't tell me where). Bill called me after about a month and asked me out for dinner. I went with him and begged him to come home! He did come home, but it was never the same again, and he never did tell me he loved me.

I was working at the bank with a young man named Murry Ginis. We both had the eleven o'clock lunch hour and ate together in the lunchroom, along with others. I was also training him to take my place as operations supervisor at the bank. Bob Hoadley, the branch manager, had asked us to attend a training session at another branch. We were returning when I told Murry that I needed to stay away from him, as I was beginning to have feelings for him. He replied, "I'm actually in love with you." My legs turned to rubber, and I didn't know what to say. We tried to stay away from each other, and I even changed my lunch hour to a later time. We still saw each other every day at work. We went to bank functions and saw each other there, sometimes sitting together, as Bill never went with me. We were *not* having an affair! I finally told Murry I had to try and make my marriage work with Bill. That evening at dinnertime, I must have cooked something that Bill did not like, as he threw the plate against the wall, spattering the food all over and breaking the plate. That certainly did not help with my decision to make our marriage work!

I soon told Bill I wanted a divorce and eventually told him about Murry. Bill said he had a girlfriend and was afraid I knew about her, and that's why I wanted the divorce. I didn't know, but I'd suspected it. I had the terrible job of telling Kim and Ron, and they were devastated. Kim was twelve and Ron was eleven. It was very hard on them. The divorce was final on June 6, 1969. We had been married for thirteen years. I only asked for fifty dollars per month for each child, which was the lowest the lawyer would let me go. Bill only paid it periodically, and then I called the court system and asked them to send him a letter. Ron asked me one time not to do that, as his dad just didn't have the money to pay it. I told Ron I used the support money for things like buying his and Kim's clothes. He still didn't want me to pursue it, so I didn't. Bill did not ask for them to visit him very much, and I told Bill several times that the kids would love to see him more often. He said it hurt him too much to see them for such a short time.

CHAPTER 11
A Marriage NOT Made In Heaven!

Murry left the bank and opened Gino's Pizza in Mesa. It was takeout and delivery only. It took about six months for it to become profitable, but he made it work, and he enjoyed the pizza business.

Murry and I started dating after the divorce. Murry was nine years younger than I. I turned thirty years old that year, and Murry was twenty-one. He was also Jewish. His parents, when they found out about me, asked him to move out of their house, since I wasn't Jewish. He then rented an apartment in Tempe. He had already met Kim and Ron, but they didn't particularly like him, and he didn't like them. We had a lot of strikes against us!

When I met and married Bill, I knew he was not a Christian, but I married him anyway. I thought I could win him over to Christ. It was ironic, as during our divorce, he became a Christian. He even took Kim and Ron to church with him, and Kim went forward and was baptized in his church. My friend Sandra said, "Didn't that bother you, since you took her to church all these years, and when she went with Bill, she went forward?" I answered that it didn't bother me, as the important thing was that she had made a decision for Christ.

When I was a teenager, I remember the pastor of our church preaching about not being unequally yoked with a nonbeliever and not to even date a non-Christian, as he/she would pull you down, not the other way around. He even illustrated it by standing on a chair, trying to pull someone up while a person below him tried to pull him down. Invariably he was pulled off the chair by the other person. However, I was in love with Murry and thought I could be a witness to him.

One funny incident that happened a year or so after we started going together was when Murry's parents had gone on a trip and needed a ride home from the airport when they returned. They couldn't locate Murry, so they called my house, asking if I knew where he was. Since Murry was working that night, I told them I could pick them up at the airport. I had met them one time, but they didn't remember what I looked like. I spotted them outside the terminal and introduced myself to them. Then I drove them home. I called Murry to let him know, and he couldn't believe it! That might have been the beginning of their acceptance of me.

We went together for two and a half years and then decided to get married in Las Vegas on January 15, 1972. I loved his family. He was the youngest of five brothers and sisters like I was. His family had finally accepted me, and all of the adults were present at the wedding. After the ceremony we had tickets to hear Tom Jones, and he sang a special song for us.

After we were married, we lived in my house for a few months. Then we bought a new house in September 1972 and had it built. It was a Suggs home in Tempe Royal Palms at 5932 South Newberry Street in Tempe. It was fun watching it being built and taking pictures of the various stages. We had an interior decorator come and help us with the furnishings and decorations. The first night we moved in, I got lost driving there from work. That was rather scary, as our phones weren't hooked up yet, and there were no address numbers on the front of the house. It was a four-bedroom home, so Kim and Ron each had their own room, plus Murry had an office. It was really a beautiful home. One summer when Kim and Ron went to Michigan to stay with Barbara and Jim for a month, we had a pool put in the backyard. We didn't tell Kim and Ron, and when they came home, we opened the curtains and showed them the new pool. They were really surprised and enjoyed swimming in it.

Christmas came, and Murry did not want us to put up a Christmas tree. I dreaded telling Kim and Ron, but they accepted it quite well. Ron said, "Mom, it's not worth fighting over or getting a divorce. It's just a Christmas tree." This was something we should have discussed before we got married, but when we were going together, Murry had taken me up north to chop down a Christmas tree. So I assumed he was okay with it now that we were married. Wrong! He said it was different—that tree was for my house, not his.

Murry did not want me to talk about my Christian beliefs with his family. Murry's sister Esther and her two children from California, Steven and Laura, were staying with us for two months. Laura had never seen a New Testament, and she asked me if she could read it. She was probably twelve years old. Of course I was happy for her to read it. I remember her telling her mom that the New Testament really made sense to her. Esther and I had some good conversations, and I told Esther I believed that when Jesus returned to earth for the

Second Coming, the Jews would finally believe in him as their Messiah. She thought that was interesting, and when the Ginis family was all together one day, she said in front of everyone, "Martha, tell the others what you believe about the Messiah!" Murry looked at me strangely, but I told them. Hopefully a seed was planted. Murry also did not want me to go to church. I watched church on TV, but it wasn't the same. After a while, when I drove by a church, I often just broke down and cried.

After three years of marriage, Murry told me he wanted a divorce (on paper only). Ron had gotten in with the wrong crowd and was quite often getting into trouble. The police had called me several times for something Ron had done. Murry was afraid of being sued and losing his pizza business. He said we could get remarried after Ron turned eighteen. He and Ron still weren't getting along. Murry and Kim were getting along well by now. I can remember sitting alone in the middle of our king-size bed, crying out to God. I had really messed up my life, and for the first time in my life, I no longer wanted to live. I would never have taken my life, but I was very unhappy and didn't know how to deal with my circumstances. I felt I was in a hopeless situation. Later God answered my prayer in ways I thought at the time would have been impossible.

In June of 1975, we sold our house, and Murry purchased a smaller one in Mesa. I bought a townhouse in the Lakes in Tempe at 5603 South Doubloon Court, Unit D. We hadn't told anyone about the divorce, which was final November 24, 1975, but of course it was in the newspaper. Murry's family saw it, and I received a call from Sheila, his sister-in-law, as we were planning on going on vacation with her and Murry's brother. So—the cat was out of the bag! Since Murry and I were still seeing each other, we did go on the vacation as scheduled with Harvey and Sheila.

I started attending Grace Community Church (GCC), since Murry and I were living separately. The first time I attended, I just sat and cried, as it was so good to be back in church. I had missed it so much!

In 1975 Kim graduated from Marcos de Niza High School in Tempe and received a scholarship to attend Arizona State University. She was ranked in the top 1 percent of her class. Kim enrolled at ASU that next fall. She was also engaged to Pat Harris, whom she'd met in high school. He had graduated a year earlier, and he was now in the US Army, stationed in Greece. They got married at Grace Community Church on April 10, 1976. Kim had asked her dad if he would walk her down the aisle, but he said no (because Murry and family would be there). Therefore Kim asked Murry. Three-year-old twins Amy and Todd Timmons were in the wedding. Kim and Pat's reception was held at the Camelback Inn. Pat returned to Greece shortly after the wedding. Kim finished her freshman year at ASU and then joined Pat in Greece.

After Ron turned eighteen in 1976, graduated from high school, and was on his own, Murry wanted to get married again. I remember thinking earlier that I would talk with him about it after his nephew's bar mitzvah in November. I was not going to remarry him, but I didn't want to spoil his nephew's bar mitzvah. However, Murry brought it up earlier that summer, and I told him I could not remarry him, as I wanted to do the Lord's will this time. He was devastated, and we both cried together.

Murry's sister Carol told me later that Murry was acting as if I had died and he was in mourning. He wouldn't go out or do anything, and he told them he wouldn't go to his nephew's bar mitzvah. He finally went, and they all cheered when he walked in. I had a chance to talk with Murry a few months later, as he was still trying to talk me into marrying him again. He said he saw something in me—a radiance he hadn't noticed before. I told him it was the Lord shining through me. I was joyful in spite of my circumstances. I told him how important Jesus was in my life and that I could no longer live without him. We talked a long time, and I hope I planted a seed in his heart.

Two years later Murry met a Jewish lady, liked her, and they got married in 1978. Ironically, she had two little girls from a previous marriage. At least they weren't teenagers! Several years later, Murry and his wife had two more children, both girls.

CHAPTER 12

Meeting Wes: An Engagement and Wedding (1977-1978)

It took me a year or two to get over Murry. Even though we had so many differences, I did love him very much. I remember getting down on my knees and praying that if God wanted me to stay single for the rest of my life, I would honor that. If he wanted a man to come into my life, then that was okay too. However, I would not even date anyone who was not a Christian. I had finally learned my lesson.

Grace Community Church was having a special outreach, which I was a part of. We wore buttons that said "I Found It." When people asked what we had found, we said, "I found Jesus." It was a good way to open a conversation about the Lord. I wore my button to work the next day, and one of my employees, Peggy Stively (now Wheatley), asked me what I had found. When I answered her, I told her where I went to church. She said she wanted to take her boys to Sunday school, and could she and the boys go with me? At that time I was only going to church, not Sunday school, but another good friend, Anne Strivings, kept asking me to come to her singles' class. I told Peggy we could all go to Sunday school together the next Sunday.

Peggy and I took the boys to their classes, and we attended the singles' class, where we met a lot of new people. A man by the name of Wes Pierce walked in, and I thought to myself, "Hmm, he's nice looking." Then my friend Anne, who was president of the class, was assigning prayer partners to each person by drawing names. Wes's and my name were drawn as partners. I thought, "Okay, God is playing Cupid!" Wes called me from time to time with special prayer requests. One of his requests was that he had applied to go to Iran for two years in the security department of AT&T, where he worked. AT&T had won the bid to rebuild and modernize the Iranian telephone system and had established an international arm called ABII (American Bell International Inc.). Wes said it would be a while before he would know if he had been chosen to go.

God also brought together Peggy and her future husband, John Wheatley, in another singles' Sunday school class. They were married a year after Wes and I got married. If it hadn't been for Peggy asking to go to Sunday school with me, I might never have met Wes, and she wouldn't have met John.

Our church had a lodge in Lakeside, Arizona. We went up there on the church bus with our Sunday school class twice. The first time was in March of 1977, and we woke up on Saturday morning to six inches or more of snow on the ground. It was beautiful! On Sunday it snowed more. It was a magical time, but we had to drive back home on Sunday afternoon. The second time at the lodge was in the summer, so we didn't have to worry about snow.

In March of 1977, Ron decided to go to Gillette, Wyoming, and get a job driving a truck. He told me later he didn't have much money, and he bought a jar of peanut butter and ate that for his meals. While he was in Wyoming, he hauled heavy equipment for a railroad, worked for an oil rig, and most importantly learned to drive a truck. He returned home in August and got a job driving a truck for Universal Rundle, hauling fiberglass bathtubs locally. When he turned twenty-one on August 26, 1979, he got his first long-distance trucking job with C & H Trucking. He left that day for Mississippi. In August 1984, he bought his first truck, a 1981 Peterbilt that he

named *Sunrise Express*. Unlike the way he kept his room growing up, this truck was immaculate! The paint on the outside of the truck faded from orange to yellow. Ron has won many best of shows with this truck, which he still has

today. I want to say here that Ron has matured and gotten away from his wild teenage years, and I'm very proud of the man he has become.

Getting back to 1977, I, along with Pat's sister Susan Harris, visited Kim and Pat in Greece. We were there for three weeks in June and fell in love with the country. They took us many places: Marathon, the Acropolis, Sounion, Delphi, Olympia, Sparta, Nafplion, the Monastiraki Flea Market, and of course Athens. We also took Pat's car and went on a twelve-hour overnight boat ride to the island of Crete. While driving on a curvy road in the country, we had a collision with a taxi. No one spoke English, not even the police. Susan and I were sitting in the car when Kim and Pat went into the police station to fill out paperwork. About fifty men from the village came to look at Pat's damaged car, which was a classic—a 1967 burgundy Chevrolet Camaro. They started pounding on the car and shaking it, not realizing that Susan and I were inside. I think they were just testing it to see how sturdy it was. They certainly scared us!

That night we rented rooms in a sparsely furnished old motel in the village. My room consisted of a single bed on a cement slab, and the floor was nothing but cement—no carpet or rug. There was a single sink in the room, and we had to go outside for the toilet and shower. All night I heard glass breaking and angry shouts. I couldn't understand what they were saying, but the word "Americans" I understood. I didn't sleep at all, as I just knew they would be breaking into our rooms soon. I also thought they were breaking the windows on Pat's car. After I got up the next morning, Pat explained that the Greeks were having a party across the road, and their tradition is to throw plates and break them on the floor. They weren't after us at all, and the car wasn't damaged either.

We continued visiting places in Greece. I began to have severe pain in my back and neck, as I had twisted my back during the accident. It felt best to walk, which was good, since the car was being repaired. Susan and I reluctantly said goodbye to Greece and Kim and Pat, and we returned home.

One Sunday morning upon our return home, I had a terrible day. The A/C in the house had quit working, I had overslept, and I was hurrying to Sunday school when I realized my car had a flat tire. Ron said I could take his pickup truck.

I had made the coffee that morning for the Sunday school class, and it was in a large coffee urn. I didn't scotch it down properly, and it tipped over, spilling the coffee and grounds all over. Ron said his truck smelled like coffee for years, and he didn't even like coffee!

After I joined the choir that next September in 1977, Wes asked me for a date. We went out to eat at Manuel's Mexican restaurant and then to an ASU football game, as he had season tickets. I had no idea how old Wes was, but when he said he'd graduated from high school in 1956, the same year I did, I knew we were close in age. He had never been married before, so I asked him if he was a confirmed bachelor. He replied that he wasn't—just hadn't found the right person. We were both thirty-nine at the time.

In December of that year, 1977, Kim flew home from Greece. Pat was discharged from the army, and he had stopped in New Jersey to pick up and drive home a new car. Kim brought home their two cats, Artemis and Kashmir. Kim, Pat, and the cats stayed with me for a few months and then purchased a townhouse in Mesa on Dobson Road.

Wes and I continued to go to all of the ASU football games and got along quite well. He didn't kiss me or even hold my hand for a long time. We went to Slide Rock in Sedona, and he took my hand and helped me over the rocks. After I got on the other side of the rock, he dropped my hand like a hot potato. I thought, "Okay, so much for holding my hand." He told me later that he didn't want to rush me! After the football games were over for the season, I wondered if he would still ask me out, which he did. He finally kissed me on November 1. I met Wes's mom, Polly, when she came to visit him from North Carolina at Christmas. Her real name was Myrtle, but her nickname was Polly because she talked a lot, even when she was young.

I started writing in a daily diary in 1977. As I was reading it recently to confirm some details, I realized I had forgotten a lot of things that Wes and I had done before we were married. Early in our dating, I had purchased two thick porterhouse steaks for grilling and invited Wes over for dinner. They cost ten dollars, which was a lot at that time. I also made a mayonnaise cake, and he thought, "Oh my, I'll have to pretend that I like it" as he pictured a glob of mayonnaise on the top as frosting. After he ate some of the cake for dessert, he said, "I thought you were going to serve a mayonnaise cake." I told him he had just eaten it. Guess what? He liked it! Ron also wanted to know why I never bought porterhouse steaks for him to grill!

Wes took me to a lot of different places: Lunt Avenue Marble Club for dinner, the A to Z Horse Show, the Phoenix rodeo, the Japanese flower gardens on Baseline Road, the Greek festival, and one of our favorite restaurants, the Magic Pan in Scottsdale. We loved their crepes and pea soup with sherry in it. Wes took me to an expensive restaurant for my birthday on February 11, 1978. We talked for four hours, and he told me for the first time that he loved me.

1978: Martha at Tlaquepaque in Sedona

Prior to asking me out, I think Wes dated all of the single ladies in the choir. When we were in Sedona, he took my picture by a large tree in Tlaquepaque, which he put in a frame. After we were married, when I took my picture out of the frame to clean it, I found he had several other girls' pictures behind mine, taken in that same spot in Sedona. I kidded him about that for years. At least my picture was on top!

Wes and I sang in the Living, Singing Christmas Tree program at GCC. The first year I sang, we sang "Still, Still, Still," which became my favorite Christmas song. A revolving illuminated ball hung from the ceiling while we sang, replicating snow. It was beautiful. We started practicing for the presentations in September and had to have all music memorized. We sang in ten performances, and it was a letdown when it was all over. Most of us did all our Christmas shopping, wrapping, baking, and so forth before our first performance, as there would be no time afterward. It was a wonderful time to witness to our friends and family by inviting them to the program. During the closing prayer at one of the performances, one of the men in the front row had a heart attack. The conductor, Keith Hill, asked us all to remain in the tree and pray while the paramedics came and took the man to the hospital.

He died the next day. For the next presentation, we left his spot open and dedicated the performance to him. Another time in the "tree," one of the ladies started screaming. Keith stopped the music and asked her what was wrong. She said she was being

The Living, Singing Christmas Tree at Grace Community Church

shocked by the electricity from the lights on the tree. Keith had the lights all turned off, and we continued on with the program. For a few years, the church had two trees with the orchestra in between. I was chosen to be the "star" at the top of one of the trees for one performance, which was exciting! When we only had one tree, Joan (Woertz) Hill was always the star.

Through the bank I belonged to the Mesa branch of Soroptimist International, a volunteer service organization for women, and had been a member for three years. In 1978 I was elected president of the club, which was similar to Rotary International but for women only. Several of us from the club flew to Calgary and Lake Louise that summer for a Soroptimist International convention. Since I was president of the local club, I had a part in the program. Lake Louise is one of the most beautiful spots I've ever seen! It didn't get dark until almost midnight, so we were able to walk around the lake late at night. As president of the club, I had to choose a theme for the year. My theme was "Look for the Silver Lining." I was also chosen to be in the 1978–1979 edition of *Who's Who in the West.*

After the convention I flew to San Francisco to visit my brother Lewie and his wife, Alene. Jack, my other brother, and Phyllis were visiting also, as they had all just returned from Hawaii. They hadn't met Wes yet, so I was telling them all about him. Jack wanted to know if Wes's last name was Coast, as in "West Coast," and asked did he have a brother with the name of East Coast? Alene was pretty gullible, and she thought Jack was serious. When I left to fly back to Phoenix, Lewie asked me, "What is Wes's last name?" When I answered "Pierce," Alene said, "I thought his last name was Coast."

Wes asked me to go to the North Rim of the Grand Canyon with him in September of 1978 and spend the weekend. I agreed only if we slept in separate motel rooms, which we did. We were walking around on the grounds and looking at the stars when Wes asked if I remembered that he had applied to go to Iran for two years. I told him I remembered, and he said, "I've been asked if I still want to go. Would you go with me?" I was shocked, as he had gone with his last girlfriend for two years, and I thought it was probably about time for him to break up with me. I said, "You do mean married, don't you?" And he said, "Of course." I replied (covering my bases), "What if you don't actually go to Iran? Would we still get married?" And he said yes. Then I blew his mind and told him I'd give him a qualified yes, but I would have to think about it, pray about it, and talk with Pastor Keith Hill at GCC, our music minister.

After we got home, we made an appointment with Keith and went in to talk with him. I told him about my concerns, since I had been married twice before and didn't want to make another mistake. He was thrilled that Wes had asked me to marry him, and he said he'd seen it coming. I asked him how he'd seen it when I didn't. He told me he saw something in our relationship that wasn't present in Wes's previous relationships. He thought we were very compatible.

We went shopping for rings and purchased them at Daniel's Jewelers in Tri-City Mall in Mesa. We had originally picked the date of Valentine's Day, February 14, 1979, to get married. We asked Keith to perform the wedding ceremony at GCC. (We later changed the date to December 23, 1978.)

Wes owned and lived in a townhouse in Scottsdale. He had just purchased a home from his good friends Wayne and Carol Ruettinger at 518 East Julie Drive in Tempe. It was about a mile from my townhouse in the Lakes. He moved there on October 6, 1978. He planned to rent out the Scottsdale townhouse.

In the meantime, things were rapidly taking shape for both of us to go to Iran in January 1979. We changed the wedding date to December 23, 1978. On October 15, we both flew to Newark, New Jersey, to learn about all of the details of the Iranian adventure. Wes was to start on November 15, 1978, and arrangements would be made for him to fly back home to get married. (Nice of them!) We were allowed to take a thousand pounds of household goods and clothing but no electronics. Since we had two homes to go through and had to sell and/ or separate things into what we wanted to take and what we wanted to put into storage, we had a lot to do before Wes left for Iran. We both flew back again to New Jersey on November 14 for a final briefing. Wes then flew to Iran on November 15, and I flew to Indiana to visit my family. Sis and Johnny had an open house for me, and I saw many of my friends and family before flying home. Wes was able to choose one place to visit prior to arriving in Iran to break up the long flight. He chose Helsinki, Finland, where he spent two days and two nights.

I knew I would have a very busy month before the wedding, so I gave my notice at the bank. I was currently the manager at the Sun Lakes branch. I told my boss, Jim Lee, I could work through the end of November. I had both houses to go through and select what we would take, and I had to sell Wes's and my cars and all electronics. The company had said not only could we not take electronics, but we should also not store them for two years while we were gone. I also had to rent Wes's home and my townhouse. Plus I still wanted to sing in the Living, Singing Christmas Tree at GCC. Then there were all of the final details of the wedding! Wes had sold his Packard before he left.

During this time the people in Iran were having serious issues with the shah, and the revolution was on the way. There was a lot of bloodshed, and martial law was in place from 9:00 p.m. until 5:00 a.m. in Tehran. Anyone caught breaking the curfew was subject to being shot on sight, no questions asked! There were pictures of looting and burning on the front page of the *Arizona Republic* newspaper. My boss kept telling me he didn't think I would be going to Iran, and he wasn't getting my replacement yet. I finally told him I could work an extra week, but I really needed time to get everything done. He consented, and I began to train Mickey Laasch, my replacement, the first week in December. I decided to take a leave of absence rather than put in my resignation, just in case things did not work out for us to go to Iran.

On December 7, Wes called me from New York. His father had had a stroke and was in the hospital in Monroe, North Carolina. Wes had made arrangements to fly to North Carolina to visit his dad before coming home. He visited his father, and he was doing pretty well. On December 15, both Wes and his mom flew to Arizona. In the meantime I was singing in the Living, Singing Christmas Tree performances at church. Wes and Polly attended a couple of them and thoroughly enjoyed the music.

On Saturday, December 23, it was time for the wedding. My sister Nancy flew in from California, along with Barbara and her son Doug from Michigan. Sis and Johnny flew in from Indiana, and Dan Johnson, Wes's best man, came from Utah. The wedding was held at GCC in the main sanctuary, now called the Davidson Center. There were one hundred people who came. Kim was my matron of honor, and Ron walked me down the aisle. One of Wes's previous girlfriends from the choir sang at my request. She sang "May My Life Reflect Thy Will" and "Wedding Prayer." Jim Stone, also from the choir, sang "Jesus, Guest at Cana's Wedding." I love the words to "Wedding Prayer":

Wedding Prayer

Words by Fern Glasgow Dunlap

Heavenly Father, hear us as we pray,

Here at thine altar on our wedding day.

Show us the path that thou wouldst have us take;
Help us to follow thee and sin forsake.

In thy sight, oh God, today,

We've come to pledge our love in unity.

Bless the sacred vows we take

And keep us one through all eternity.

Give us strength in sorrow, want, or pain,

Always steadfast to remain.

And when clouds shall fill our skies of blue,

Help our love to see us through.

Oh God, until we reach life's ebbing tide,

May we in perfect love and peace abide.

And when life's sun shall set beyond the hill,

May we go hand in hand, together still.

Amen.

We had a reception afterward on the church campus, with cake and punch. Wes and I took Dan Johnson and my sister Nancy to the airport after the reception. Then Wes and I left to eat at Chez Louis in Scottsdale. After a delicious lobster dinner, we checked into La Posada hotel in Scottsdale for a short, one-night honeymoon. The next morning we went to church with the family. After church we invited a few people over to Wes's house for a buffet, provided by friends Norm and Irene Clark. We opened our wedding gifts and enjoyed visiting. We then all went to the Christmas Eve service at church. On Christmas Day, we got together again with the family. I took Barbara and Doug to the airport, and all of the guys went to the Fiesta Bowl.

CHAPTER 13

The Iran and Greece Adventure

On December 28 our ten boxes weighing a thousand pounds were picked up and would soon be shipped to Iran. On December 29 the movers came to pick up and store our furniture. Polly also left that day to fly back to North Carolina. Since we no longer had any furniture in the house, Wes and I stayed at the Mazona Inn in Mesa until we could leave for Iran. Sis and Johnny stayed at the Lakes townhouse.

We were originally supposed to fly to Iran on January 1. However, with all of the unrest in Iran, we were told to call the AT&T headquarters in New Jersey every other day and see what the latest instructions were. In the meantime we had to rent a car in order to get around. We all got sick with the flu (Kim, Pat, Sis, Johnny and me). Wes had gotten it earlier (and obviously gave it to us!).

On Friday, January 13, Wes received a call from New Jersey, telling us we were not going to Iran after all. However, they wanted us to fly to Athens, Greece, to help evacuate the telephone employees from Iran. Everyone would gather in Greece until it was safe to return to Iran, if ever. My flight and expenses would be paid for also. Our airline tickets would be waiting for us at the ticket counter at the airport on Monday morning, January 16.

Since the bank was now closed for the weekend, and I was still considered on leave of absence, I called personnel on Monday morning, just prior to boarding the plane, and resigned from the bank. One advantage was that I got paid for three weeks of vacation, since I was still employed in the new year. Our family all came to the airport to see us off, as we were presumably going to be gone for two years or more. Kim and I hugged each other and cried for a long time, trying to say good-bye.

We had a nice flight to Athens, although it was long. We stayed at the Amalia Hotel in downtown Athens, a very nice place. While Wes went to work, I met some of the other ladies, and we went out for lunch or walked to the flea market in the Plaka. One day I tried to find a laundromat to wash our clothes. Our maid, who didn't speak English, tried to give me directions. I started out walking, carrying two bags of dirty clothes, hangers, and laundry soap. I never found the laundromat, so I went into a small grocery store and asked how to get back to the Amalia Hotel. He said, "It's too far away to walk. You need to take the bus." I wasn't about to take the bus, as I could end up on the other side of the city! He pointed me in the right direction, and I started walking. By this time I had been walking for about three hours and was exhausted. I finally hailed a taxi and was driven to the hotel. What an experience! The next day I tried again and found the laundromat. I had an English map, but the street signs were all in Greek for some reason!

We had wonderful experiences in Greece and met a lot of nice people. Many times a group of us went out to eat at a nice restaurant. One of the most memorable ones was Dionysus Restaurant on top of Likavitos Hill in Athens. Likavitos Hill was the highest point in Athens and had panoramic views of the city. We took a cable car called a funicular up to the top. At the restaurant I ordered the jumbo prawns wrapped in bacon, and they were delicious. I thought the prawns had cloves on them, and I said something about the cloves looking like eyes. The others started laughing at me, and they said, "Those *are* eyes!" After that I wasn't sure I could eat the prawns. (But I did!) At another restaurant, Gerofinikas, we had to pick out what we wanted to eat from a meat counter. Nothing looked very appealing, and I decided on what I thought was a large portobello mushroom. The butcher said, "Madam, that is not a mushroom. It is brain." I ordered something else!

We soon learned that no one was going back to Iran. Wes called George Fielding, his previous boss in Phoenix, and discovered his job in marketing had been filled. George said he would make some calls and see what was available. Wes received a call the next day, and he was given a choice of Orlando or Denver. We talked it over and chose Denver, Colorado.

Now that we would soon be leaving Greece, we wanted to buy some souvenirs. We went shopping at the flea market in Athens, and Wes bought a brass Russian samovar for $125, used to heat water for tea. He was looking at various statues, which were about twelve inches tall, and he had them all lined up on a shelf in the shop, trying to decide which ones he wanted. He finally said, "I'll take them all." I asked Wes how he thought he was going to get them home, and he said he would ship them, along with the samovar. We no longer had a home address to ship them to, so Wes shipped them to Mountain Bell in Denver. We had a hard time finding enough old newspapers for wrapping the items and boxes for shipping. We also sent some of our clothes and other gifts we had purchased. If I remember right, we shipped ten boxes home, which cost seventy-five dollars in postage. We waited a long time for these boxes to arrive in Denver. One of the main problems was that Wes had put the wrong address on the boxes! I finally called the Denver post office, and I discovered they had the boxes and had placed all of the contents on shelves in a large warehouse. I went to the warehouse in downtown Denver and picked out all of our things. Many of the statues were broken; in fact, most of them were in pieces, and the samovar had a huge dent on the side. Wes spent many hours gluing the statues back together. He said it was a good winter project. We later took the brass samovar to have the dent removed. We also had it covered with a coating so we wouldn't have to polish it.

Before returning to the States from Greece, we decided to go on vacation. Wes said I could choose two countries to visit, and so could he. I chose Portugal and Switzerland, and Wes chose Denmark and Norway. Before we flew to these countries, we rented a car and drove to Olympia, Greece, where we viewed the original Olympic Stadium and both ran the length of it. We visited Tripolis, Argos, and Nafplion before returning to Athens and visiting the Parthenon.

1979: Wes and Martha in front of the Parthenon, Athens, Greece

We reluctantly said farewell to Greece and our new friends, and on February 8, 1979, we flew on Olympic Airlines to Geneva, Switzerland. We stayed in a very quaint hotel with a canopy bed. It rained the two days we were there, but we walked in the rain under an umbrella. We estimated that we walked about five miles the second day. We rode on a bus to Chamonix-Mont-Blanc in France and took a cable car up the mountain. It was snowing and so picturesque! At the top we indulged in a French pastry and hot chocolate. What a beautiful memory!

We left Switzerland in the late afternoon and flew to Lisbon, Portugal, where we checked into the Hotel Tivoli in downtown Lisbon. The next day, February 11, was my forty-first birthday. We celebrated that evening with a wonderful dinner of chateaubriand and wine. We took several tours in the area. They were having a lot of rain and flooding, and there was no water in the hotel. They brought us bottled water to drink and a large trash can full of water to use for flushing the commode.

We left Portugal on February 14 for Copenhagen, Denmark. Wes gave me a beautiful card and a box of chocolates for Valentine's Day. In Copenhagen we stayed at the Royal Hotel. The next day, while we were touring the royal palace, the queen came out of the palace to take her dog for a walk. We also visited the famous Little Mermaid statue.

On February 16 we flew to Oslo, Norway, where we encountered lots of snow on the ground. It was beautiful! It was very dry with no wind, and although it was zero degrees, it did not seem very cold. We bought heavy gloves and scarves, and Wes bought some furry boots. We attended a Norwegian Lutheran church service on Sunday, and even though it was all in Norwegian, we felt the presence of the Holy Spirit. We went to the front and took communion. They let the children run up and down the aisles prior to church starting, and then the children settled down when the service began.

We visited several places in Oslo. I particularly enjoyed the Vigeland sculptures and the Folk Museum, which depicted medieval Norway. The Vigeland sculptures consist of 212 bronze and granite statues, all designed by Gustav Vigeland. The sculptures culminate in the famous monolith, with its 121 figures struggling to get to the top. That evening we both ate reindeer for dinner. As we were walking through the royal palace, two mounted royal guards rode by on their horses. They suggested that I stand between them and have Wes take my picture with them.

Our European vacation was over, and we packed up and flew to the United States, changing planes in London. We were supposed to fly to Boston and then on to JFK in New York City. However, due to bad weather, the flight was canceled between Boston and JFK. We were soon able to get on another flight to JFK and were met by a representative of ABII and taken by limo to New Jersey. What class! And there was fifteen inches of snow on the ground! Wes called his new boss in Denver, and he learned his tentative starting date was March 18.

CHAPTER 14

A New Start In Denver, Colorado (1979–1980)

After Wes's debriefing with ABII and getting a cash advance on his earnings, we flew to Phoenix through Chicago, arriving in Phoenix on February 23, 1979, at 7:00 p.m. We rented a car at the airport and drove to Kim and Pat's home for dinner. We stayed at the Best Western motel in Dobson Ranch in Mesa.

We purchased a 1977 Toyota Celica Hatchback—bright yellow! We visited lots of friends while we were home and went to our old singles' Sunday school class at church (even though we weren't single anymore). Everyone was thankful we were back safely!

Wes and I had our first argument, and it was about taking my dog, Peanuts, to Denver with us. Kim and Pat had watched her while we were gone, but Pat said he would have her put to sleep if we didn't take her. So, of course, I wanted to take her with us. Wes did not like house dogs, so this became a problem. He finally relented for Peanuts to go with us.

On Friday, March 2, we left early in the morning and started driving to Denver. Wes did not want to take the easy way, which would have been on I-40 to Albuquerque and north on I-25 to Denver. He wanted to drive the "scenic" route, going through Kayenta, the Navajo Indian reservation, and into Colorado through the mountains. I reminded him it was winter, and we could get into snow! It didn't matter. When we arrived in Pagosa Springs, Colorado, that evening, the ground was covered with snow. We also found out Wolf Creek Pass was closed, which was the way we had planned to go. We rented a room in a motel and spent the night. Peanuts had never seen snow before, so she would not go to the bathroom when I took her for a walk. We walked and walked, and no luck! I finally gave up, and we all went to bed for the night. During the night, Peanuts got up and went to the bathroom on the floor near the toilet. (At least she had the right idea!) But guess who stepped in it during the night? Wes, of course! He was not very happy!

We had to buy chains for the car before we could continue on through Wolf Creek Pass. Even with the chains, we ended up in a seven-foot snowdrift due to the icy road. While we were wondering what to do, a car from Arkansas stopped with two big men inside, and they pushed us out of the embankment. Thank you, Lord, for sending them at just the right time!

We continued on our journey, stopping in Alamosa, New Mexico, where there was no snow on the ground. Peanuts was so happy that she did her business immediately.

We arrived in Denver and checked into the Ramada Inn. We stayed there several nights and then rented a two-bedroom, two-bath townhouse on a monthly basis, much cheaper than a hotel. The townhouse was completely furnished, with dishes, small appliances, telephone, even wood for the fireplace. There were a lot of townhouses in a row, and they all looked alike. When Peanuts went outside, she often returned to the wrong townhouse. She finally learned which one was ours. She absolutely hated the snow and sometimes would not even go outside.

Wes and I had our second disagreement: I put the toilet paper "under," and he wanted it "over," so he changed it! Then I changed it back! Finally, since we had two bathrooms, I suggested that he could do it his way in one bathroom, and I did it my way in the other bathroom. Eventually I gave in, and it's now "over" all the time!

We began looking for a church. We attended a couple and didn't care that much for them. We kept driving by Denver First Church of the Nazarene (DFC) and wondered what they believed. Wes called and talked with one of the pastors, and it sounded as if they basically believed the same as we did. We stopped by one afternoon and had a tour of the church. It was a very large church and quite modern. We were invited to attend a dinner drama being held there the next day. We went and thoroughly enjoyed the meal and the play. We attended the Sunday service that same weekend and were greeted about five different times before we went to the suggested Sunday school class. We were very impressed! We liked the Sunday school teacher (Pat Wellman, the pastor's wife), and the music and Pastor Don Wellman's sermon were excellent. Wes wanted to join the choir right away, but I wanted to wait at least a week or two.

We met Keith Showalter, the choir director, and he came out to the townhouse to visit us. We told him we wanted to join the choir. The choir consisted of about two hundred members, with each person having their own microphone and sharing the music with an assigned partner. The church had three music ministers: Jerry Nelson, the pianist and music writer and arranger; Les Stallings, director of the orchestra; and Keith Showalter, choir director. They only held one morning service, as the sanctuary held four thousand people, including a large balcony. We had just found our church home!

We spent several days getting acquainted with the Denver area. We visited the state capitol building, McNichols Sports Arena, and Mile High Stadium. Wes declared right then and there that he was *not* going to become a Denver Broncos fan—*ever!* (Which, by the way, was not true! He became a *big* fan when John Elway was the quarterback!)

Monday, March 19, was Wes's first day at work. He spent the day reviewing the products, which he would start teaching in April.

We started looking at homes on the west side, near Wes's job. After about three days of looking, we found the one we wanted at 7337 West Fremont Drive, Littleton, Colorado, in Columbine West. It was a trilevel, 1,942 square feet, with four bedrooms, two baths, two-car garage, upstairs outside deck, and nice landscaping. Our offer was accepted, and we moved in on April 16. We ended up buying a lot of new furniture. The thousand pounds of items that were originally slated for Iran arrived a week later, along with the items that had been in storage in Phoenix. It was scary watching the movers haul the piano up the steep steps of the outside deck into the living room. I kept busy opening boxes and putting everything away.

In June 1979 I started working two days a week as a volunteer in the music department at church. I did a lot of filing and helping the other secretaries. After a few months, Les Stallings, the orchestra director, asked me to work for him (and get paid) three days a week. I talked it over with Wes and told Les I would be glad to work for him. I had to be careful to call them the right names (Wes versus Les). Les did most of his own arranging and wrote a lot of his own songs, especially for musicals. I ended up learning how to take a director's score and transpose or copy the various instruments to their individual music sheets. I also made lots of copies from the originals and learned how to run and repair the large copy machine. The orchestra and choir were already rehearsing, and I was hurrying down the aisle of the sanctuary, carrying a huge stack (about one foot deep) of music, when I tripped and scattered the music all over! (I've always been kind of a klutz!) Everyone watching just gasped and tried to help me gather it all up. Of course, now it wasn't in any kind of order and had to be sorted again.

Wes tried out for the next dinner drama at DFC, which was *God's Good Man*. Wes was chosen for the lead part, a church pastor. After that a lot of people called him Parson. In later dramas he was an old man named Gamper in *No Time for Heaven*, and he was Ananias the high priest in *New Moon Rising*.

Wes wanted a big dog, so he started looking at the ads in the newspaper. He saw an ad for a six-month-old Dalmatian. He had pedigree papers, and his full name was Royal Blue's Sam Hubbard. I wasn't sure I wanted a Dalmatian. When we went to check him out, he came and actually wrapped his front legs around my neck while I was sitting next to him! I couldn't help but like him, so we bought the dog, a chain, and a doghouse for sixty-five dollars. Wes renamed him Thor. On the drive home in our car, the doghouse took up the space in the back, so Thor had to sit in the front seat on my lap!

I kept saying Thor was deaf. Wes said he was just stubborn. We both decided he needed training, so I called various dog trainers in the area. One time I was asked what kind of dog he was, and when I said "Dalmatian," he asked if he was deaf! He told me that one-third of Dalmatians are deaf, and if we chose him to train Thor, he would have his vet check his hearing. Sure enough! Thor was diagnosed as being deaf and was trained with hand signals. We didn't have to worry about him being afraid of fireworks or loud noises. We noticed that when I played the piano, his ears would perk up, and he would come over to the piano. He must have felt the vibrations. He and Peanuts played together quite well, although Peanuts wasn't playing, and Thor thought she was. It was funny to watch Peanuts chase him around the yard, as Thor was so much bigger than she was. Peanuts was part dachshund and part terrier.

We had a lot of trouble with Thor. He chewed on everything—trees, boxes, garden hose, and the wooden beams in the garage. We tried Tabasco sauce, lemon juice, and other things, but nothing stopped him. We finally crushed garlic and brushed it on everything. He didn't like garlic, so that finally took care of his chewing! Dogs are *so* smart! Peanuts kept eating Thor's food, so we bought a large metal bucket to use for Thor's food. It didn't stop Peanuts! She simply dumped the bucket over and continued eating Thor's food.

We soon needed a second car, and Wes found a used 1973 Mercury station wagon for $400. It was cheap because it had a huge dent in the left rear fender, but it drove well, so the dent didn't matter to us. It came in handy to have another car, since we were both working in opposite directions. I also started selling Avon products and had to periodically attend meetings.

1979 in California: Martha, Nancy, Jack, Lewie, and Sis

In July 1979 I flew to San Francisco for my niece Diana's wedding to Al Hagerstrand. As my brother Lewie was picking me up at the San Francisco airport, Sis walked up and surprised me. She had originally told me she wasn't coming. All five of us brothers and sisters were together for the first time in twenty-four years!

Diana and Al had an outdoor wedding. As the "Wedding March" was playing and Diana was walking down the aisle, Jack put his arm in front of me and said, "I'm holding you back, as you're so used to walking down the aisle." He was so ornery! Speaking of orneriness, we were staying at Lewie and Alene's house in a small trailer in their yard. Jack, Phyllis, Nancy, Sis, and I were all in the trailer. The first night, I couldn't seem to get under the covers and kept trying to straighten them. Jack had short-sheeted my bed! So the next night, Jack just "happened" to find empty soda cans in his pillowcase. The third night, Jack's pajamas were tied in knots, and there were uncooked noodles in his bed. The rest of us found rubber worms in our sleeping quarters! I also stuffed newspapers in Jack's shoes. We had a great time, laughing and teasing one another. Jack and Phyllis flew to Colorado with me and stayed for a few days. They fell in love with Thor, and they soon bought a Dalmatian by the name of Dutchess. You'll hear more about her later.

In February 1980 Kim called from Phoenix and said she was two months pregnant. However, it wasn't but a few weeks later that she had a miscarriage. Then she had a second miscarriage. In May Kim called and said Pat wanted a divorce. We were all devastated and of course wanted to help Kim as much as we could. I flew to Phoenix and stayed with her for a week. Pat's mother, Inge Harris, felt very sad about the divorce, as she thought so highly of Kim. To this day she's still part of our family and comes to all of the family gatherings. (She's Grammama to the kids.) Ron moved in with Kim to help out.

I kept very busy between working at church and selling Avon. DFC put on many musicals, and I was always in charge of making all of the copies for the orchestra and seeing to all of the details. I really learned a lot from working in the music department.

Our church was featuring Larnelle Harris, a well-known Gospel singer, at SNID (Saturday Nights in Denver). My boss, Les, couldn't pick him up at the airport, so I was asked to do it. Larnelle didn't know what I looked like, but I knew what he looked like. I found him and took him back to the church. Since he didn't have a car to get around, I called Wes and asked if I could loan him our Toyota. Wes agreed, and I got a ride home with someone else at church. I gave Larnelle the Denver map, which he didn't return. I relied on that map, and a few weeks later when I had to drive in downtown Denver, I got lost. I looked for the map, and of course, it wasn't in the glove compartment. I drove around quite a while. It was beginning to snow, and I pulled over and started to cry. (That always helps!) I found a phone booth and called Wes, asking for his help. Downtown Denver streets are all on an angle and most are one way, and I couldn't get "out." I finally got home, with Wes's help!

We had visits in the summer of 1980 from several people. Sis and Johnny came in June, and we took them to Colorado Springs to visit the Air Force Academy, Estes Park, Evergreen, Morrison, and Red Rocks Park. After they left, Nancy flew in for the weekend. Two weeks later Kim came. Ron was driving through with his truck, so he stopped by. We loved having company, and there's so much to see and do in Colorado.

As a side note, on November 4, 1979, the US embassy in Tehran, Iran, was taken over, and forty-nine hostages were taken captive. Wes had been in that embassy many times! The hostages were freed on January 20, 1981, after 444 days.

Joel, Wes's dad, with all his musical instruments

In August Wes and I flew to South Bend to visit family. Then we flew to North Carolina to visit his family. I had only met his mother, so this time I met the rest of his family. His dad had just gotten out of the hospital following three major surgeries, and he seemed to be doing well. Wes's parents

126

were divorced, and his dad's home was in Monroe, a few miles from Polly's home in the country. Wes was working on genealogy, and we spent a lot of time in various cemeteries getting family names and dates. I kidded him and said, "When people ask what we did on vacation, we can tell them we visited cemeteries!"

In September, shortly after we arrived back in Colorado, Wes flew to Minnesota to purchase and drive home a bright pink 1956 Packard. He paid $2500 for it. It was a beautiful car.

During the school year in the fall of 1980, we had an exchange student from Helsinki, Finland come and live with us. His name was Jaakko Laurikainen. We bought him a bicycle so he could ride it back and forth to Columbine High School. He even rode it to school in the snow. His best friend was another exchange student—Philipp Blomeyer from Germany. We took Jaakko to Arizona over Christmas and went to Sedona and the Grand Canyon before visiting Kim. Jaakko was a great photographer, and he was taking many, many pictures. As we were leaving Sedona, he realized he had forgotten to put film in his camera! He was just sick about it! We told him we had a lot of pictures of Sedona, and we would get some made for him.

Jaakko liked to play jokes on people. I always used Sweet'N Low in my iced tea, and Jaakko spent a lot of time replacing the sweetener with salt! He kept watching me at dinner that evening. It took me a while before I took my first sip of tea. I made an awful face, and Jaakko just burst out laughing! I knew then he had pulled a joke on me!

Wes and Jaakko went hunting several times. Wes had a cousin who lived in Steamboat Springs, Colorado, and she and her husband

1980: Martha, shooting the rifle

owned a ranch with many deer and elk. The second time Wes and Jaakko went there, I went along. Wes taught me how to shoot a rifle on that trip. Jaakko kidded me and said I had just killed a tree!

We purchased season tickets for the University of Colorado football games in Boulder, Colorado. They did not have a very good team that year. We also bought partial season tickets for the University of Denver hockey games. We only went on the weekends.

1980: Jaakko, Martha, and Wes in Steamboat Springs

CHAPTER 15

Return to Phoenix
(1981–1985)

In January of 1981, Wes requested a transfer to Phoenix when something became available. He was soon offered a job as manager of the coin phones as of April 27. We put the house on the market, and I gave my notice at church.

In the meantime we continued to visit places in Colorado. One weekend we drove to Aspen and Vail. On the way home, we hit black ice on I-70, and the car spun out three times, hitting the guardrail each time. We ended up on the side of the highway, facing the right way, when traffic behind came barreling by. It was a miracle that we ended up where we did and not in the middle of the road. Our car only had a broken headlight. Thank you, Lord!

Ronald Reagan was our new president. On March 30 he was shot at the Washington Hilton hotel by a twenty-five-year-old man from Evergreen, Colorado. Reagan was hit on the left side and in the lung. Three other men were also shot.

On April 21 we received an offer on the house. We countered and they accepted, with a closing date of May 25, 1981. Both the church and Mountain Bell had going-away parties for us. We said good-bye to our Sunday school class, neighbors, and Jaakko, who went to live with one of the other exchange students. We started packing up all of our things, and the movers came on May 13. Wes drove the Packard with Thor sitting upright in the passenger seat, and I drove the Mercury station wagon with Peanuts snuggled up right next to me. We arrived in Phoenix on May 15 in the evening and slept at Kim's. Thor chased the cats; they were afraid of him and went into hiding.

A few days later, our furniture was delivered and set up. Wes and I and the dogs slept in the house at 518 East Julie Drive in Tempe. This is the house Wes had purchased from his friends and rented out. We had too much furniture for the amount of space, so it was back-to-back furniture, especially in the living room.

One evening we took the dogs for a walk at nearby Kiwanis Park. Thor fell in the lake, and as we were laughing at him, Peanuts fell in also. We got them both out of the water, and Peanuts fell in a second time! They were soaking wet, and of course, we did not have anything to dry them off. Neither of them liked water, especially after that! One afternoon both of the dogs were in the backyard, barking at something. When we investigated, they had dug up a dead poodle encased in plastic. Evidently the renters had buried their dog in the yard. I can't remember what we did with it!

We had no sooner settled down in Phoenix when Wes had to fly twice to Denver for meetings. While there, he picked up our Toyota, which we had left with friends, and he traded it in for a 1981 Volvo. After the week-long meeting in Denver, he drove the Volvo home. We also purchased a 1981 Isuzu pickup truck in Phoenix, trading in the Mercury station wagon.

In August we flew back to Indiana for my twenty-fifth Mishawaka High School class reunion and had a wonderful time. A few days later, we flew to Roanoke, Virginia, for Wes's TKE convention, and then to North Carolina to visit Wes's family.

I was hired back at The Arizona Bank and started on August 31, 1981, as a relief branch manager. I was sent to various branches in Ahwatukee, Sun Lakes, Chandler, Mesa, Tempe, and Casa Grande. I loved that job and met a lot of new people at the branches.

Wes and I both rejoined the choir at Grace Community Church (GCC). We put on a musical, *The Day That Never Ends*, by Otis Skillings. Wes was chosen to be the narrator and did a great job. We not only did the musical for our church, but we went "on the road" and performed it at the marine base in Twentynine Palms, California, and also at Palm Springs Community Church.

In September we looked at model homes in Ahwatukee, not thinking we would buy a new house. We liked the Paiute model. They just happened to have a partially built model that a buyer didn't qualify for. We decided to put the Julie house up for sale and signed a contract on the new Ahwatukee house. We sold the Julie house in November and moved to 11829 South Coconino Street in Ahwatukee on December 5, 1981.

Wes hadn't been feeling very well for several weeks. At first the doctor thought he had pneumonia. After further testing, he was diagnosed with valley fever, a fungal infection caused by inhaling spores from the soil. He had a very bad case and was off work for about six months. Some days he didn't even get out of bed, and other days he was able to open boxes and put things away in the new house.

Wes's dad died the first part of 1983. He was sixty-nine years old. Sis and Johnny were visiting us at the time, and we were on our way to California to visit Nancy and her husband, Dirk. Wes flew back to North Carolina for the funeral, but he told us to continue on to California. I've often regretted not going back in respect for Wes and his dad.

In January of 1984, I had to have Peanuts put down. She had gone blind, and we didn't actually realize it until we moved to the new house, where she kept bumping into things. In the previous house, she knew where everything was. We had some landscaping put in the backyard of our new home, and one day Peanuts fell into a large hole. Thor kept barking for someone to come and help her. Finally the landscaper saw what had happened and pulled her out. At a later date, Peanuts was in a lot of pain and kept crying and moaning all night. When I got up the next morning, I took her to the vet on my way to work and had her put to sleep. I didn't stay with her, and I've always regretted that decision. Kim called me after I arrived at work and asked how Peanuts was. I said, "Don't ask," and I started crying. Peanuts was seventeen years old.

I worked as relief branch manager for a year. Then my boss asked me if I would take over as manager at the Broadway/Greenfield office in Mesa. As much as I liked that branch, I loved my current job. However, I agreed and actually switched jobs with the other manager. I enjoyed Broadway/Greenfield and the staff very much. The bank was having a contest in 1983 and 1984 regarding ATM usage. Whatever branch had the highest increase in ATM usage, that branch manager would win a trip to the Bahamas. There would be fifty winners. Since our branch customers were basically seniors over sixty, they hadn't felt comfortable using the ATM. The staff made up a sign that said "Send our Manager to the Bahamas." When customers asked what it meant, we told them and showed them how to use the ATM. I ended up being one of the winners! The bank flew us to the Bahamas on a chartered plane, and we had a wonderful time. The bank president, Bob Matthews, was also there.

To J. Wes Pierce
With best wishes
Ronald Reagan

Spouses were invited to go to the Bahamas also, but Wes had a dilemma. That same weekend, he and the Tau Kappa Epsilon (TKE) officers were invited to have lunch at the White House with President Reagan, who was also a TKE. I suggested that Wes fly to Washington, DC, first, have lunch, and then fly to the Bahamas, which is what he did. When Bob Matthews asked me where my husband was, I answered, "Oh, he's having lunch at the White House with President Reagan." When Wes arrived in the Bahamas for dinner that evening, he was quite the celebrity!

In May of that same year, Wes and I and forty others traveled to Europe with XYZ (Xtra Years of Zest) from Grace Community Church. The main emphasis of the trip was a special 350th anniversary of the Passion play presentation in Oberammergau, Germany. We were gone two weeks and also visited London, Belgium, Switzerland, and France. We were by far the youngest ones on the trip. The leader, Pastor

Jim Rentz, had divided everyone up into "families." We were assigned to be "parents" of six much older people. Pastor Rentz had a Rotary meeting in London after the tour, so he asked if we would escort the group home from London to Phoenix. That may have been the beginning of our travel leadership experiences.

 An important thing happened on October 6, 1984. Kim and Mike Rinke were married in Las Vegas, Nevada. Kim had met Mike at his sister Carrie's wedding. Kim and Carrie were good friends in high school. It was a small wedding with mainly family present. I was Kim's matron of honor, and Wes was the "official" photographer. Everyone had a good time. Mike owned a home in Glendale, so Kim and Mike lived there, and Kim rented out her townhouse in Mesa.

In April 1985 Kim told us she was pregnant for our first grandchild! We were so excited. The baby was due in January 1986. One day soon after that, Wes called me at work and told me the AT&T security department, where he now worked, was shutting down in Phoenix and moving to Denver. We would be transferred within the next few months. Wes said this would be a permanent move. All I could think about was that we would not be here for the birth of our grandbaby! Wes assured me I could come back for the birth and stay as long as I wanted in order to help Kim with the new baby.

CHAPTER 16

Back Again to Denver (1985–1987)

In June of 1985, Wes and I flew to Denver to look at houses. We found one we liked located in Ken Caryl Ranch at 11167 Wildhorse Peak, Littleton, Colorado. It was a two-story house with a full basement. It also had a *beautiful* backyard with a vegetable garden and lots of flowers. Our offer was accepted, and we flew back to Phoenix. We flew again to Denver on August 27 to sign the closing papers, returning to Phoenix to get ready for the move. Since AT&T was covering all of the costs, they paid to have packers come on September 3 and pack all of our belongings in boxes. The next day the moving van came and transported our things to Littleton, arriving on September 8. In the meantime we drove to Denver, along with Thor, our Dalmatian. He wasn't happy with the move, and his security was the car. He stayed in the car and watched as all of the furniture was taken into the new house. It was a good way to keep him out of the way. Two people came the next day and unpacked everything for us. That was nice, except everything was scattered all over, as I wanted to be the one putting things away.

We had several visitors that fall. Kim and Mike came the end of September when we had twelve inches of snow fall while we were eating dinner at the Fort Restaurant, which was in the mountains. When we tried to leave, we were stuck in the snow. We called AAA, and they wouldn't come out that far. The waiters all got together and pushed our car out of the parking lot and into the road. We drove home *very* slowly and carefully!

Sis and Johnny visited us in October for two weeks, and Wes's cousin Blaun and her family came for Thanksgiving. We always enjoyed having company.

I did not want to find a permanent job in Denver, as I wanted to be able to fly to Phoenix when our grandbaby was born. I got a job with Kelly Services, where they placed me on temporary assignments. I also told them when I wanted to work and how often. They basically sent me to banking jobs, which I enjoyed. It was a good way to tell which bank I wanted to work for when the time came for me to get a permanent job.

CHAPTER 17

The Birth of Lindsey, Our First Granddaughter (1986)

On Saturday, January 18, 1986, I received a call from Kim, telling me she was having labor pains. I called the airlines but couldn't get a flight out until Sunday. We had tickets to a hockey game that evening, so we went ahead and attended the game. When we got home, I called Kim, and she was at home but still having pains. The next morning Wes took me to the airport, and I flew to Phoenix. Inge picked me up at Sky Harbor Airport in Phoenix, and we went right to Kim and Mike's home. It wasn't long after that when Mike and I took Kim to Good Samaritan Hospital in Phoenix.

Lindsey Nicole Rinke was born at 10:41 that evening after many hours of severe back labor pains for Kim. Mike and Kim were so excited and full of energy. Lindsey was a beautiful nine-pound, one-ounce baby girl with dark hair and a round face. She was chunky for a newborn. Wrapped tightly in a blanket, we said she looked like a papoose. Mike and I finally left at 2:00 a.m., but it was hard for either of us to sleep that night. The next day Kim had lots of company, as Mike has a large family. I, of course, called Wes to let him know, and I told him how pretty Lindsey was. He said, "All babies are ugly right after they're first born." I sent him a picture of her, and he agreed that she was beautiful! Since Mike had to work, I picked up Kim and Lindsey on Tuesday the twenty-first and drove them home from the hospital. Kim kept telling me to drive safely, as we had precious cargo in the car! Mike's parents were waiting for us on the doorstep. Mike's mother's name is Martha also. In order to differentiate between the grandmas and papas, all of the grandchildren in Mike's family added their dog's name. We were Grandma and Papa Thor.

As a side note, on January 28, the space shuttle *Challenger* exploded a minute after takeoff, killing all seven aboard, including a schoolteacher from New Hampshire.

Martha, Kim, and Lindsey, eight weeks old

I stayed with Kim and Mike off and on for two months. Mike told me he was glad I was there, because since Lindsey was their first baby, they didn't always know what to do. (That's a nice compliment from a son-in-law!) Wes flew down for a few days and loved to hold Lindsey on his lap and talk to her. I think she liked his deep voice. When Kim had to go back to work, I stayed with Lindsey for about a week, which made Kim feel better about leaving her. Lindsey was dedicated at Grace Community Church on February 16 by Pastor Davidson. Wes's mother wrote this poem about Lindsey:

Memories of You, Lindsey
by Myrtle (Polly) Pierce
June 1986

I know a baby so radiant and good;

She smiles and chuckles like
a good baby should.

Her name is Lindsey Nicole—she's
more precious than gold.

At her grandparents' home in
Littleton, Colorado—

Where for a month I did roam—

I saw, held, and caressed this
"living doll" galore.

She was merry, like the "song of a lark,"

Brilliant as the "evening star."

Her antics pleased us all—

Recognized her name upon call.

Memories lead me to you, with
pleasurable thoughts—

And priceless hugs too.

Seems I see you, dear,

When photos of you are near.

Like the nightingale, you cooed,

Much like an angel—wooed,

A more darling child is yet to be found,

Though many are sweet the world 'round.

Lindsey's first piano lesson
was enjoyably conducted

When at the instrument,
she was inducted.

*1986: Polly with Lindsey,
four months old*

A "Lullaby" she
played well, as
Great-Grandmother can tell.

These memories are beyond measure,

Greatly cherished and a priceless treasure.

Shortly after this, I was ready to get a permanent job in Denver. I went shopping and purchased a navy-blue suit for my interviews. (Denver wasn't as casual in the work arena as Phoenix was.) Wes then told me the Denver location for his job wasn't working out as well as the boss thought it would, and we might possibly be returning to Phoenix. Wes had to do a lot of traveling for his job, and his areas included Arizona, Utah, New Mexico, and Montana. It did not even include Colorado, where we lived! Therefore he was almost constantly flying somewhere. It was very expensive to pay for airline flights, car rentals, hotel rooms, and food. It would be cheaper in the long run to pay for office space in Phoenix.

It didn't happen immediately, so I continued working for Kelly Services to earn a little extra money. I basically worked at the First National Bank of Englewood, which I enjoyed. I started working in the trust department, which I knew very little about. Their books were out of balance by several thousand dollars, and I asked if I could try to find it. I kept asking the supervisor questions so I could understand the procedure better, and she kept ignoring me. (I don't think she understood either.) I was finally able to balance the books and typed up instructions on how to balance each day. They then asked me to work in the accounting department. The secretary was pregnant and would soon go on maternity leave. She trained me on the basics, like writing checks and balancing accounts. When she left and had her baby, she decided to stay home with the baby, and she gave her notice to the bank. I did not want to take the job, so they hired someone new and asked me to train her.

I kept having really bad sore throats. The doctor took a throat culture and told me I had strep throat. After this kept happening several times, he sent me to a throat specialist, who said I needed to have my tonsils out. I had previously thought it was great that I never had to have them out when I was young! In May of that year, I checked into Porter Hospital in Denver and had my tonsils taken out. I woke up in the recovery room with all the little children who had just had their tonsils out. They were all crying, and I knew just how they felt! I went home that day at 5:00 p.m. and hurt all night. I also hemorrhaged, and Wes called the doctor. She said to put ice on the outside of my neck, which stopped the bleeding.

One Sunday morning we were backing out of the garage to go to church. I didn't realize I was sitting on the garage door opener, and I accidentally closed the garage door. We backed into it, breaking the door and denting the pickup. Wes was not very happy! The sermon that morning was on stress. It couldn't have come at a better time!

Our neighbors across the street, Jim and Susan Hillan, became very good friends. They had four boys: Gerod, Jimmy, Justin, and Joel. Justin especially loved to come over and help Wes in the garden or play with Thor. I started giving Justin piano lessons, and we had a recital one Saturday for his family. Justin was nervous and asked me to sing while he played. I'm not a soloist, so I know it didn't sound very good. After that the other boys wanted to take lessons also. I ended up teaching them all, and Jim and Susan bought a piano for them.

We had several visitors that year who stayed with us. Polly came for a month, and Wes's brother, Larry, and his wife, Ruth, flew in from Florida for two weeks. My son, Ron, was driving through Denver in his truck and stopped by. Sis and Johnny came for a week in May, and Kim and family came from Phoenix on several weekend trips.

September 1986: Lindsey, eight months old

In August of that year, 1986, we flew to South Bend, Indiana, for the wedding of Pam (my grandniece) and Ken in Michigan. Kim and Lindsey flew to Denver from Phoenix, and we boarded the same plane with them and flew together. After arriving in South Bend, we drove to Detroit for the wedding. Lindsey was seven months old, and we put her in a baby walker to keep her happy and out of trouble. Pam let her try for the wedding bouquet at the reception. I was in charge of Lindsey, and by the time the wedding and reception were over, I looked a mess! Lindsey had wet on my dress and thrown up all down the front of me. When Wes took my dress to the cleaners the next day, he said, "It has pee, puke, and who knows what else on it."

In October Wes and I took a driving trip to South Dakota to see Mount Rushmore. We also visited Crazy Horse Memorial, an unfinished Indian monument being carved in a mountain. I thought it was fascinating. We went to Glacier National Park, where we hiked with no one else around. I kept waiting for a bear to be just around the corner, but we didn't see any. In Missoula, Montana, we got tickets for the University of Montana and Montana State University (from Bozeman) football game, a fierce rivalry. U of M won 59–28. We had been rooting for them. We really liked Missoula. After that we drove to Yellowstone National Park and saw lots of wildlife (elk, buffalo, chipmunks, and ravens), Old Faithful, waterfalls, and geysers.

We drove on to Jackson, Wyoming, and then to the Grand Tetons, where we ran into a lot of snow. We arrived back home on November 1, after spending the night at Little America in Cheyenne, Wyoming.

You may recall when Wes said he would *never* become a Broncos fan. But he really liked John Elway, the quarterback, and we both became big fans of the Broncos. Wes purchased season tickets to the Broncos football games in November of that year. The seats were on the second row from the top and were back to back, not next to each other. Otherwise we would have had a long wait for season tickets.

I flew to California in November to visit my sister-in-law Alene, who was dying from cancer. Her cancer had been in remission but had now returned. She was taking chemo again, and I wanted to spend some time with her. I wanted to encourage her, and she ended up being an inspiration to me! I was pleased to find out she had been watching several ministers on TV and had made her peace with God. She had confidence she was going to heaven when she died. Alene died on August 17, 1987, at the age of sixty-four.

We ended the year by flying to California and going to the Rose Bowl in Pasadena. Arizona State University (ASU) beat Michigan 22–17. It was a great game! We flew home that evening and got in bed at 1:00 a.m.

The very next day, January 1, 1987, I flew to Indiana for Sis and Johnny's fiftieth anniversary celebration, which Barbara and I hosted. Nancy, Debbie, and Manda came from Chicago on the South Shore train. Barbara and Jim drove down on Saturday from Michigan. We had an open house for Sis and Johnny on Sunday afternoon at First Christian Church. Sis's grandson, Doug Armstead, sang the songs that were originally sung at their wedding: "I Love You Truly" and "O Promise Me." Everyone had a good time, and we saw a lot of people we hadn't seen for a long time.

Two weeks after I got home from Indiana, I flew to Phoenix for Lindsey's first birthday. Barbara, Jim, Sis, and Johnny were already there. Thirty people came to Lindsey's party, and she was awestruck! We put a small cake in front of her, and she stuck her finger in the frosting, but that was about all. Lindsey took her first steps a week later, and by January 31, she was walking back and forth between us. She was so excited! We put her in the knitted pink dress my mom had made for me, and Lindsey just strutted around in it. She thought she was so pretty in it, and she was!

Wes and I flew back to Denver. Wes's cousins, Blaun

1987: Blaun, Martha, Wes, and Sylvia

Bennett from South Carolina and Sylvia Little-Sweat from North Carolina came to visit us for a week in May. In July we went to the Billy Graham Crusade at Mile High Stadium in Denver. There were forty-three thousand who attended that night, and three thousand went forward to accept Christ as their Savior.

Wes got the official word that our relocation to Phoenix had been approved. We went to Phoenix on July 21 to hunt for a house. Our Phoenix Realtor took us several places. There was a new section south of where we'd lived before in Ahwatukee, where Wes used to take Thor walking on dirt trails. A new subdivision now occupied this area and was called Mountain Park Ranch. We looked at one of the models, which was decorated in blue, my favorite color! We really liked the model, and there was a sign on the wet bar saying this model was for sale. We made a very low offer, and when we returned to Denver, we received a call from our Realtor, who told us the offer had been accepted! We also purchased all of the furniture and appliances for $4000. The address was 3850 East White Aster Street, Phoenix, Arizona, which is still our current address.

We put our Denver house up for sale. The housing market was pretty bad, and interest rates were very high. At the house inspection, we found out our basement had radon gas, which we had to have taken care of. We sold the house for less than we wanted, so AT&T made up the difference.

We still had another trip lined up, and on August 15 we flew to Nashville, Tennessee, where we visited Ray and Bernie Lipinski, whom we hadn't seen since 1979 in Greece. After visiting them, we went to the TKE convention in Washington, DC, and stayed at the Grand Hyatt hotel. We had a tour of the White House and visited Mount Vernon. After the convention, Wes and I flew to North Carolina to visit his family. We always enjoyed eating at the fish camps with Wes's cousins Joe and Helen Thomas. Wes always ordered catfish, and I ordered flounder. It was all you can eat and so good! We did some preparing for Polly's upcoming eightieth birthday open house in October.

CHAPTER 18

Another Move to Phoenix (1987–1988)

The packers came to our Denver home on September 26 and 28, and the moving van came the next day. We sent the Packard in the moving van, and we drove the Volvo with Thor to Phoenix. We closed on the house on October 2. The moving van was already at the house, waiting for us. They thought they were at the wrong house, since it was full of furniture we had purchased with the model. They helped us put the furniture we weren't going to use in the garage. Ron later took a lot of the extra things for his place, and we used a lot of the furniture at the cabin we purchased later.

The house was actually pretty dirty! There were dead bugs in the kitchen and bathroom cupboards, and no one had moved the furniture and vacuumed under any of it. We woke up the first morning to water all over the carpet in front of the wet bar. A water pipe had broken. When I hung up the towels on the towel rack, the rack fell onto the floor. The doorbell rang one morning at 5:00 a.m., as the sprinkler system had sprung a leak and was shooting water fifteen feet in the air in our front yard! The drapes fell apart when I washed them.

Thor was bitten by a scorpion on his face that first night, and since it was Friday evening, we had to find an emergency vet to take him to. We were told to put ice on his face, which he didn't like. We didn't have any heat for several days, either, and the weather had turned very cold. The repairman couldn't come for a couple days, so I wrapped myself in an electric blanket until we could get it fixed. I told Kim that I hated the house! I'd never buy a model home again! We finally made a list and called a handyman to come and fix everything. In case you're wondering, we bought the house "as is."

In the midst of all of this, we flew to North Carolina for Polly's eightieth birthday celebration on October 11 at her church, Mill Creek Baptist Church, in Unionville, North Carolina. Her actual birthday was a week away on October 19. Blaun, Wes's cousin, brought a hundred roses from her garden in South Carolina for decorations; Aunt Juel served punch; Aunt Myrtle was in charge of the guest book; Cousin Judy cut the cake; Cousin Sylvia played the piano for background music; and Wes was the emcee. Polly was pleased with everything and played "Perfect Day" on the piano. It really was a perfect day!

We flew home to Phoenix, and Kim and Mike went on vacation to the Caribbean while we watched Lindsey, who was one and a half years old. Inge, Kim's previous mother-in-law, wanted Lindsey to come over and spend the night with her, so I took Lindsey to Inge's house. The next morning Inge called and said that her dog had bitten Lindsey, and she wanted to take her to the doctor. Since I had the necessary medical paperwork, I drove over, and we both took Lindsey to the doctor. The doctor gave her a shot and said she'd be okay. Now who was going to tell Kim and Mike? All of the grandmothers got together—Martha (Mike's mom), Pat (Mike's stepmother), Inge, and me. We decided we wouldn't tell them until they arrived home, or it might ruin their vacation.

Lindsey was a lot of fun to take care of. She loved peas and ate three or four helpings one evening for dinner. When it was time for her bedtime snack, I asked her if she wanted some ice cream. She shook her head no. A cookie? No. I finally showed her the peas, and she nodded. She just didn't know what they were called.

Kim and Mike arrived home a few days later, and Wes and I picked them up at the airport. This was the era when we could actually meet them coming down the Jet-way from the plane. They were both running to see who would get to Lindsey first. Mike won, and he took one look at Lindsey and said, "What happened?" (Since the bite was on her cheek, it was very noticeable.) Of course, I told them what had happened. They took it pretty well.

Ron was still living in Kim's townhouse in Mesa. The renters in my townhouse in the Lakes had just moved out, so Ron decided to buy the Lakes townhouse from us. He assumed the mortgage, and we wrote up a promissory note for the balance. He never missed a payment.

Sis and Johnny came in January of 1988 to stay with us for three months. They celebrated their anniversary on January 17. We honored them at church with flowers. We all went to Lindsey's second birthday party on January 19. She was so cute and had such an outgoing personality!

February 11 was my fiftieth birthday. Wes surprised me with a restored 100–150-year-old pump organ, which he'd bought in New Mexico and had brought to Phoenix by a friend. What a nice surprise! Then my brother Lewie surprised me by flying here from San Francisco. We all went out to eat that night at Pinnacle Peak Patio and had steaks. When we arrived home, there were fifty people in our living room who all said, "Surprise!" Kim had planned the party. We were late leaving the restaurant, and everyone was anxiously waiting by the time we walked through the front door.

Martha with her surprise antique organ.

I had recently interviewed for a job at The Arizona Bank—in fact, two different jobs: manager at the Ahwatukee branch (I preferred this one, as it was so close to home), and manager at the Apache Wells branch in Mesa (fifty-six miles round trip). Well, you guessed it—I was offered the Apache Wells office, along with the title of assistant vice president. I took the job and started on February 17, 1988.

When we were in Denver, Pastor Wellman had recommended that we visit Dobson Ranch Church of the Nazarene in Mesa, which we did. We liked it and the pastor, Mark Fuller, but we also liked Grace Community Church. Pastor Davidson had left GCC by this time. Pastor Mark visited us and said he would certainly like it if we decided to come to his church; however, we needed to pray about it and do what the Lord told us to do. That was the deciding factor for us to join his church. Eventually we also joined the choir.

On Wes's fiftieth birthday (May 25), I surprised him by taking him on a hot-air balloon ride. I awakened him at 4:30 a.m. and drove him to Fifty-Ninth Avenue and Bell Road, still not telling him what it was all about. (He actually had no clue!) After we arrived and he saw what it was, he said he had always wanted to go up in a hot-air balloon. It cost ninety dollars per person, and it lasted for an hour. We saw beautiful scenery, and it was nice and quiet. Then, upon landing, we hit a large cactus, and the basket tipped over. We skidded for about fifty feet, stopping just short of a wire fence. I happened to be on the bottom of nine people. No one was hurt badly, but I had bruises and a broken rib, which hurt for days! What an experience! We've never been in a hot-air balloon since.

In July Wes and I drove to Flagstaff, as we wanted to buy a cabin in that area. We hired a Realtor, and she showed us many places. We had given her a limit of $30,000, and we soon realized we would have to increase that amount. We really liked one of the places she showed us in Mountainaire, about eight miles south of Flagstaff. Kim and Mike told us they wanted to go in with us to buy the cabin, so we all went up the next weekend to look at more places. We told our Realtor to show us the bad ones again and then this one we liked. Someone else was looking at it, so we had to wait to show Kim and Mike. After we looked at it, Kim said, "I think we should make an offer on it, as those other people may be doing the same." We countered a couple times, and finally our offer of $57,900 was accepted. We closed on September 9, 1988. While

we were still working, we went to the cabin on weekends and enjoyed the cooler weather. Kim and Mike owned a third, and we owned two-thirds. We named it Pine-Oak because of the sixty-five pine trees throughout the property and a clump of oaks in the front.

In September Wes's brother, Larry, and his wife, Ruth, moved in with us, as they couldn't make it financially on their own in Florida. We had already helped them financially many times. Ruth had many health issues and couldn't work, and Larry had just lost his job. They had lived with Ruth's parents in Florida for several years, and they needed a change. They lived with us for five or six months. Then Wes and Ruth had an argument, which was the cause of them moving out. Ruth grabbed her purse and said she was leaving; Wes tried to stop her, they struggled, and Ruth fell. She was okay, but she left and called the police, and an officer showed up at our door. I was working, and Wes called to tell me all about it. Larry and Ruth filed an assault charge against Wes, and Larry told us they were suing us for everything we had. We lived in fearful anticipation for a while. After praying about the situation, we had real peace and decided if we lost everything, they were just "things." Nothing ever came of it, and we reconciled with Larry and Ruth.

CHAPTER 19

Michelle's Entrance Into The World (1989)

On February 19, 1989, Michelle Stephanie Rinke was born to Mike and Kim. Wes and I, along with Sis and Johnny, had gone to the cabin for the three-day weekend. Mike was skiing in Utah, and Kim was concerned the baby might come that weekend, even though her due date wasn't for a couple of weeks. Sure enough, the phone rang at 3:00 a.m. at the cabin, and Kim was in labor. I told her I would drive down when it got light. Fortunately we had two cars in Flagstaff, as Wes had been in Flagstaff on business and had the company car. At 6:00 a.m., I tried to start the car, and the battery was dead. We had forgotten to turn off the headlights the night before! We called AAA, but it was 8:30 before I finally left for Phoenix. By this time Kim had called Inge and Martha, Mike's mom. Inge took Kim (and Lindsey) to the hospital, and Martha met them there. By the time I arrived at the hospital, Michelle had just been born. The nurse came out and asked if Kim's mother was there, and if so, to come into the delivery room. Kim was crying, and she said the doctor thought Michelle had Down syndrome. I took one look at her and said, "Yes, she does." We cried together; then I told Martha and Inge. We all went into the delivery room, and the nurse put Lindsey on the delivery table and put Michelle in her arms to hold. Wow! That was really a bonding moment! Lindsey was three years old at the time.

Kim had already called Mike and told him she was in labor, so he was on his way home from Utah. We had it all planned that when he came, I was to take Lindsey aside, and Martha would tell Mike about Michelle. When Mike arrived (he flew from SLC), Martha took him aside, but Lindsey had other thoughts! She ran to him, telling him about holding the baby, and that broke the ice. It was much better than our plan!

Kim asked me to call all her friends and tell them. She and Mike didn't want sympathy; they wanted to be treated as if Michelle were a normal baby. People brought gifts, sent congratulatory cards, brought balloons, and so on. I remember when Mike's sister Carrie came to the hospital and brought balloons. Kim was crying, and Carrie said, "I want to see Michelle!" Then she cooed over her and said how pretty she was. That was a big help and a changing point!

Lindsey, 3, holding Michelle, one week old

I took off work the next week to be with Kim. Michelle was born without a wall between the two upper heart chambers, and when we put our ears down to her chest, we could hear the blood rushing through. She didn't have any energy and couldn't nurse. We cut a bigger hole in the nipple of her bottle and let the milk drip into her mouth. It sometimes took two hours to feed her four ounces of milk. The doctor said she

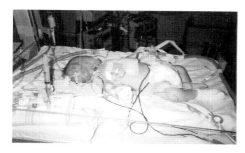

Michelle, right after her first surgery.

Michelle, shortly after two surgeries; eight weeks old

would need surgery to repair the heart, but he wanted to wait as long as possible. She was six weeks old and weighed a mere eight pounds when she had the surgery. Kim stayed at the hospital the entire time, and Lindsey said, when she and Martha, Lindsey's other grandma, drove by one day, "That's where my mommy lives now." Michelle was hooked up to a lot of wires and was in critical condition. I stayed at the hospital overnight twice to keep Kim company. The heart surgeon did a second surgery to correct the tightness of the valves. The second surgery worked, and after a total of ten days, Kim took Michelle home. It was Mother's Day and a wonderful Mother's Day gift for Kim.

After recuperating for a couple of months, Michelle was dedicated at our church, Dobson Ranch Church of the Nazarene, in Mesa. Mark Fuller was the pastor, and he had been with us at the hospital during both surgeries. He dubbed Michelle "the Miracle Baby." That she was!

"The Rinke Girls Two"
by Winifred Rea
July 30, 1989

The Rinke Girls Two, and oh what a pair!

Lindsey and Michelle—each of
them so lovely and fair.

Lindsey has beautiful curls and eyes of brown,

The prettiest three-year-old in Glendale town.

Michelle is pretty, plump, and cuddly too,

A real sweet little baby—that is true.

We call her our "Miracle Baby,"

For she survived two surgeries just like a lady!

We knew she would, for she was in God's care,

As many prayers went up for
her from here and there,

God saved this sweet little gal,

So Lindsey could have a real little pal.

May Mommy and Daddy be
given wisdom from above,

To raise these girls in Christian love.

May they walk through life in sunshine bright,

Ever led by God's guiding light.

We love these little girls so far away,

And wish we could see them more each day.

May God bless them and
always keep them too.

This is our earnest prayer for
the Rinke Girls Two!

1989: Kim; Lindsey, three years old; Michelle, seven months old

CHAPTER 20
Family Deaths,
A Wedding, and
Retirement (1989–1992)

It was necessary for Wes to make several trips to North Carolina to help his mother. Polly broke her hip twice and had successful surgery both times. We both visited her for her eighty-second birthday in October. She was still living at home but with full-time live-in help.

Wes wanted to sell the 1956 Packard Caribbean, and he listed it in the Packard Club newsletter. We received a call from Geoff and Cathy Ralls, who were from New Zealand. They were visiting in Michigan and saw Wes's ad. They wanted to fly to Phoenix and look at our Packard. We picked them up at the airport and brought them to our home. They liked the Packard and decided to purchase it. We invited them to stay with us for the night. They ended up staying several nights, and we became good friends. Wes helped them make arrangements to ship the car to New Zealand. I ended up having to drive the car to the shipping company, as Wes had to go out of town that day. I had never driven the Packard, so it was rather scary.

In December Wes retired from AT&T at the age of fifty. He was offered a package called 5-5-5, which gave him five more years on his age, five more years on his service, and a retirement income incentive for five years. It had only taken him about thirty seconds to decide! We both had originally said we wanted to retire from our jobs when we turned fifty-five. However, we hadn't really thought that out too well, as our income would have taken a big hit all at once! God knew better, and we had five years to adjust to the loss of Wes's income before I retired.

Nineteen ninety was another busy year for us. Wes visited Polly in January and in May, and we both visited her for her eighty-third birthday in October. Wes's cousin Tad Tadlock and Tad's wife, Gretchen, from Scottsdale, went with us, and we all had a wonderful time. Tad was born on February 2, the same day as Wes's dad, making them nephew and uncle. While Wes was staying with his mom, I drove into Monroe to buy a birthday gift for Polly at the mall. I also drove to the Food Lion to purchase candles for her cake. While I was in the store, the lights went out, and someone yelled, "Tornado! Get to the back of the store now!" I stayed in the back for ten minutes and then ventured to the front of the store. There were cars piled up on top of each other in the parking lot! Since our rental car seemed to be okay, I jumped into the car and drove out of there before the fire trucks came and blocked me in. I had to drive home a different route, and since this was my first time driving alone to Monroe, I wasn't sure I would be able to find my way back to Polly's. I made it just fine and thought Wes and Polly would be so worried about me. I was anxious to let them know I was okay. However, they knew nothing about the tornado, which was a little disappointing! I never did find the candles in the store.

When we returned to Arizona, I started working long hours at the bank, which was now Security Pacific Bank, as The Arizona Bank had merged with Security Pacific Corporation from California. It was nice having Wes at home to do grocery shopping, laundry, and even some cooking. He refused to do the ironing, though! We celebrated Lindsey's fourth birthday in January and Michelle's first birthday in February. Sis and Johnny came out for three months and stayed with us. Johnny started having some heart problems in late March, so he and Sis flew home instead of driving their car. Upon arrival in South Bend, he was taken to the hospital, where he had heart surgery. In the meantime, Wes and I drove their car back and stayed with Sis for a few days before flying home. One week later we had to fly back for Johnny's funeral. He had died suddenly from a heart attack after returning home from surgery.

We survived the record 120- and 122-degree heat in June. The planes were grounded in Phoenix because the manual didn't go that high for flying instructions! Wes and Thor left that morning to go to our cabin, and I was thinking how glad I was that they were in the cooler temperatures. When I got home from work, there were Wes and Thor! They'd had car trouble on the way and had to sit out in the hot weather, waiting for AAA to come and help them. So they weren't cooling off after all.

One of the highlights of 1990 was an East Valley branch manager's two-day seminar in Sedona, Arizona. A lot of it was outdoors, and several of the women were concerned about that. We had to climb a net, do a trust fall, repel down a cliff, and perform other physical exercises. The emphasis was about trust and teamwork. It ended up being a wonderful experience.

We weren't in town very long in 1991 to go to work very often. First of all, we celebrated Lindsey's fifth birthday in January. She was in kindergarten, and she loved it. She came home very disappointed the first day and said she didn't learn how to read yet! At Lindsey's graduation from kindergarten, the class put on a play, *Who's in Rabbit's House?* Lindsey knew her lines well; in fact, she also knew everyone else's part and prompted them when needed. When the teacher asked the students what they wanted to do during the summer months, Lindsey said she wanted to help her mom with Michelle, as her little sister needed a lot of attention. Michelle turned two years old in February and took her first steps. Once she was confident in walking, she walked and ran all over. We had trouble keeping up with her!

Wes visited his mom in March. We were thankful that he did, as she went to be with the Lord on June 10. She was eighty-three and died peacefully in her home in North Carolina. We flew back and planned her funeral according to the instructions she had written out and put in her Bible. She had even chosen the music and who she wanted to sing. It was a very nice service.

1991: Martha, Nancy, Jack, Lewie, and Sis

In May and August, we made two trips to Indiana. The first was for the funeral of my sister-in-law Phyllis, Jack's wife. She had died suddenly from a heart attack. We five siblings were together again for the first time in twelve years. We had a good time together in spite of the circumstances.

Then again, in August, we flew to Indiana for my thirty-fifth high school reunion. More exciting than that was the wedding the next day of Sis and Kenny Rea. Kenny was Johnny's best man at his and Sis's wedding in 1937, and Kenny and his wife, Phyllis, now deceased, were good friends over the years. Sis and Kenny were married at First Christian Church in Mishawaka, immediately after the regular church service. Barbara was matron of honor, and Phil Rea, Kenny's son, was the best man. Sis's grandson, Doug, sang "The Hawaiian Wedding Song." Doug and Pam, Sis's granddaughter, walked Sis down the aisle. A lot of people came to the wedding and wished them well. Little did Sis know that on her wedding day back in 1937, both of her future husbands were facing her. Kenny had six grown children and many grandchildren, so Sis inherited a new family. One of Kenny's grandsons, Jeff Rea, was the previous mayor of Mishawaka.

In July Wes and I flew to Denver to attend the Drums Along the Rockies concert. In August we flew to New Orleans for a TKE convention. Afterward we went with Wes's cousin Blaun and her husband, Joe, to Mississippi where we stayed in old antebellum homes and toured Confederate battlegrounds and cemeteries.

Nineteen ninety-two was another busy year for us. Wes flew to North Carolina in January to oversee the sale of Polly's house and arrange for an auction for her furniture. While he was gone, I kept getting a phone call in the middle of the night. It started out with heavy breathing, and I quickly hung up. Night after night the same call came and progressed into a man talking dirty. I quit answering the phone in the middle of the night, but he called one evening at ten. Not knowing who it was (this was before caller ID), I answered the phone, and the same voice called me by name. I quickly hung up and called Kim, and she told me to come over to their house immediately! I was scared to even open the garage door to back the car out of the garage! Wes came home a few days later, and when the phone rang, he answered it. The man finally stopped calling after that!

Sis and Kenny visited us for two weeks in February. In April Wes and I joined XYZ Seniors at Grace Community Church for a two-week trip to Greece and Turkey. I'll talk more about the trip later.

The most important thing that happened in 1992 was my retirement from the bank. I'll go into more detail in the next chapter. My last day was September 12, and we left on September 21 for a two-month-long trip to New England. Blaun and Joe joined us for the first part of the trip. We all drove in our new 1992 GMC conversion van with captain seats, which made it very comfortable. On October 12, as we were driving in Vermont at dusk, we hit and killed an eight-hundred-pound moose! A baby moose had already crossed the road, and a bull moose was waiting to cross. We had just killed the mother moose! In the accident Wes severely sprained his right ankle and couldn't walk on it. The windshield was shattered, and the front of the van was badly damaged. Our CB radio wouldn't work, so a passerby called the state police. By this time it was dark, and we were on a two-lane highway with no streetlights. The man who called the police stayed and shone his headlights on the dead moose so other cars would not run into it. Soon the highway patrol arrived, paramedics came, and an ambulance drove up, along with several police cars. The word had gotten out that a van had hit a moose and all four passengers were injured. Another story was told that two people were dead! The paramedics checked all of us to make sure we were okay.

Wes chose not to go to the hospital. The moose was taken away by the game warden, and we were towed to the next small town of Waitsfield, Vermont, where there was one filling station and one motel. We rented two rooms there for the night, and Wes was in a lot of pain all night. The filling station had a station wagon that we rented the next morning and drove to Burlington, which was about fifty miles north. We took Wes to urgent care. He had a four-way sprain of his right ankle and needed to wear a cast. He also bought a cane so he didn't put his full weight on the ankle. We rented hotel rooms in Burlington, and Joe called around and found a van for us to rent. We drove back to Waitsfield to return the station wagon and to transfer everything into the van. Wes had made arrangements for our damaged van to be towed to the GMC dealer in Burlington. We were told it could cost up to $6,000 and possibly take a month to get it repaired.

We continued on our vacation to view the colors. We drove to New Hampshire and Maine. The leaves were gorgeous. We ate a lot of lobster while we were in Maine. In fact, Blaun and I got tired of it, but the guys didn't. One evening, Wes and Joe each ordered twin lobsters for $14.95, and they ate every bit of it. Blaun and I had pizza!

Our last stop on the vacation before Joe and Blaun flew home was Boston. We went to the old cemetery where my ancestor John Endicott was buried. He was the first governor of the colony of Massachusetts. That next morning we drove Joe and Blaun to the Boston airport, and they flew back to South Carolina. I did most of the driving after that.

My nephew Gary and his wife, Cam, lived in a suburb of Burlington. We called them, and they invited us to stay at their home until the van was fixed. They said we could stay there as long as needed. I had never met their children; Christine was seven, and Jeff was four. They were both beautiful children and very well mannered. We watched them a couple of times while Gary and Cam went out for dinner or to a movie. Cam had purchased a new sewing machine, and since she didn't know how to use it, she asked me to show her. You may remember I was not a very good seamstress, but I was able to show her the basics.

Since the van wasn't going to be ready for a while yet, we did day trips to visit various places in Vermont and New Hampshire. We even drove up to Canada one day. We had originally planned to go to Indiana on the way home to visit Sis and Kenny. I suggested we go while we were waiting and come back when the van was ready. We stopped at Endicott, New York, on the way to Indiana and bought some things that had "Endicott" on them. We took turns driving.

Barbara and Jim were at Sis's when we arrived. After they returned to Michigan, Sis, Wes, and I drove to Champaign, Illinois, to visit family there. We just stayed a couple of days and drove back to South Bend. We had dinner one evening at a restaurant with Jack and family. A couple of days later, we woke up to snow on the ground! We were leaving that afternoon to drive back to Vermont. The van still wasn't ready, but the mechanic said it would be soon. We stopped and spent a couple nights with Barbara and Jim and then drove to Detroit to visit Pam and Ken before heading back to Vermont. We drove back through Canada, which took three days.

After we arrived in Burlington, we picked up the van. It was finally finished, and I transferred things from the rental van to our van. We returned the rental van, which cost $900 for the eight weeks we drove it. We had driven 4,250 miles. Everything we bought for the next couple of years had a moose on it. Wes had a cane made with a moose head on the top. It was partially made of moosewood. He still gets many comments regarding the cane. We said good-bye, thanked Gary and family, and drove to Greenville, South Carolina, to Joe and Blaun's home. After visiting there for a few days, we started out for Arizona.

We stopped at our cabin in Flagstaff, and as soon as we walked in the door, I smelled gas. There was a blue haze in the air and soot over everything. Things were very dirty, and an oily film was on the cupboards and walls. When I turned on the gas heat, we could see flames on the outside of the furnace. I quickly turned off the furnace. The next morning we called the furnace repairman, and he was able to come out that same afternoon. Our furnace was in the floor, and he climbed into it and told me to turn on the furnace. When I did, he said, "Oh my gosh! Turn it off!" He said it was completely clogged, and the gas wasn't getting to the proper place. He said it could have caught on fire at any time. After he repaired the furnace, we left for the final leg of our journey, arriving home in Phoenix on November 19. We had been gone two days short of two months.

CHAPTER 21

My Banking Career and Retirement (1955–1992)

I've talked a lot about my job at the bank, but I thought I would go into more detail in this chapter. As I mentioned in an earlier chapter, Sis got me a job at First National Bank of Mishawaka in the summer of 1955. I also worked there after school in 1956 before I graduated and full time after graduating. I worked in the bookkeeping department. I was always good at math and liked it, so banking was a good fit for me.

After Bill and I married and moved to Sault Ste. Marie, Michigan, I worked at First National Bank of Sault Ste. Marie in the bookkeeping department. I was also the "walking clearinghouse," as I took the checks to the other two banks in the city and picked up the checks they had for our bank. In Phoenix this was called the "clearinghouse," and checks were delivered by armored car. I could have been robbed, but I never really thought about it.

When we moved to Phoenix, I started working at The Bank of Douglas in February of 1960 at the Stockyards branch. The

Bank of Douglas soon changed its name to The Arizona Bank. When the stockyard with the cattle was still nearby, the flies in the branch were terrible! Each desk was given a fly swatter, and we really needed it. The flies were very annoying!

I was promoted several times, from bookkeeper to return items clerk, to notes and collection teller, and then to operations supervisor. One afternoon I was balancing the branch's financial ledger, and I noticed that it was off by $1500. I discovered after checking several items that cash was out of balance. We had a relief teller working that day, and she had evidently lowered the amount of cash on her beginning ticket, which made her cash drawer balance, but not the overall branch cash figures. I called the manager right away, and we started investigating all the facts. We called the FBI and internal auditors. I later went to court and testified against the relief teller. The jury found her not guilty because of too many other circumstances and procedures that weren't being followed. The FBI agent told me later he thought we really had strong evidence against her, but the jury just didn't understand banking procedures.

When I was the note teller, I had become good friends with Walt, the operations officer, and his wife. One day Walt was called downtown for a meeting, and he didn't come back. Later that afternoon our manager called a branch meeting and informed us that Walt had been arrested for embezzling at another bank prior to coming to our bank. We were all pretty shaken up, as he was our supervisor and friend. While I was getting ready to leave for home, the phone rang, and it was Walt's wife, wondering why he hadn't come home yet. I didn't know what to tell her, so Vern, the assistant manager, and I drove to Walt's home and told his wife in person that he had been arrested and was in jail. We didn't know how she would react, and we were prepared for the worst. However, she said she didn't believe he had taken any money and thought he would get it worked out. The next day I was checking our bank books and discovered cash was off by $500. He had evidently started embezzling from our bank also.

When I was the notes and collection teller, I was in charge of all of the livestock drafts that came into the bank. Since we were the Stockyards branch, there were many livestock companies who were our customers. Part of my job was also issuing and cashing US savings bonds. One day, when I closed my teller window and counted the cash, I was $112.50 short. I knew it had something to do with three savings bonds that I had issued at $37.50 each. I finally realized the customer had never paid me for them. I contacted him, and he came in the following day and gave me a check. That same evening I came up one hundred dollars short in my cash drawer. I knew two days being out of balance was going to reflect poorly on my record. I prayed about it that night, and the next day, a customer came in and said that right before he'd gone to bed at eleven o'clock (the exact time that I was praying), he'd decided to check his wallet to see how much money he had. He had a hundred dollars too much! He came to my window and asked me if I had balanced the previous day. I told him I was short one hundred dollars, and he took out his wallet and started counting out five twenty-dollar bills! It was close to Christmas, and I told him that was the best Christmas gift I ever received!

Banking was changing quite a bit. When I first started, we had to alphabetize all of the checks by hand and post them in alphabetical order. We soon assigned account numbers to each checking and savings account, and the numbers were imprinted on the checks with magnetic ink and sorted by machine. I'm still pretty good at putting things in alphabetic order.

My manager thought I had a good sense for approving credit. One of the things I did as operations supervisor was to approve or disapprove each customer for a check guarantee card. This meant whenever a customer wrote a check and showed the card at a store, the bank had to pay the check whether it was good or not. He asked me if I wanted to transfer into the loan department, as there was a job opening. At first I said I wanted to think and pray about it for a few days, as I enjoyed my current job. That week I had the most frustrating things happen in the operations area, and I decided that was the answer I was seeking. I started working in the installment loan department the following week.

I stayed at the Stockyards branch for eleven years and had just about every position there with the exception of the manager and the agricultural loan officer. I even went out on some cattle inspections with the manager, Bob Hoadley. My job description at that time was just to approve and manage loans, and it really wasn't considered an official officer title. The person prior to me had the title of "assistant manager and loan officer." My previous job as operations supervisor was taken over by a man, and he was promptly named "assistant manager and operations officer." I was furious, as I felt because I was a woman, I wasn't getting my officer's title! Mr. Hoadley agreed and said there was a senior vice president in charge of our area at the home office who didn't believe in promoting women as officers. He sent me to the home office for six months of training in the credit department. I was then assigned (in a different area) to Camel Square branch as assistant manager and loan officer. Finally, I received my officer's title!

The Camel Square office was located at Forty-Fourth Street and Camelback in the heart of the Phoenix financial district. We had a lot of very wealthy customers. I enjoyed the branch and the employees there. One event I'll never forget. I set the time on the vault one afternoon before I left, and I must have set it wrong, as the vault would not open the following morning. It was time for the branch to open, and the vault was still locked. A lady came in to get her passport out of her safe deposit box, as she had a plane to catch in a few hours. We had to tell her the vault wouldn't open and we didn't know when it would! I felt bad, but there was nothing we could do about it. I told her I would call her as soon as the time expired on the time clock and we were able to get inside the vault. Thank goodness it wasn't very long before we were able to open it, and she got her passport. After that we had two people check the time on the clock prior to closing the vault each evening.

I took a leave of absence in 1973 and was going to stay home for a while. That didn't last long, maybe six months, and I was assigned to the Rural and Baseline branch as an assistant manager in the loan department. I took a lot of real estate loan applications and really enjoyed working with that type of loan. The branch had a large fountain in the middle of the lobby. We were so tired of hearing it all day we could hardly wait until the bank closed to turn it off. You would think the sound of water would be soothing and peaceful, but it was pretty loud and got on our nerves.

After being at Rural and Baseline for about six months, I was asked to become the branch manager at the Mesa Country Club branch. I was the second woman to be promoted to a branch manager. I started there in 1974 and had a good staff. I interviewed and hired Peggy Stively (now Wheatley) as the notes and collection teller, and we've been good friends ever since. One time Tim, one of my customers, invited me to lunch at the Scottsdale Airport in his small airplane. The girls at the branch each wrote a poem about this trip and presented me the poems in a notebook. They were very concerned we might crash (and about his motives). They were happy when I got back safely! Here's one of the poems:

That Day
Anonymous

As our leader goes forth and
assumes her duty,

Men enjoy her company and her beauty.

There is one fellow, though, who
wants more than lunch.

What it could be—now, I have a hunch.

So, Martha, as you make this business trip,

Be very careful—don't make the first slip.

The flight plan could be more
than you bargain for;

Watch your pilot and where he will soar.

A prayer we will say for you that day,

That the skies will be clear and not a dull gray.

Keep our manager safe as she
represents our branch;

Keep her out of the arms of
this naughty mensch.

After three years at Mesa Country Club, the branch was made into a facility where there would be no loan activities and would thus no longer need a manager. I was transferred to Mesa Main in June of 1977 as assistant vice president. Harvey Prezant was the branch manager there, and I was second in charge. My area manager, Jim Lee, thought it would be a good move for the bank, as all of the existing loans would be transferred and new loans made at Mesa Main, not Mesa Country Club. I had many customers who were doctors at Mesa Country Club, and they would (hopefully) come in to see me for their loans instead of leaving the bank. It basically worked well, but I was unhappy at Mesa Main. I had taken the place of a well-liked man who had been sent to another branch to make room for me. The two secretaries resented my being there and really gave me a hard time. Whenever I asked them to type up a loan document, they quite often told me I must wait until they had time. Since I was a good typist, I started doing my own typing. One day I was talking on the phone with my boss, Jim, and he asked me if I was happy at this branch. I told him that I wasn't, but I couldn't talk about it over the phone. He asked me to come to his office in Scottsdale and discuss what was going on. After I told him, he said he would work out something for me.

After a week or so, Jim called me into his office and offered me the position of manager at the Sun Lakes office. I didn't even know where it was, but I accepted. I was to start in a month. Wes drove me there that weekend. I could only peek in the windows, as of course the bank was closed. My first day was January 30, 1978. It was a small branch with a secretary, one teller, and an operations supervisor who also did teller work. Everyone there was a Christian, so we decided to come in fifteen minutes early each day and have devotions. It was my all-time favorite branch to work!

The Sun Lakes development had only one housing section at that time, called Phase One. All of the homes were mobile homes. There was a small grocery store, Bashas, next to the bank, doctor and dental offices across the sidewalk, and the Sun Lakes Community Church was at the end of the street, along with the clubhouse and offices. I especially liked working with seniors and enjoyed visiting with them and helping them.

This was the branch where I worked when Wes and I were preparing to get married and presumably go to Iran. I gave my notice for November 30 to be my last day, but I ended up working one more week.

Earlier in 1978, on January 3, Kim started working for The Arizona Bank in the data processing department. When she was little, Kim had heard me talk about interesting things that happened in the bank, and she had always wanted to try banking. Up until this time, the bank did not hire relatives, but they had just changed their policy. Since I knew the personnel director pretty well, I called her and put in a good word for Kim. She already knew Kim and hired her right away.

Kim stayed in this position for one year, but she still wanted to be in a branch. She was soon transferred to Rural and Baseline branch as a teller. Since I had previously worked there, she was introduced as "Martha's daughter." Years later, when she had worked longer and I had just returned to the bank from Denver, I was introduced as "Kim's mother."

Kim ended up working for the bank for over forty-two years and retired on July 6, 2020, with the title of vice president. She was thought of very highly in the bank. When I retired after thirty years, I was an assistant vice president. I told her if I had worked for over forty-two years, I would have become a vice president also!

When Wes and I returned from Denver in 1981, I was hired by The Arizona Bank as a relief manager in the East Valley. While I was gone, the bank had become automated. Everyone had been trained on how to work the computers. Prior to this, we had printouts that gave us all of the information that we needed. My first day back, I couldn't even answer the phone, as I couldn't help anyone. Everything was on the computer, and I hadn't been trained. I started writing everything in a steno notebook when an employee would explain something, like how to get a balance and so forth. I soon learned just about everything that I needed to know, just by trial and error. I really enjoyed being a relief manager, as I was like a babysitter at the branch. I didn't have to do loan reports, the branch budget, or make big decisions that affected the branch.

The employees at the Broadway/Greenfield office in Mesa were having trouble getting along with their manager. They must have complained to the area supervisor, as he asked me to switch positions and become the manager at that office. I really wanted to stay where I was, but I consented. Before starting at the branch, I had to have a hysterectomy and was off work for six weeks. What a way to begin a new position!

One day, after a customer had gotten her safe deposit box and gone into a side room to look inside, she started screaming. I ran to see what was wrong, and she informed me that someone had gotten into her box and replaced her expensive jewelry with fake jewelry. She said it was dull, and it used to be shiny. I knew no unauthorized person could have gotten into her box, but I called the bank's security department to see what we should do. I was told to tell her we would check all of our entry records, but I shouldn't let her take the jewelry out. Then we put a freeze on her box. After checking all of our records, I was sure there was no possibility that someone other than those authorized could have gained entrance to her safe deposit box. After checking with the bank's attorney, we asked her to come in and open the box. We took pictures of the jewelry and then requested she take the jewelry to a reputable jeweler and have it appraised. We had her sign an affidavit before allowing her to do this. She then realized that after jewelry sits in a box for a very long time, it sometimes loses its sparkle and becomes dull.

Another time, we were all dressed up for Halloween. I was a vampire with a black cape, black pants, and red blouse. My phone rang, and a muffled voice said he had placed a bomb in our branch and we had just a few minutes to get out. I called bank security immediately, and I was told that it was probably a hoax, but it was my decision whether to vacate or not. I chose to be cautious and vacate the premises. The tellers put their money in the vault, and we hurriedly closed the vault door. In the meantime I called 911, and the police were on their way. Since we probably would already be outside when the police arrived, I was asked what I was wearing so they could identify me. I chuckled and told him I was a vampire. Fortunately he laughed also. After the bomb squad came and checked out the branch, finding nothing, we went back inside and resumed our work for the day.

I worked at Broadway/Greenfield branch for three years. Wes called me at work one afternoon and told me the security department at AT&T in Phoenix was planning to merge with security in Denver, and he was being transferred. I then gave my notice. I was given a nice going-away party—the second of three going-away parties, as I was hired again in the future.

While in Denver, as I mentioned before, I worked for Kelly Services, which used to be called Kelly Girls. I was sent to many banks to work, since I had experience. I quite often worked as a teller at Intra West Bank in the mall, ten minutes from our home. I hadn't worked as a teller for many years, but the procedure came back quickly. The first few days, I balanced to the penny. After that I was off a few cents, and then a few dollars. I've always been a perfectionist, so I always wanted to balance to the penny!

The bank I worked at the most and liked the best was First National Bank of Englewood. Colorado at that time did not have branch banking, which I was used to in Arizona. The voters kept voting it down on election day. I don't think they understood branch banking at all. Each bank in Colorado had to have its own president, trust department, accounting department, and so on, whereas in branch banking only the home office or a central location needed separate departments. Customers also had to go to each individual bank to make deposits and cash checks, even though the name might be similar. Later, after we left Colorado, they finally approved branch banking.

When I was working in the trust department at the Englewood Bank, I became pretty good friends with a woman named Pearl. She asked me if I wanted to go "out" for lunch with her the next day. I agreed, thinking we were going to a restaurant. She actually meant "out walking." Since I had to eat something for lunch, she agreed to stop for fast food, and we continued walking while I ate. I chose not to go "out" with her for lunch anymore!

When we returned to Arizona, I waited awhile until we got settled before applying back at the bank. I've already mentioned that I was hired at the Apache Wells branch in Mesa.

In all of my banking career, I had never been at a branch that was robbed. When I was at Broadway/Greenfield, we had an attempted robbery, but the lady robber didn't get any money. A woman came into the branch with a gun and pointed it at our vault teller, who had just put the vault money away. The teller told the robber she didn't have any money to give her, so the robber turned around and left. The teller yelled, "She has a gun" and tried to follow her out the door to get a glimpse of her car and license plate. I had to grab the teller and hold her back, as we had strict instructions not to follow the robber outside.

Shortly before I retired from the bank, the Apache Wells branch was robbed. I was sitting at my desk within plain view of the teller windows when two masked men came into the branch. They robbed one of our new tellers and got quite a lot of money from her. I pushed the button on my desk that notifies the police and wrote down their complete descriptions. About two weeks later, we were told they had been apprehended, and we breathed a sigh of relief and weren't quite so nervous. In actuality, only one of them had been caught. The second robber came back again that next Friday at lunchtime. We had a lot of young men in line from McDonnell Douglas Helicopter, waiting to cash their payroll checks. When one of the men in line saw the masked robber go up to the teller, he knew he was up to no good and didn't want us to be robbed again! He slammed into the robber from behind so hard that the robber flew forward, breaking the teller window. I happened to be in the lunchroom when I heard the noise and the teller's scream when the robber came flying toward her. I started to go out into the lobby, but something told me not to go! I would have been right in the path of the robber. At this point the robber turned and ran out of the building, and several men in line ran after him, tackled him, and held him on the ground until the police came. I would have loved to have gone outside to see what he looked like without his mask, but I knew that I shouldn't.

That evening, while driving home on US 60, I was stopped by a patrolman for speeding. I was deep in thought about the robbery, and I mentioned that to the policeman. He went back to his patrol car, and I'm sure he checked on my story. He didn't give me a speeding ticket, but he gave me a ticket for using excess finite resources (gasoline). If I remember correctly, the ticket cost seven dollars.

Shortly after the second robbery, we had a counselor come and talk with our group, as we were all pretty nervous. The supervisor had put all of the phones on hold while we were in the meeting, which we weren't supposed to do. Someone from home office was trying to get in touch with me, and the phone kept registering as busy. They were concerned and called the police. After the counselor left, I happened to look out the window and saw a man with a shotgun looking in. I told everyone not to leave the branch. One girl was just walking out the front door, and I pulled her back inside. Then I saw a man in the front of the branch, also with a gun. After everyone settled down, we realized they were plainclothes policemen there to protect us and to see what was going on. Everything that the counselor had told us just went down the drain.

One day we received a call from McDonnell Douglas that their outside ATM was spitting out twenty-dollar bills and wouldn't stop! I drove over there in a hurry and also called the ATM repairman. Thank goodness for the honest person who called us! I think we only lost $200.

I was asked by the Lions Club of Mesa to speak at their monthly breakfast. I spoke on changes in banking. A few years later, they asked me to speak again, so I must have done okay. I spoke on the same subject, as banking was always changing. They gave me a small lion paperweight as a gift.

In 1989 the bank's name was changed from The Arizona Bank to Security Pacific Bank. We had to put a note on every telephone to remind us to now say, "Thank you for calling Security Pacific Bank." Our opening hours were also changed to 9:00 a.m. until 6:00 p.m. Monday through Friday, and

Saturday from 9:00 a.m. until 2:00 p.m. There went our weekends going to Flagstaff!

I worked at Apache Wells for five years, from 1987 to 1992. Security Pacific Bank was just merging with Bank of America, and there were too many branch managers, as some of the branches were merging. I told my boss I was planning to retire when I turned fifty-five, and I was now fifty-four. He was able to get a package for me to retire early and get paid my full salary until I turned fifty-five. (I've always wanted to get paid while staying at home.) There was another going-away party for me at the branch and at a restaurant, where other employees came to say good-bye. One of the branch managers at another branch did not tell her supervisor she planned to retire when she reached fifty-five, as she was afraid she would get fired. When she discovered I had gotten a package, she was very upset. I've always felt being honest is the best policy.

CHAPTER 22

Life After Retirement (1993–1997)

It was now 1993. Time was flying by! Ron purchased a home in Ahwatukee with his girlfriend, Karen. Nancy and Dirk bought Wes's Scottsdale townhouse. Wes and I and nineteen others from New Hope Community Church attended John Maxwell's church growth seminar in San Diego. John Maxwell asked what our spiritual gifts were. We didn't know. When we returned to New Hope, we attended a class on spiritual gifts. Wes's gift was leadership, and my gift was service. Wes started teaching spiritual gifts at New Hope and later taught it at Grace Community Church. In April Wes and I were in charge of registration for the Nazarene Laymen's Retreat at Pine Rock in Prescott, Arizona. There were 183 who registered and attended. We were registrars for several years for the laymen's retreat.

At the first of the year, Ron Rogers, associate pastor at New Hope Community Church, announced that he and wife, Leslee, were going to Las Vegas to plant a church. A few weeks later, Wes felt the Lord was calling us to go with them. I just felt sick when he told me, and I told Wes before I would agree to go, I must feel the same calling and get excited about going. Over the next few days, I felt somewhat better about it and tentatively agreed to go. However, I prayed very specifically that if God did not want us to go, he would not send a buyer for our house. That was my "fleece."

We put our house up for sale and drove to Las Vegas to buy a home there. We looked at models in a new subdivision and found one we liked. We put $1500 down as earnest money. It was to be completed on October 10 and was contingent upon the sale of our Phoenix home. We met with Ron and Leslee numerous times, reading up on how to plant a church. We were going to meet in a school, and the name of the church would be Circle Church.

Ron and Leslee rented a home in Las Vegas and moved there. We were waiting for the sale of our Phoenix home. Many people looked at it and liked it, but we did not get any offers to buy it! We received a call from the builder of our Las Vegas home, and it was time for us to make a decision. Ours was the last home left in the subdivision, and he had a buyer for it if we weren't going to take it. We had to turn it down and believed that God had closed the door on Las Vegas. Ron and Leslee were very disappointed, but they understood.

As I was reading in my diaries to get dates and specifics for this writing, I came across one page that I'm going to copy verbatim. We were up at Pine-Oak, our Flagstaff cabin, with my sister Nancy, her husband, Dirk, daughter Debbie, and Debbie's two children, Glenna and Alison. We also had Michelle, our granddaughter.

Monday, May 31: "Had a horrible night! We had all gone to bed at 10:00. Phone rang at 11:00 p.m. (It was a wrong number.) Allison cried twice in the night. Deb put Allison in bed with her. At 4:30, Thor had a bowel movement in our bedroom. I cleaned it up. Then Michelle messed her pants, and I changèd her. At 6:00 a.m., Thor lost control again. I cleaned it up and had to bathe him outside, as he had rolled in it. (I stayed up after that.) We left at 3:00 p.m. for Phoenix. Had a tire blow out (right rear) on the way home near Happy Valley Road. A highway patrolman stopped and helped. Glenna was with us and had to go to the bathroom. She couldn't wait and wet all over the seat in the van!" So—it was a rough day and night! At least we got help with the tire blowout.

Ron asked us to watch his dog for a few days. Both dogs were in our backyard eating their dinners when I left to go to the store. Wes was still at home to make sure they got along okay. When I arrived home, there was blood all over the living room carpet, couch, and chair. I followed a trail of blood into the bedroom and outside into the backyard. Wes and the van were gone; I went into the back to see which dog was still alive, and it was Ron's chow. I knew then that something terrible had happened to Thor. I found a note from Wes that the dogs had gotten into a fight, and he had taken Thor to an emergency vet. I called the vet, and he told me Thor was going to be okay, even though he had lost a lot of blood. Wes soon brought Thor home. Thor had a huge bandage wrapped around his neck! I tried to clean up the blood, but there was too much. Our insurance company replaced most of the carpet and the couch and chair. Thank goodness for good insurance!

In July we had to put Thor to sleep, as he was losing complete control of his bladder and bowels. He had given us nearly fifteen years of great companionship and pleasure. We stayed with Thor while the vet gave him the shot.

Kim was working as operations supervisor at the Nineteenth and Thunderbird branch at Bank of America in July. Wes and I were at Pine-Oak in Flagstaff, and I called Kim before the branch opened to ask her a question. I was told she couldn't come to the phone. I felt something was wrong, so I waited awhile and called back. The branch had just had a take-down robbery! As Kim was having a meeting with the bank officers before the branch opened, two robbers, who had spent the night on the roof, came down through the ductwork in the kitchen. They held guns on everyone and forced Kim and another person to open the vault, where they promptly cleaned it out. They took over $140,000 in cash that morning, and they've never been caught, as far as we know. Of course, everyone was very upset. I sent flowers to the branch the next day, and I suggested they hire a security guard to be with them. Kim said later that the security guard was unarmed. Kim was involved in so many bank robberies, she was an expert on handling them. However, this one was the worst and scariest one!

We made several trips to Los Angeles to check on the 1954 Packard Cavalier that Wes had purchased for $1500 from a man in Anaheim. Wes had taken the car to a restoration company in Santa Ana to have the car restored. About $20,000 later, we picked it up and drove to San Diego, where we were promptly rear-ended. We drove the car back to the shop; they were just sick, along with us. We left the car there to be fixed and drove back home.

In October and November, we took the trip of a lifetime to New Zealand and Australia, which I will talk more about in a future chapter.

We did a lot of traveling in 1994. In March fifty of us from Grace Community Church went on a sixteen-day tour to Israel. Seeing where Jesus walked and talked in Nazareth, Galilee, and Judea was a great spiritual experience. Reading the Bible was never the same again! Half of us went to Egypt for five days and enjoyed the pyramids, rode camels, and sailed down the Nile River. We met a couple in Jerusalem, George and Wilma Weber, who worked in hospitality for a tour company called Educational Opportunities (EO). They lived in California and worked as volunteers for EO two or three months a year. (See the travel chapter for more details.)

In the meantime the directors of XYZ were retiring, so we applied for that position. We were getting ready to leave on a driving trip to Alaska, so we asked the pastor to call us and let us know whether we got the job or not. We never heard from him and found out in the Sunday bulletin when we returned that the church had hired another person for the job. God had closed another door.

We then applied for hospitality jobs in Israel with George and Wilma Weber. We had stopped at their house while on vacation, and they put in a good word for us. In September we received a call saying we had been chosen to go in January and February. We were very excited! God had just opened a new door!

My son, Ron, moved in with us for two months, as he and his girlfriend had broken up. She bought the house from him. Ron bought the Lakes townhouse from me and moved in as soon as the renters moved out. Lindsey turned eight years old and was in third grade. She and her mom were negotiating a weekly allowance. Kim suggested two dollars; Lindsey wanted three. They went to get Dad's opinion. Before waiting to hear the amounts in question, Mike said, "How about five dollars?" Lindsey yelled "Yeah, Dad!"

Michelle was five now and was attending a special ed class. She was given a happy-face or a sad-face sticker each day at school. One day she came home with a sad-face sticker and a notation saying Michelle had called everyone, including the teacher, a butthead! So much for new words that she was learning every day!

Wes's sister-in-law, Ruth (Larry's wife), died on October 30 after a long battle with hepatitis C. A memorial service was held for her at Grace Community Church. She was fifty-seven years old.

In February 1995 we worked in Israel as hospitality staff for EO at the Holiday Inn Crown Plaza in Jerusalem. It was quite an experience, and we loved it. It was hard work, as we put in long hours. We were volunteers, but all expenses were paid. We had a desk in the hotel lobby and helped the passengers with any problems they might have. The following two years, we worked in Israel for two months.

When we returned home from Israel, we drove to Santa Ana, California, to pick up the restored 1954 Packard. It had been there for two years. Wes drove the Packard home, and I followed in our Lincoln.

The end of May, we drove to Minnesota to attend the wedding on June 3 of Wes's brother, Larry, and his fiancé, Wilma. Wes was Larry's best man, and I was a bridesmaid. It was a nice service with a small reception afterward. While we were on our upcoming driving trip, Larry and Wilma planned to stay at our house.

After we left Minnesota, we drove to Sault Ste. Marie, Mackinaw City, and Mackinac Island in Michigan before visiting

Barbara and Jim in Lansing. We then drove to Mishawaka and visited Sis and family. Sis lived in a three-story house with a finished basement across from Mishawaka High School, from where I graduated. I took Wes for a tour of the high school. Kim, Lindsey, and Michelle flew to South Bend from Phoenix in order to attend our first Endicott reunion at Barbara and Jim's in Michigan. We had twenty-two people there and had a good time. Wes and I, along with Kim and the girls, returned to Sis's for a few days. While Kim was visiting a friend in Indianapolis, I was in charge of the girls. Michelle, now six years old, loved to climb up and down stairs. With me following behind her, she climbed from the basement to the third floor and back again. Unfortunately Lindsey pointed out that there was also an attic. We then climbed another flight of stairs!

While we were in Mishawaka, we all attended an open house for one of Johnny's nephews. His mother, Katie Stayton, had always liked Wes. She jokingly told him he should run for president of the United States. Whenever anyone new arrived at the open house, Katie introduced Wes and told them he was running for president. We told her she could be the campaign manager. We even made up a slogan: "Vote Yes for Wes for Pres."

Kim and the girls flew home, and Wes and I drove to North and South Carolina to visit his family. We stopped at Western Carolina University in Cullowhee, North Carolina, where Wes graduated from college. During this same trip, we also visited friends in Illinois, Tennessee, and Colorado. We put 9,500 miles on the van and were gone two months.

Wes and I worked in Greece in October and November in hospitality with Educational Opportunities. EO is a Christian travel company headquartered in Lakeland, Florida, that plans trips to various countries based on Biblical teachings. The Greek trip was called "The Journeys of Paul." We were based in Athens but also traveled to Thessalonica, Philippi, Kavala, Meteora, Delphi, and Corinth. (See the EO hospitality chapter for more details.)

During the time we were working in Greece in 1995, and shortly before we were to go home, Kim called and told me Michelle had been in the hospital for a week but was now home. She had been diagnosed with viral spinal meningitis and was very, very sick! Kim stayed with her while in the hospital. She didn't call and tell me because she knew I would get on a plane and fly home. After hanging up the phone, I just sat and cried. Thankfully Michelle was okay.

When we returned home, we discovered that Larry and Wilma had separated. Wilma was staying with a friend, and Larry and our van were nowhere to be found. Wes's rifle, a few of our checks, a debit card, and other items were also missing. We changed the locks on our doors and started looking for Larry (and our van). We called his last place of employment, and we learned he no longer worked there. We started calling local trucking companies and discovered where he was working. We drove there and saw our van in the parking lot. We talked with the manager, telling him the situation. We left a note in the van, asking Larry to call us and return the van to us. We told him we would not file charges against him. He did not respond or bring the van back. We waited two weeks and then returned to his place of employment, notified his supervisor, and took the van. We lost track of Larry for a few years and finally located him in Mississippi. During this time, Wes always forgave him and helped him financially.

We started out the new year of 1996 by volunteering in Israel again for two months, working for EO. We personally greeted and helped 5,500 passengers during our stay. We helped with problems from lost luggage to sickness and hospitalization. After our "tour of duty," we took a much-needed five-day vacation to the country of Jordan, and we saw where John the Baptist was imprisoned and beheaded, and where Moses saw the Promised Land from Mount Nebo. We toured the ancient city of Petra and took shelter in a Bedouin tent during a rainstorm. We watched as camels and burros meandered by the tent. We returned home on March 13. (See the travel chapter for more details.)

Our granddaughter Lindsey belonged to a group through Glendale Public Library called My Kids in Sign, which was part of the American Sign Language program. In May Lindsey and sixteen other students ranging from ages seven to sixteen put on a concert of popular songs from Broadway musicals and motion pictures. They "signed" nine songs, which included "So Long, Farewell" from *The Sound of Music* and "Singin' in the Rain." It was very enjoyable to watch.

During the summer months, we went on several more trips. We drove to Indiana to attend my fortieth class reunion and to visit relatives. We also went to Florida, South Carolina and North Carolina, El Paso, and Brownsville, Texas.

A wonderful wedding took place on October 27, 1996. My son, Ron, married Jan Muschong on the Dolly Steamboat at Canyon Lake. Ron asked Jan's eleven-year-old son, Chase, permission before asking Jan to marry him. I thought that was very thoughtful! There was only one problem with the wedding: Wes and I were working in Greece for two months and could not attend! I tried to send a telegram but couldn't find a telegraph office in Greece.

1996: Ron and Jan's wedding with Chase on the right.

Fast-forward to 1997. Israel was again our "home away from home" in January and February. We generally spent our afternoons off in the "Old City." One day we hired a Palestinian guide and driver and went to Hebron, where we saw the tombs of Abraham, Sarah, Jacob, Leah, Isaac, and Rebekah. From Israel we flew to Athens, Greece, where we worked for the month of March. (See the travel chapter for more information.)

This was our last time working with EO in Israel and Greece, as we were planning on starting a new senior adult ministry in early 1998 at Arizona Community Church (ACC) in Tempe. Pastor Guy Davidson was the founding pastor, and the six church buildings were being built. He was hoping to open the church on Christmas, but it wasn't quite ready yet.

We were still involved with XYZ at Grace Community Church, where we planned and led some of the trips.

My brother Jack died while we were visiting in Indiana in June 1997. My oldest brother, Lewie, had driven from California and was taking care of Jack, who had esophageal cancer. Jack and his son Larry, who was dependent on Jack because of the brain damage he had suffered at birth, were getting ready to move to a new location. Barbara, Jim, Wes, and I had been painting the new house and getting it fixed up. Lewie called me early the next morning and said Jack had died in his sleep. Wes and I were asked to pick up Larry from the bus stop and tell him that his dad had passed away. Larry was devastated and told us he wanted to stay in the house and keep Dutchess, his dog, with him. Larry wasn't capable of living alone, so the state of Indiana put him in a group home. Jack had told us he had a last will and testament, which would outline where Larry should go. Barbara and I tore Jack's house apart looking for a will, but we never found it.

Wes, Jim, Barbara, and I decided to clean Jack's house. The mice had taken over the kitchen—there were mice in the oven, the microwave, and the cupboards. Wes opened an old portable record player, and four mice jumped out. Things in his refrigerator had expired months and sometimes years ago. Several large dumpsters were rented for items to be thrown away.

Lewie wanted to take Dutchess, the Dalmatian, home with him to California. Lewie later told us some funny things that happened between him and Dutchess. Prior to leaving Jack's house, Lewie dropped his partial dental plate, and Dutchess caught it in her mouth, breaking the tooth. On the drive home in the car, Lewie and Dutchess stopped for the night at a campground. Lewie put up a tent, and they were settling in for the night when it started raining. Dutchess knocked down one of the tent poles, causing the tent to collapse. They were both drenched by the time Lewie was able to get the tent secured! They stopped at McDonald's or other fast-food restaurants quite often on the way home. Lewie ordered two hamburgers: one for Dutchess and one for himself. Dutchess sat upright in the front passenger seat just like a person!

After they arrived back home in California, Lewie realized he couldn't have a dog in his apartment. We had told Lewie if it didn't work out for him to keep Dutchess, we wanted her. He called us, and we drove to Pleasant Hill, California, and took Dutchess home with us.

Dutchess was accustomed to sleeping with Jack and then Lewie in their beds. We did not want her sleeping with us or sleeping on the furniture! We broke her of sleeping with us, but I don't think we ever won the battle of her not getting on the furniture. She stayed off while we were home. When we left and returned home, we noticed there was an indentation in the middle of our bed. We soon bought a leather couch and love seat and discovered she didn't like leather; therefore she never got up on the leather furniture. (We did outsmart her there, but just by accident.)

CHAPTER 23

Arizona Community Church and IN-JOY Seniors (1998)

Wes and I were attending Grace Community Church and XYZ, where we were helping with the events and trips. We heard that Pastor Guy Davidson, the founding pastor of Grace Community Church, was back in town, and he was talking about starting one last church. We saw him and his wife, Martha, at a friend's fiftieth anniversary party. We asked him if it would be possible for us to start a seniors' group similar to XYZ at the new church. He said to contact him and we'd get together and talk about it.

We contacted Pastor Guy, and we met several times over breakfast. He wanted to make sure we had a calling from God, which we felt we did. Then he wanted us to put our thoughts and plans in writing, which we did also. After reading our proposal, he said, "Let's go for it!"

First, I'll give you some background information on the church, which they named Arizona Community Church, or ACC. Pastor Guy and Elmer Bradley, former Tempe mayor, planned the church on a napkin over lunch at Coco's Restaurant in Tempe. They bought the land, built the buildings, hired the staff, and then opened the doors to the congregation. Wes and I were there for the groundbreaking and the first Sunday service.

While ACC was being built, the future congregation met occasionally on Sunday evening at Corona Del Sol High School, just across the street from the church. We set up a booth with information about the seniors group and asked people to sign their names, addresses, and phone numbers if they were interested. We had an organizing committee that met to discuss details. We decided to name the group IN-Joy! John Maxwell, from California, was a mentor to us, and he had a leadership club called Injoy Life Club. The name was copyrighted, so we thought we would have to get permission to use it. Pastor Guy said, "Add a dash and an exclamation point, and you'll be all set." The new name became IN-Joy! Seniors. (We've just recently taken off the exclamation point and made the name all capital letters). Most people never spelled it correctly anyway. I'll try to remember to type it the new way from here on.

On Easter Sunday, April 12, 1998, Arizona Community Church held its first two services at 9:00 and 10:30. Wes was an usher and I was a greeter that Sunday. We had no idea how many to prepare for. About 8:30, the parking lot was full, and drivers were beginning to vie for the few remaining parking spots on the street. People kept coming...and coming...and coming. Wes and some of the men went to the other buildings to get more chairs. There were people sitting in the choir loft (no choir yet) and in the lobby. For the two services, twenty-five hundred people attended. The sanctuary actually held eight hundred to nine hundred. Thirteen hundred bulletins had been printed, and they were all used for the first service. Pastor Guy asked people to turn in their bulletins so they could be used at the second service.

Gradually various ministries started. The first meeting for IN-JOY was held on Tuesday, May 5, 1998, at 10:30 a.m. Debbie Swanson, the cook for XYZ, had offered to cook for our group, and we quickly hired her. We offered a free lunch to anyone who came to the first meeting, and we had seventy people attend. Pastor Guy said, "Take an offering." When we took the offering, it almost covered the lunch cost! Pastor Davidson was our speaker for our first meeting, and Bonnie Peterson sang several songs. Randy Lucas led the singing and opened with our theme song, "Joyful, Joyful, We Adore Thee." Marcie Lee (now Whaley) played the piano, Norm Peck made the drinks, Ruth Coutts was in charge of decorations, Priscilla Gittus was our greeter, and Debbie Swanson made baked ziti for our first luncheon. Wes was the emcee, and I was in charge overall. We celebrated Mother's Day that Tuesday and gave each mother a carnation. We had no committees set up yet, just volunteers to help. Wes and I cleaned up after the meeting, went home exhausted, and took a nap! We met in C-1 until 2003, when we outgrew C-1 and moved to the community center.

Even before the church opened, Pastor Guy asked us if IN-JOY would be willing to sponsor and run a group that could clean the C building and sanctuary every Monday. Virgil Mathews became the leader of TLCC (Tender Loving Campus Care). The name was later changed to Dust Angels. It used to start at 9:00 a.m., but several people started coming earlier and earlier (like 4:00 a.m.). After cleaning, we always had a time of fellowship and refreshments. After Virgil retired as the leader, Gene Woods took over and was the chairman for many years. A couple of used vacuum cleaners were originally donated to us for cleaning. Gene Woods was always repairing one of them. I purchased an electric broom so Gene didn't have to use a regular broom on the bathroom and kitchen floors. Everyone had their specific job to do. If someone else came in and did the job, the original person often got upset and said, "Hey, that's my job!"

Ivan Welty was our oldest Dust Angel. We loved Ivan. He died several years ago at age ninety-five. When he was in good health, he insisted on vacuuming the entire lobby in the sanctuary. When he was unable to continue vacuuming, he sat at a table and stamped IN-Joy! on old church offering envelopes that would have otherwise been thrown away. (We always tried to be thrifty.)

On one particular Monday, I did the vacuuming. As we were sitting afterward having coffee and snacks, my chest started hurting. I couldn't breathe very well either. I became very quiet, and one of the ladies asked me what was wrong. I told her what was happening, and she hollered for Wes. (The men always sat together at a different table.) He took me to urgent care, and they in turn transported me by ambulance to Chandler Regional Hospital. After running various tests, it was determined my heart was just fine, but the vacuuming had caused my ribs and diaphragm to become sore and bruised. So lesson number one: no more vacuuming!

ACC's choir started up in June of 1998, and I became a charter member. Eventually I was asked to be in charge of the robes. We had different sizes and lengths, and I could look at someone new and tell just what size they would take. We originally had maroon robes that zipped up the back. At first, these being our first robes, everyone loved them! We had gotten them just before Christmas in 1998. They were quite warm in the summer months, so I was in charge of looking at some cooler summer robes. We voted on a white robe with a purple yoke and stripe on the sleeve that was made with lightweight material. I made sure they zipped in the front! When we wore the maroon robes in the winter, we unzipped the robe of the person walking in front of us (after we got out of public view). We used to kid about that. The choir now wears different-colored street clothes each Sunday. I'm sure we were the only choir to have two sets of robes! I continued to sing in the choir until about three years ago, when I had to drop out due to health issues.

Our first IN-JOY event was a tour of Bank One Ballpark (BOB). We had twenty-nine people attend, and it was very interesting. That was the first year for the Diamondbacks baseball team, and Wes and I had season tickets. We ate lunch at the VIAD Tower on North Central, followed by *Everest* at the IMAX Theater at Arizona Mills Mall in Tempe. Our first overnight trip was October 29 and 30, when ten of us drove to Flagstaff in two private vehicles. We stayed at Little America and toured the Riordan Mansion and Lowell Observatory and, of course, had pie and ice cream at Rock Springs. December 3 to 5 was our first out-of-state trip, when seven of us attended the *Glory of Christmas* musical performance at the Crystal Cathedral in Garden Grove, California. We also toured the *Queen Mary.* Wes drove our GMC conversion van.

For the first few months of IN-JOY, we had no computer. I typed everything on an electric typewriter. That fall Wes and I purchased our first computer and tried to figure out how to use it. We started making name tags in October, and I made flyers for trips and events. Randy Lucas printed words for various hymns that were in the public domain. He hand-printed twenty different song sheets with four songs on each sheet, plus various holiday sheets. I then typed up each song sheet on different-colored paper, and we sang from a different song sheet each week. "Joyful, Joyful, We Adore Thee" was our theme song, which we sang each week. We also put together our own IN-JOY brochure, which I did on the computer.

In January of 1999, we became very excited when we learned a lady from the church was donating a fifteen-passenger van, mainly to be used by IN-JOY. Another person donated money to buy a second fifteen-passenger van for the church. We could now use both vans for our trips and events. I generally drove one and Wes drove the other one.

As more and more people started to help with the setup and cleanup, we started forming committees. As we grew larger, we needed a visitation committee for the sick and hospitalized. Other committees were formed, and we currently have over thirty. Summer lunches were started, as people wanted to see each other during the long summer months. Each Thursday several ladies got together for a sack lunch and to play dominoes. We were small enough at the beginning that Wes called people if they missed IN-JOY. He also called some of the husbands of the attendees who weren't coming yet. He called Bruce Kick and Ken Ellerbrock so many times that they came just to make him quit calling. They both liked IN-JOY and started coming regularly.

Our average attendance in the first full year was forty, with a high of fifty. By 2002 the average was eighty-one. Wes and I divided the duties to make it more efficient. Wes did all of the programming, and I did the monthly events, trips, and paper-work. I planned hundreds of events during our eight years of service. I won't name them all, but a few were Biosphere 2 in Tucson, Sedona, Branson, Canaan in the Desert, Prescott and Jerome, Verde Canyon Train, the Dolly Steamboat, Palo Verde nuclear power plant, Canyon de Chelly, Monument Valley, and four mystery trips.

On longer trips, we generally booked through Educational Opportunities (EO). We did all of the marketing and meet-ings with the group. We went to the Holy Land twice, Greece twice, and Alaska three times. We took them on six cruises, (Panama Canal, Russian riverboat, Hawaii, South America, Canada/New England, and Greece/Turkey.) Two years ago, when Wes was unable to help me any longer, Peggy Wheatley offered to help with the trips. I've now trained her, and the last trip in 2019 to Atlanta, Savannah, and Charleston was all hers. She did a great job.

Our mission statement was "Fun, Food, Fellowship, and Spiritual Renewal" in the middle of the week. We also sup-ported missions and gave support money to Peter Pincu, a missionary to Romania. After he passed away, we support-ed his wife, Ileana, and then their son Daniel and his wife, Ramona. We also supported Sunshine Acres, Cambodia, and Mexico when the youth from ACC went there on a mission. Attendance at IN-JOY has continued to increase. Our record attendance recently was 220 for the Liberty Quartet from Idaho, an all-time favorite Gospel music group.

In 2006, after being the directors of IN-JOY for eight years, Wes wanted to retire. (I still wasn't ready, but I agreed to give it up.) We were given the privilege of selecting the next directors, with approval from Pastor Jeff. We invited

Pete and Sandy Peterson over for T-bone steaks one evening, and after talking for a while, we told them we were planning to retire. We asked them if they would be willing to be the new directors of IN-JOY. They were shocked! We asked them to pray about it and commit for at least three years. Pete called the next day and said they'd accepted and would commit for five years! We were thrilled! Pete and Sandy took IN-JOY to new heights, and it continued to grow under their leadership. We turned everything over to them with the exception of the longer trips. Sandy took over the monthly events.

2006: Martha, Joan, Keith, and Wes

We were given a wonderful retirement party, hosted by the social committee. Sandy Waldron and Lynn Van Ausdle were cochairs and did a great job. Our friends Keith and Joan Hill from California surprised us by attending. Joan sang, accompanied by Keith on the piano. The theme was a Mexican fiesta, and we were given big sombreros to wear. However, when we put them on, people behind us couldn't see, so we had to remove them. Pastor Guy interviewed us, and people told some funny stories. It concluded with a Mexican buffet lunch.

Pete and Sandy started "IN-JOY the Night," especially for those people who still worked and couldn't come on Tuesday morning. Many of the regular members came also. If I remember correctly, it only met once a month. One of the annual programs was "IN-JOY's Got Talent." The first one was a takeoff on the Arthur Godfrey show. Three of us, Jan Main, Laura Tipton, and I, were the McGuire Sisters, and we mouthed the words to the song "Sugartime." We closed the program by singing "Goodnight, Sweetheart, Goodnight." We were all dressed alike, and many people thought we were actually singing. The next year we sang "Sincerely," also by the McGuire Sisters. We no longer have "IN-JOY the Night."

When Pete and Sandy retired after five years, Pastor Richard Hatfield became the interim director for one year. That's when I started doing the monthly events again, as I knew one person couldn't do everything. Arnold and Merry Karraker did a wonderful job as directors for the next two years. They just didn't do it long enough! Running IN-JOY was a big job for one person or even two people. Pastor Jeff talked with Gayle Molenaar about taking over but having teams to help her. Thus the concept of having several couples as team directors was born. Del and Laura Tipton, and Larry and Lynn Van Ausdle, along with Gayle, were the new directors for 2016 and 2017. Prior to the start of the fall season of 2017, Pastor Bill Meiter asked if I would come alongside Gayle and be a director. I agreed, and we were both in charge for one year. In the fall of 2018, Gayle took over on her own. As of the writing of this book, she is still the director. I've just recently agreed to be the assistant director. We have an advisory team that includes all the past directors, who help as much as possible. The director's job is a full-time job with no pay! Wes used to say, "Of course we get paid. Not with a salary but by the friendships and knowledge that we're helping others."

Wes and I made photo albums of each trip and each year of IN-JOY. During the first few years, Randy Lucas made up the albums, and then we took over. We have at least twenty-four photo albums on our shelves, and a few more yet to be done. I'll talk more about trips in another chapter.

The IN-JOY ministry has meant a lot to people, especially the widows. We have people who are in their nineties still serving on one or more committees, and they are so faithful. Most of the committee members have been serving on the same committee for years and only give it up for health reasons. We put out a roster once or twice a year. There are over two hundred people on the roster. The average age is eighty-one. We've had 170 deaths since IN-JOY started in 1998.

CHAPTER 24

Ecuador, Trips, and the Packard Adventure(1998-1999)

1999: All of us in the back of the truck, heading to the Village of Mulintimi in Ecuador

During February 1998 Wes and I spent two weeks in Ecuador on a Work and Witness mission with twenty others from Flagstaff Church of the Nazarene. We built two churches in a village in the Andes mountains at 10,500 feet elevation. What a great experience as we helped carry and pour concrete, cut and soldered rebar, and played games and sang songs with the village children. To honor us, the villagers served guinea pig one day for lunch! I could only eat two bites and then gave it to one of the workers. We went back to Ecuador again in February of 1999, and made a third trip in 2000 to help build a gym. On one of the trips, we played with a pet llama

Charlie the llama and one of the natives

named Charlie. We soon found out that the locals were going to butcher Charlie, who became our meal for the day. I could *not* watch as they killed him. It was also hard to eat the meat!

The summer months found us traveling by van—first to California in July, where my family had a West Coast Endicott reunion, and then to Indiana for another Endicott reunion. While we were on our way to Indiana, Jim Armstead, my niece Barbara's husband, died of myelofibrosis, a rare cancer of the bone marrow (which is what Wes had also). He was sixty-three years old. We arrived in Michigan just in time for Jim's funeral. In April of that same year, Jim and Barbara had gone with us on an XYZ Hawaiian cruise. We were so glad Jim was able to go and enjoy himself. Before leaving Indiana, we visited a pastor friend's church in Alexandria and were thrilled to meet and talk with Gospel musicians Bill and Gloria Gaither. Bill and Gloria's granddaughter was being dedicated at church that evening, and we sat behind them. We also drove to South Carolina and North Carolina, where we helped with the Pierce reunion. (This

1998: Deane and Larry Pierce's Wedding

was the year for reunions!) Then on to Mississippi, where we attended the wedding of Wes's brother, Larry. He and his new wife, Deane, were working at the Baptist church in Pass Christian, Mississippi.

In June Lindsey was chosen to travel with the People to People Student Ambassador Program for two weeks. They traveled to England, Wales, and Scotland. People to People is a cultural exchange program where students tour various educational sites, and it is offered to middle and high school students. All students had to complete an application and be interviewed to see if they possessed the maturity and social skills needed.

In March of 1999, we were in an automobile accident, which totaled our 1991 Lincoln. A sixteen-year-old girl turned left in front of us at the corner of Forty-Eighth Street and Ray Road in Ahwatukee. Wes and I were bruised, and Wes received burns and cuts from the airbag. Sis was with us, riding in the back seat (without her seat belt, unknown to us, as we were only going a short distance). She was hurt the most and ended up going to the ER in an ambulance. The young girl who hit us was very distraught, as the car she was driving was her mother's brand-new car. She said her mother was going to kill her and was sobbing uncontrollably. I put my arms around her and told her that her mother was going to be so happy she wasn't hurt. Later I received a letter from the girl and her mother, thanking me for being so kind to her.

Just before the accident, we had been out to eat with friends, Don and Connie Bowman, and they had invited us to their house for brownies and coffee. When the police came, I said we needed to call our friends and tell them we weren't coming. It was before cell phones, so the policeman called them. When Don answered the phone, the policeman said, "I hear there's coffee and brownies at your house." Not knowing who it was, Don hung up on him. Then I called and told Don what had just happened. Don and Connie drove over right away and took us to the hospital to be with Sis. It took several weeks for Sis's arm and shoulder to heal. Now *no one* rides in our car without their seat belts fastened!

On April 20, 1999, you may recall that two twelfth-grade boys at Columbine High School in Littleton, Colorado, killed twelve students and one teacher on what is known as the Columbine High School massacre. As we were in that school district when we lived in Colorado in 1981, I remembered that some of our neighbors had babies that year, which would have made them eighteen years old at the time of the shooting. I checked the newspaper for names, and one neighbor boy was listed as one of the "jocks" who might have been an intended victim but was not hurt. I wrote to our next-door neighbors, Charlie and Jean Herndon, whose daughter, Laura, would have been that age. Jean wrote back, telling me Laura had decided to stay home that day, as she wasn't feeling well. However, Jean was at work and did not know Laura was at home. Jean spent hours in a panic until she was able to find and talk with her daughter. The two boys who did the shooting and attempted bombings took their own lives. Columbine High School was where Jaakko, our Finnish exchange student, went to school in the fall of 1980 and spring of 1981.

That same year, we drove our 1954 Packard to Warren, Ohio, for the week-long Packard centennial celebration. We arrived in Warren trouble-free and had a wonderful time at all the festivities. Over one thousand Packard cars were there. Wes entered our car in the judging, and it took second place in its category. After driving to Indiana for the annual Endicott reunion at Potawatomi Park, we headed for home.

1999: Endicott Reunion in South Bend, Indiana

Unfortunately, our forty-five-year-old car started rebelling. In Illinois the fuel pump went bad. (Fortunately Wes had bought a fuel pump at the car show.) Two days later we were on our way again. After only two hours, the fan belt snapped. While Wes was changing it, two Illinois transportation workers stopped and helped. After that it took us a week to drive through Kansas, as the carburetor had to be rebuilt, and then the generator went bad. A voltage regulator also had to be installed. In spite of this, we enjoyed the state of Kansas and visited the Eisenhower Museum, home, and visitors' center; the Greyhound Hall of Fame; the Russell Stover candy outlet, where we purchased fifty small boxes of chocolate to give to IN-JOY members; the Swedish town of Lindsborg; several museums, the Heritage Center Monument Rocks (also called the Chalk Pyramids); and many car repair shops! Quite often we checked out of the motel very early in the morning to beat the heat and would start driving on the highway when the car started to act up again. We would just turn around, go back to the hotel to pick up our key, and go back to bed until the repair shop opened. This happened twice. It was very frustrating!

We finally made it through Kansas, hobbled into Albuquerque, New Mexico, and had more problems. I wasn't sure we would ever get home! We stopped at our cabin in Flagstaff for the night and finally arrived at home in Phoenix.

Some bad news! In December my niece Diana called and said my brother Lewie was very sick with the flu and was in the hospital and not expected to live. Sis and Barbara were visiting for Christmas, so we all decided to drive to northern California to see and be with Lewie. We were there several days, and he seemed to be doing better. We decided to drive home in order to be home for Christmas. We checked out of the hotel and were eating breakfast when Diana called us on December 23 and told us he had just passed away. We checked back into the hotel and stayed through Christmas for his funeral on December 28. He was seventy-seven years old. Shortly before he passed away, I talked with him about accepting Jesus as his Savior, which he did!

CHAPTER 25

Trips, Cancer, and Grandchildren (2000-2005)

On May 15, 2000, we left for Kufstein, Austria, where we spent two glorious months working in hospitality for Educational Opportunities (EO). You may recall we used to do this in Israel and Greece. We had never been to Austria, and we just fell in love with the beautiful countryside and the friendly people. We were able to go once or twice a week with the passengers on their day trips. The highlight of the trip was getting to attend the Passion play in Oberammergau, Germany, which is performed every ten years.

Pastor Guy Davidson, our senior pastor, had heart surgery in July 2000 and a massive stroke a few days later. God performed a real miracle in his life, as he learned how to walk and talk again and was able to finally participate again in the Sunday services. He couldn't talk immediately after the stroke, but he started singing "Jesus Loves Me" after a few days.

One advantage of getting older is that Wes and I received our first Social Security checks in 2000. We started buying hearing aids and other items needed as a person gets older.

In 2001 our lives took on a new twist. Wes was diagnosed with rectal cancer. The surgeon suggested chemo and radiation be done prior to surgery, hoping to shrink the tumor. I don't think Wes missed any IN-JOY meetings during that time. When Wes had the surgery, the doctor couldn't find any evidence of a tumor. It was completely gone! It was a real miracle!

In March we took twenty-six people to Greece on a ten-day land tour and three-day Greek island cruise. After the group trip, Wes and I stayed nine days on our own, relaxing and visiting Greek friends. After spending some time at Pine-Oak, we set off on a six-week driving trip to visit friends and relatives. We stopped in San Antonio to visit the Alamo and the River Walk. We decided it was *not* the best time of the year to vacation in Texas! Off to Mississippi, where we visited Wes's brother and wife. Also not a good time to visit—it was hot and humid! After spending a week with relatives in South and North Carolina, we headed to Indiana and attended my forty-fifth high school reunion. It was fun to see how old everyone else looked!

In May we had a great five-day trip to San Diego with thirteen others from IN-JOY. Eighteen of us rode in the two church vans in November to Williams, Arizona, where we boarded the train (first class, no less) for the Grand Canyon. We had a nice sunny day to view the canyon's beautiful colors.

September 11, 2001! Sound familiar? Everyone remembers what they were doing on this date. I was babysitting our grandchildren, Lindsey (age fifteen) and Michelle (age twelve), at their home in Glendale, Arizona. Wes had just taken Kim and Mike to the airport for a trip to Egypt and Spain. I turned on the TV to check on the weather and saw the first plane hit the north tower of the World Trade Center in NYC. Then the second plane hit! I called Lindsey in to watch it and told her not to worry, as Kim and Mike were still at the Phoenix airport. They were actually waiting in line to get on the plane when the Jetway door was closed, and the flight was canceled. Kim called me, as they couldn't find out what was going on. They of course canceled their trip that day but ended up going just to Spain the following week. I didn't want them to go then, but they did.

This was also the year for the Diamondbacks to win the World Series. We had given up our season tickets that year, as we were too busy to attend eighty-two games. Of all years to give up the tickets and not be able to attend the World Series games! As you may recall, we beat the Yankees in the bottom of the ninth inning in the seventh game of the series! Such excitement! One of Wes's favorite Diamondback players was southpaw Brian Anderson. He was sitting at the counter of a local coffee shop when Wes entered and ordered coffee. Wes accidentally spilled his coffee on Brian and then realized who he was. Wes was always looking for speakers or singers for IN-JOY. After apologizing to Brian, Wes asked him if he would come and speak at one of our Tuesday meetings. Anna, Brian's wife and agent, said, "Yes, he would be glad to do that." Both Brian and Anna came. Everyone enjoyed hearing Brian speak, and he signed autographs after the meeting.

Time marched on, and in January of 2002, thirty of us from IN-JOY went to Palm Springs, California, for three days. Wes was unable to go, as he was having side effects from the chemo and radiation. We enjoyed the Oasis Date Gardens, the Aerial Tramway, Air Museum, a city tour, windmill tour, and the Fabulous Palm Springs Follies!

We flew to Montreal on Halloween, where Wes purchased a 1954 Packard Clipper with only twenty thousand miles on it. We already had a 1954 Cavalier. Both cars were the same color—two-tone blue. We drove the Clipper from Montreal to Barbara's home in Michigan, where we had the car transported back to Phoenix.

2002: Our family picture: First row: Kim, Martha, and Jan; Secord row: Michelle, Lindsey, Wes, and Chase: Back row: Mike and Ron

We celebrated New Year's Eve with a group from IN-JOY by attending the Gaither Jubilate concert at America West Arena. It was a five-hour concert. What a way to bring in the new year!

Two thousand three was another busy year. In April I had surgery on my left shoulder for torn ligaments. The surgery went well, and recovery was successful as long as I remembered to do the physical therapy at home.

I kept running into people who were from Mishawaka, Indiana, my hometown. Someone suggested I have a reunion for those who had graduated or attended Mishawaka High School (MHS). In May of 2003, I mailed out invitations to fifty people to attend the first Arizona MHS Alumni Luncheon at Monti's La Casa Vieja restaurant in Tempe. The first year, thirty-five attended; the second year, we had seventy-two. After the first year, we held it in March to catch the winter visitors who came to Arizona for the Cubs spring training games. Our high school has an MHS alumni club that meets for lunch once

2008: Martha leading the MHS luncheon at Monti's restaurant

a month in Mishawaka. About three hundred alumni attend. The club has a membership of almost five thousand, and we receive a monthly newsletter with interesting information about the alumni. I have continued the luncheon each year since. We had it at Monti's until it closed in 2015. We've had it at various places since then. For the 2020 reunion on March 7, I mailed out 160 invitations, and thirty-three responded. We just made it under the wire for meeting in groups because of the pandemic rules. Two thousand twenty-one will be the nineteenth annual luncheon, if we have it.

We led several trips and events for IN-JOY. We took eighty-two people to Barleens Arizona Opry, and we also visited Champlin Fighter Museum and Taliesin West, attended several plays at the Hale Theater, and ate at Organ Stop Pizza. We took them on a three-day trip to Kartchner Caverns, Bisbee and Douglas, and a four-day trip to northern Arizona.

Wes and I celebrated our silver wedding anniversary by flying to Hawaii for two weeks. Our son, Ron, and his wife, Jan, joined us at our time-share on the island of Kauai. We all had a great time! We even had time to play some dominoes and cards.

Michelle graduated from the eighth grade and was now in special education classes at Peoria High School as a freshman. She was learning how to read and write. She was at a first-grade level academically and a fourth-grade level socially.

Lindsey wrote a beautiful essay about Michelle in her senior year at Ironwood High School in Glendale. Here are a few excerpts from Lindsey's article:

Lesson of Acceptance
by Lindsey Rinke
2004

I only have one sibling, my sister, Michelle Stephanie Rinke. She is now fifteen years old and has Down syndrome. Her disability slows her mind's process. It took her twice as long to accomplish things most babies start to do at an early age. It took her three years until she was able to say words in sentence form. But now, being fifteen years old, she can speak clearly and continues to surprise us each day with new vocabulary. She is a neat freak and has made my life a pain, since her room is always cleaner than mine. She is obsessed with movies and has a collection of over four hundred videos and DVDs.

Having a sister with Down syndrome has changed my life. At first I hated introducing my sister to my friends. I thought others would look down on me because of her. But looking back, I realize that I got so much more than a retarded sister. I got a sister that would always love me no matter what. I'll always be her big sister that she looks up to, and I'm happy to be there for her. Though she hated coming to my basketball or volleyball games, she always came up to me after each game and asked, "Sissy, did we win?"

I have never been prouder of having a sister with Down syndrome than I am now. Though she may never be able to drive a car or get married, and will probably live with my parents for the rest of her life, she has done so much that has made our family as close as it is. There have been so many times that we have doubled over laughing from some cute line she said or something she has done.

Though my sister has a disability, it sure hasn't held her back. She has participated in dance concerts and Girl Scouts, has played on baseball teams, and has been involved in track and swimming in Special Olympics. Just the smile of accomplishment on her face makes me the proudest sister in the world. I wouldn't trade it for anything.

Lindsey ended her essay with this quote from an unknown source: "When a person has Down syndrome, it's the only thing they have that you don't. They still have a house, a family, friends, favorite pastimes, hobbies, and dreams."

When Lindsey talked about Special Olympics, I remembered the time that Michelle had won two medals for track, and her friend Christine was crying because she didn't win a medal. Michelle gave one of her medals to Christine. Then there was the time Michelle and her friend Amanda were running in the same race. Michelle stopped running because she was tired, and Amanda, who was farther ahead, came back to help Michelle.

Lindsey, #22, in her volleyball uniform

Lindsey played both basketball and volleyball during her high school years. An article in the school paper featured Lindsey. Her volleyball coach said, "Lindsey is funny, hardworking, very aggressive, and a good kid. She's had a huge impact on the team. She's a leader by example on the court." In her senior year, she was a straight-A student, student body president, and homecoming queen. There was an article about Lindsey in the *Arizona Republic* in the sports section on January 23, 2004, with the headline "She's the stabilizer." The article quoted the basketball coach as saying, "Lindsey is more of a complete player and tries to do everything to help the team."

Lindsey and Kim were checking out Christian colleges for Lindsey to attend after she graduated. Michelle was quite upset when she learned Lindsey might be going away to college soon. However, she perked up when Kim told her she could have Lindsey's room. Ron and Jan's son, Chase, graduated from Peoria High School and attended DeVry Technical Institute in the fall.

The year 2004 proved to be a good year but a busy one for us. IN-JOY Seniors' attendance had grown to 115 or more each week. Throughout the year we took the group to Barleens

Arizona Opry (a favorite every year), a Diamondbacks baseball game, a mystery trip, and several plays at the Hale Theater.

Barbara visited us in January, and she told us she had met a man named Paul Kerekes, and they were dating. They both worked at the local hospice facility as volunteers and had met there. Paul did not seem to understand the time difference between Michigan and Arizona. We woke up many mornings with the phone ringing at 5:00 a.m. Unfortunately, the phone was beside my side of the bed. I sleepily answered the phone and told Paul to call back in a couple of hours. Barbara returned home to Michigan, and she and Paul were married on Valentine's Day, February 14, 2004.

During the summer months, my sister Nancy was diagnosed with the West Nile virus. She and Dirk had been in Chicago, where she was bitten by mosquitoes. On the flight home, Dirk said she started acting and talking very strangely. The next day Dirk took her to the emergency room, and she was promptly put into the ICU. They did not know what was wrong with her, as there had been no cases yet of West Nile virus in California. Her left side was paralyzed, so their first thought was a stroke. Dirk called me, and I told him that the symptoms of WNV were in our paper, and it sounded similar to what Nancy had. After a spinal tap was done, she was definitively diagnosed with West Nile virus. She was so sick that she didn't want to live any longer. Dirk called me and asked me to talk with her and encourage her, which I did. She finally pulled through, but she had to go to physical therapy and learn how to walk and talk again. Nancy had previously had a brain tumor and kidney cancer. With God's help she was able to pull through these health issues. Nancy was deeply grateful for all of the hundreds of people who "stormed the prayer gates of heaven" to ask for her healing and recovery.

Our granddaughter Lindsey graduated from Ironwood High School and received a basketball and an academic scholarship to Vanguard University, a Christian college in Costa Mesa, California. Wes and I drove there in the fall to watch her play, meet her new friends, and see her dorm room. She was enjoying her first semester and also got all A's on her report card. Michelle was a sophomore at Peoria High School and was involved in track and swimming in Special Olympics. She also joined a special needs cheerleading class. She had her first date! Ron and Jan's son, Chase, turned twenty and went out on his own. He was working nights as a security guard.

In September we flew to Germany and Austria for two weeks with good friends Larry and Lynn Van Ausdle. We had a wonderful time. One of the highlights was attending the festival of the cows in Kufstein, Austria, the town where we stayed. Each fall the cows, decorated with flowers and bells, return from the mountains where they've been grazing all summer. The cows actually parade through the town, and the people have a big festival with food and crafts. There's more information in the travel chapter.

The year 2005 was rather quiet. Wes sold *both* of his 1954 Packard cars! He said it was time to start "simplifying life." Now there was room in the garage for both of our regular cars.

Wes and I drove to Costa Mesa, California, again this year to watch Lindsey play basketball. Vanguard University was rated number one and were undefeated in their division. Vanguard played Arizona State University girls' basketball team as a preseason game. Many of our friends went to the game with

2005: Our friends at the ASU-Vanguard game

us. Jan's son, Chase, moved back home again (children have a tendency to do that). Michelle continued to have a few dates with boys and enjoyed her social life.

We were still directors of IN-JOY. We "injoyed" several local events, including *Gypsy, The Buddy Holly Story, Camelot, Nunsense, No Time for Sergeants,* and *The Sound of Music,* all at the Hale Theater. Longer trips included five days in Branson, a trip to Kartchner Caverns to tour the "Big Room," and a major cruise through the Panama Canal, on which we hosted fifty-two seniors for fourteen days. More on that in the travel chapter.

On our own we made a four-week driving trip to Illinois, Indiana, Michigan, North and South Carolina, and Mississippi to visit relatives. No problems with our old 1992 GMC van with the exception of two blowouts on our way home. Wes was getting good at changing tires! The rest of the summer was spent in Flagstaff at our cabin, cooling off from the intense Phoenix heat.

CHAPTER 26

More Trips, Deaths, and Surprises (2006-2011)

The year 2006 was another busy year. In May we retired as directors of IN-JOY after eight years of leadership, which I discussed previously in the chapter on ACC and IN-JOY.

We had a whirlwind summer. In May Wes and I flew to New York City for five days with our church choir to sing at Carnegie Hall. I sang, and Wes toured. Maryellen Hawkinson, from ACC, did most of the planning, and I helped with some of the airline details. There were sixty-five who went on the trip. We checked into the Hyatt hotel next to Grand Central Station. Since it was Wes's birthday, I took him to a Greek restaurant for dinner. In between rehearsals we visited the Statue of Liberty, Ellis Island, the Empire State Building, and attended *Beauty and the Beast*. Wes and I attended a Yankees baseball game with Jan and Del Main. The Yankees beat the Kansas City Royals 15-4. The next day was dress rehearsal in the morning and the concert in the afternoon. We sang with 250 other choir members and a full orchestra. We sang

Requiem, which was in Latin. The composer, John Rutter, directed the choir and orchestra. It was quite an experience to be in that historic concert hall.

In July we went on a three-day Alaska cruise and nine-day land trip to the Yukon and Alaska. It was a great trip! In August we flew to Indiana to attend my fiftieth high school class reunion. I saw many fellow classmates I hadn't seen for years. The next day Barbara and I hosted a ninetieth birthday open house for Sis. Sis's stepgrandson, Jeff Rea, who was the mayor of Mishawaka, declared October 25 "Winifred Rea Day" in Mishawaka.

In November Wes and I flew to Tennessee, where we attended our granddaughter Lindsey's basketball tournament. Her team, Vanguard University from Costa Mesa, California, won all three games. They were then in first place, as they had beaten the number-one-ranked team, Union University from Jackson, Tennessee.

This was the year Michelle started going steady with her boyfriend, Casey Bagley. Kim and Nancy (Casey's mom) took them to movies and other places, but they weren't allowed to sit with Michelle and Casey! As of this writing, they are still going together, a total of fourteen years.

In 2007 Lindsey turned twenty-one. Wes and I, along with Kim and Mike, were in California at one of Lindsey's away games with Azusa Pacific University. Vanguard won, and right after the game, everyone in the crowd sang "Happy Birthday" to Lindsey. Kim and Mike told her she could ask a few of her friends out for dinner at a nearby Mexican restaurant. I called and made reservations, and twenty of her friends, plus a few adults, showed up. Among them was a new friend, Bryan Binninger. We noticed that he sat next to Lindsey at the head of the table. We soon learned that Bryan had asked Lindsey out for Valentine's Day. (He's now her husband.)

Two thousand seven was another year for big trips. In March Wes and I, along with our pastor and his wife, took a group of forty-five people on a ten-day pilgrimage to Israel. This was our sixth trip to Israel, and we once again came home on a spiritual high. I'll go into more details in a future chapter. In May we flew to North Carolina, where we attended Wes's fifty-first high school reunion. This was the first reunion Wes had attended (they only had two), and we both had a fabulous time. In July we joined a group from a Lutheran church in California for a two-week Russian riverboat cruise. Details on this trip are in the travel chapter. We once again flew to Tennessee to watch Lindsey play in the NAIA basketball tournament. We then drove to Gulfport, Mississippi, to visit Wes's brother, Larry, and his wife, Deane. Larry was now in a nursing home, and he was blind and couldn't use his arms or legs, but his spirits and attitude were positive. Our last trip for the year was an after-Christmas, eleven-day driving trip to California with our dear friends Larry and Lynn Van Ausdle. We attended the Tournament of Roses Parade and viewed the floats before and after the parade, toured the Reagan and Nixon Museums, and traveled to San Diego, where we enjoyed four days of sightseeing. The trip ended in Costa Mesa, where we visited Lindsey and attended her basketball game.

2007: Seated: Dirk and Debbie; Standing: Tim and Manda

Some sad things happened in 2008. My sister Nancy Nelson died in May from kidney cancer, which had traveled to her lungs. I made several trips to Apple Valley, California, to visit her prior to her death. She was seventy-five. It was nice visiting with her son Tim, daughter Debbie and granddaughter Manda at Nancy's memorial service. A week after we visited Wes's brother, Larry, we received a call from Deane, informing us that Larry had passed away. We were glad we had visited him the previous week. In December, after Christmas, we had to put Dutchess, our fourteen-year-old Dalmatian, to sleep. She had a cancerous tumor on her paw, and the vet said he would have to cut off her paw and possibly the leg. We did not want her to go through that. We stayed with her and comforted her while the vet put her down.

2007: Elyshia and family at her quinceañera in Arizona

We had a mini Phoenix family reunion in October when our great-grand-niece, Elyshia Armstead, had a quinceañera on her fifteenth birthday. Relatives came from Michigan, Indiana, and Texas for the big event. The next day we had a surprise fiftieth birthday party for Kim. We also celebrated Sis's ninety-first birthday a little early. The quinceañera was beautiful, and Elyshia was absolutely stunning. The celebration was similar to a wedding.

Ron and Jan purchased a new five-bedroom home in Avondale, Arizona, with a finished basement. Ron finally had his "man cave." He quickly filled it with his marble collection, kaleidoscopes, and model cars and trucks.

In the travel realm, we made ten trips to California in 2008 to watch Lindsey play women's basketball at Vanguard University in Costa Mesa. In March we flew to Jackson, Tennessee, along with Kim and Mike, for the NAIA Division One Women's Basketball National Championship. Vanguard beat

the number-one-ranked, undefeated team, winning the national championship. We were all on cloud nine! We were so proud of the entire Vanguard team, and we felt Lindsey had played an important part in winning the championship. This was Vanguard's first national championship.

Two thousand eight was a year of surprise parties! It all started in February for my seventieth birthday. My family surprised me by inviting family and friends for dinner at my favorite restaurant, Monti's La Casa Vieja. Then in May it was Wes's turn for a surprise party with family and friends on his seventieth birthday. In August our son, Ron, turned fifty, and his wife, Jan, surprised Ron by having a party at their home.

2008: Wes, Lindsey, and Martha at Lindsey's graduation from Vanguard University

Lindsey graduated in May from Vanguard University with an accounting degree. She was hired at KPMG, an accounting firm, in Costa Mesa. Michelle's cheerleading team (and mothers) went to Atlanta to compete against seven other special needs cheer teams and many regular teams. Michelle's team, Lightning, was announced as the national champion in their category. She and Casey also took ballroom dancing lessons during the year. We traded in our old 1992 GMC conversion van, which had really served us well, with 172,000 miles on it. We bought

2008: Michelle's cheer team (she's in the back row, second from the left)

a 2008 Chrysler Town & Country van, which was our gift to each other for our thirtieth wedding anniversary on December 23.

Travel was still a big part of our lives in 2009. In March we took twenty-seven people on a fifteen-day cruise and land tour of Greece and Turkey, which included three days on our own in Athens. In August and September, Wes and I drove 7,200 miles and were gone six weeks. We visited friends and relatives in Texas, Mississippi, Georgia, Tennessee, North and South Carolina, Indiana, Michigan, Illinois, and Colorado. We rode the narrow-gauge train from Durango to Silverton, which was an awesome experience. The fall colors of the aspens were just magnificent! In November we took thirty-one people to see Christmas shows in Branson and then toured the Precious Moments Chapel in Carthage, Missouri. Everyone had a good time, and the weather was chilly but nice.

Wes and I drove to Palm Springs, California, to watch Michelle in a cheerleading competition. Her team, all with disabilities, took first place.

We stayed busy in 2010. Our church choir had two Gospel hymn sings during the year, and we presented the musical *The First Noel* at Christmas. The next Sunday we performed five songs from Handel's *Messiah*. We were busy practicing for months! I was on the board of directors for AZBAR (Arizona Bank of America Retirees), and we planned quarterly lunch meetings with various speakers. We purchased a partial season ticket package to the Arizona Coyotes hockey games, along with good friends Ernestine and Murchie Hatt. We enjoyed attending the games and going early to eat at Johnny Rockets restaurant.

In February I flew to Indianapolis, rented a car, and drove to South Bend (150 miles one way) to escort my now ninety-three-year-old sister back to Phoenix on the plane. Sis stayed for about three weeks, attended the high school luncheon at Monti's, and then I flew with her back to Indiana. In August Wes and I flew to Portland, Maine, rented a car, and drove to Beaver Harbour, New Brunswick, to visit Murchie and Ernestine Hatt at their summer home. After enjoying our stay there for five days, we drove to Bartlett, New Hampshire, where we stayed for a week in a time-share and did lots of hiking and sightseeing. We returned home for a few weeks and then led a group of thirty-three to Germany, Italy, Austria, and Prague. We all attended the every-ten-year Passion play in Oberammergau, Germany. Everyone fell in love with the Tyrol area of Austria. (See the travel chapter for more details.)

During the hot summer months in Phoenix, we escaped to our cabin in Flagstaff. We had several out-of-town visitors, which we always enjoyed. We found a wonderful church in Flagstaff—Victorious Life Christian Center, which had become our summer church. Pastor Tim Masters and his wife, Jewel, became very good friends.

On New Year's Eve in 2010, Wes and I hosted twenty-two of our friends for a New Year's celebration, which we continued each year until our health didn't permit it any longer. We celebrated at 10:00 p.m. with New York City, where it was midnight.

In January and February of 2011, Sis visited for five weeks, escaping the snow and cold in Indiana. In March we enjoyed the Phoenix Coyotes hockey games. I hosted the ninth annual Mishawaka High School reunion at Monti's. In May we traveled with Larry and Lynn Van Ausdle to Washington, DC, and surrounding historic highlights, including Mount Vernon, Jamestown, Williamsburg, Gettysburg, Philadelphia, and the Naval Academy in Annapolis, Maryland.

In June we flew to Indiana and then drove to Michigan for the bat mitzvah of great-grandniece Sarah Finegood. After the service in the synagogue, a big party was held on a chartered boat on Lake St. Clair near Detroit. Everything was first class!

In August we drove to San Antonio for the TKE convention, Wes's social fraternity. Wes's first job was as a traveling rep for TKE in Indianapolis, Indiana. We also spent several days with our friends Tim and Linda Doll in the Texas hill country of Kerrville. Tim was my classmate at Beiger School in Mishawaka. A small herd of deer greeted us at the Doll home. After leaving there, we visited my grandnephew, Mike Armstead, and family in El Paso and went to see the outdoor drama *Viva El Paso!*

September meant back to Indiana for the MHS alumni meeting of some five hundred people that gather every month; then to my fifty-fifth high school reunion. I also planned and hosted the first Beiger Junior High reunion at a local restaurant. It was rather hard to do it from a distance, but it all worked out. Some of the people who attended Main Junior High School, our rival, wanted to come, but I had already closed the reservations. Barbara and I had organized a ninety-fifth birthday celebration for Sis, attended by eighty people.

Pastor Richard Hatfield of ACC was asked to become the director of IN-JOY for the coming year. I offered my help with the committees and once again planned the events. Events included the Poinsettia Festival, Christmas caroling, a play at Hale Theater, and the leadership party. I was also in charge of the IN-JOY Christmas program, which was built around the song "The Night Before Christmas." Over fifty people participated in the production. I had allowed too much time between numbers, and we had too much time left over at the end. We sang some carols until lunch was ready.

CHAPTER 27

Good Years and Bad Years (2012–2016)

We had some wonderful things happen in 2012. In May we went on an eight-day trip to Los Angeles with Dewain and Sharol Cisney. We visited Catalina Island, the Reagan and Nixon Presidential Libraries, and ate lots of good seafood.

In July Wes and I led a two-week Russian riverboat cruise with twelve people. We thoroughly enjoyed the Russian people and the beautiful countryside. (See the travel chapter for more details.)

The highlight of the year was our ten-day trip to New Brunswick to visit Murchie and Ernestine Hatt. We had a small group of fourteen friends from our church, whom I called "the gang." When Wes and I previously visited the Hatts, Ernestine said, "Wouldn't it be fun if our gang could all come to New Brunswick?" I took her up on that at the time and started planning the trip. All but Tom and Sandy Waldron were able to go. We flew into Portland, Maine, and spent the night at Comfort Inn. We rented two six-passenger vans; Wes drove one van with Dewain and Sharol Cisney and me, and Del Main drove the second van, which carried his wife, Jan, and Larry and Lynn Van Ausdle. Roger and Lorna Scott, from Canada, drove their motor home and met us in New Brunswick.

KING SQUARE IN SAINT JOHN   AUGUST 13, 2012   NEW BRUNSWICK CANADA

Front Row: Lynn VanAusdle, Ernestine Hatt, Lorna Scott, Martha Pierce, Jan Main and Sharol Cisney   Back Row: Larry VanAusdle, Roger Scott, Murchie Hatt, Wes Pierce, Del Main and Dewain Cisney

The next morning we drove to New Brunswick. A friend of the Hatts loaned them a home nearby, where Wes and I and the Mains stayed. The Cisneys and Van Ausdles stayed with Murchie and Ernestine, and Roger and Lorna slept in their motor home. We all ate together at Murchie and Ernestine's.

We had a wonderful time. We visited Prince Edward Island, Hopewell Rocks, and Campobello Island (summer home of Franklin Roosevelt); drove to Green Gables Heritage Place, said to have inspired the novel *Anne of Green Gables*; and enjoyed playing games together. We stayed one night at a bed and breakfast, where we took over the entire house. It was a magical time! They lived right on the Bay of Fundy, and the scenery was gorgeous.

The year 2013 was busy with monthly events and travel, of course. In January we took fifteen from IN-JOY to tour the Tovrea Castle in Phoenix. For many years the castle had not been open to the public, so this was a very popular event. The castle resembled a wedding cake and was surrounded by many acres of desert land, with lots of saguaro cacti. It was a beautiful building, but not much was inside. The maximum we could take was fifteen, so I set up several different dates and times to tour the castle.

I also flew to Indiana in January, as Sis was in the hospital. Both Barbara and I flew in to Indianapolis, where we rented a car and drove 150 miles to South Bend. We weren't sure if Sis, at age ninety-five, was going to make it. When she saw Barbara and me walk into her hospital room, she perked up and was soon feeling good enough to go back to St. Paul's retirement home. I drove in snow, which I hadn't done for a while.

Ron loved to cook. For my seventy-fifth birthday, he invited us and twelve of our close friends ("the gang") plus Kim's family to his and Jan's home for a birthday dinner. It was a delicious dinner of fajitas and all the trimmings. Believe me, he didn't get his cooking skills from me! He tries to have a birthday dinner for me every year. We all look forward to it.

July 2013 was a very special month for our family, as Lindsey and Bryan Binninger exchanged their wedding vows at the Newland Barn in Huntington Beach, California. Lindsey had twelve bridesmaids, which included her sister, Michelle. Michelle was thrilled to be in the wedding. Michelle's boyfriend, Casey, was a groomsman and afterward walked Michelle

2013: Left to right: Jan, Ron, Mike, Bryan, Lindsey, Michelle, Kim, Martha, and Wes

back down the aisle. Michelle even caught the bridal bouquet, and Casey caught the garter. (I think it was a setup.) They were excited that they could possibly be the next to be married! Casey's dad told him to wait until he was forty years old, and they would talk about it then. Casey and Michelle seemed to be content with that.

Everything about Lindsey and Bryan's wedding was perfect! Even the weather cooperated—important since it was an outdoor wedding and reception. Bill, my ex-husband, and his wife were there for the wedding. I hadn't seen him for years, so I was a little nervous. I decided to go up to him, talk with him, and meet his wife. When I greeted him, he said, "Who are you?" I didn't think I had changed that much! I recognized him!

My niece Barbara and her daughter Pam had flown to California from Michigan for the wedding. The day after the wedding, we were walking on the Redondo Beach pier. Barbara was walking next to me when all of a sudden she fell to the ground. The security guards patrolling the pier tried to help her stand, but she promptly passed out. The paramedics were called, and she was taken to the hospital. Pam was a nervous wreck! It was determined that Barbara's leg was broken. Since her flight for home was the next day, the hospital released her to fly home as long as she was in a wheelchair. We went to a local store and purchased a wheelchair for her and made sure she and Pam got on the flight the next day. When they got off the plane in Detroit, the wheelchair collapsed. Either we hadn't put it together correctly, or it was faulty. They were able to return it to the local store in Michigan.

In early December of 2013, Wes was diagnosed with myelofibrosis, a very rare blood disease. After we had visited the cancer doctor and he told us the diagnosis, I called Barbara in Michigan. I said, "He has something called myelofibrosis, and I don't really know what that is." There was silence on the other end of the phone, and Barbara said, "That's what Jim died from." I knew then it was very serious, as I knew firsthand what Jim had gone through before his death. Wes's bone marrow was producing too many platelets, and the main problem at first was extreme fatigue. His prognosis for living was about eight years. Wes had such a good attitude, and he said he would beat the odds and live eleven years. We knew God was in charge! One of the Bible passages we claimed was Philippians 4:4, 6–7: "Rejoice in the Lord always. I will say it again: Rejoice! Do not be anxious about anything, but in everything, by prayer and petition, with thanksgiving, present your requests to God. And the peace of God, which transcends all understanding, will guard your hearts and your minds in Christ Jesus" (NIV).

The health issues kept piling up in 2014. Not only did Wes have myelofibrosis, but he was also diagnosed with Parkinson's disease (PD). He was now dealing with a double whammy! I was diagnosed with spinal stenosis and severe degenerative disc disease in my back. I had a series of three epidural shots in my spine in June and July. We still planned to do as much as we could for as long as we were able.

I continued planning the monthly events for IN-JOY. We saw four plays at the Hale Theater in Gilbert. Other events included an Arizona Coyotes hockey game, a Diamondbacks baseball game, Barleens Arizona Opry, Salt River Brass, and two Christmas programs. We also caroled at a nursing home and went to the Dutton Family musical show.

On a personal note, Wes and I flew to Nevada in May and spent five days in a time-share at Lake Tahoe. It snowed while we were there and was beautiful. For two weeks in June, we shared our time-share in Kauai, Hawaii, with good friends Dewain and Sharol Cisney. We all had a very relaxing time with wonderful weather. We toured in the mornings and played cards in the afternoon and never tired of being together. Both Dewain and Wes had serious health issues. We were glad Dewain was able to go with us, as he passed away the following year.

Twenty fifteen was quite a year! Wes was still dealing with myelofibrosis and Parkinson's disease. He took medicine for both diseases to help control the symptoms. He had good days and bad days, and lots of doctor appointments. I had bladder surgery in July and cataract surgery in December. Both surgeries went well—just couldn't lift or bend.

In March we took forty-seven people to Tucson and Kartchner Caverns, and in October we led twenty-eight people on a Canada and New England cruise. Wes did well on the cruise, as he could go to the cabin and rest whenever he needed to.

Sis wrote the following poem about Barbara and me, although we weren't so little anymore:

Two Little Girls
by Winifred Rea
September 20, 2016

Two little girls went to Beiger
School every day.

They laughed and talked all along the way.

One liked music and piano lessons she took,

Even liked practicing from her music book.

Both liked the Chicago White
Sox baseball team,

Collected their cards and
cheered for the team.

They graduated from MHS on the honor roll

With dreams of a productive
future as their goal.

Fine young ladies they turned out to be,

Living Christian lives for others to see.

They both got married and
moved out of our state,

Moving to others whose states were great.

They had happiness for many years,

Yet some sorrow and many tears.

God was good to them and right by their side,

He stopped their frustrations
and calmed the tide.

Now Barbara has made me
a great-grandmother,

I'm happy to say,

And I'll pray for their families every day.

I've loved these little girls, Barbara
and Martha, all of my life,

In spite of some struggles and strife.

May God bless them and keep them in his care,

For them that is my earnest prayer.

In spite of severe health issues, 2016 was a good year. We found out we were going to be great-grandparents. Lindsey and Bryan were expecting twin girls in March of 2017. Too bad they lived in California! Kim and Mike were excited to be grandparents for the first time, and Michelle was anxious to be an aunt.

Sis wrote this poem about them and the upcoming birth of their twin girls. Sis died two weeks before the twins were born.

Lindsey and Bryan
by Winifred Rea
2016

Lindsey and Bryan were quite a pair,

They were seen by everyone everywhere,

Soon they decided to become a team,

And wedding invitations were
everywhere to be seen.

The wedding was lovely in the afternoon,

And the weather was generous too.

They wanted to take a honeymoon far away,

So they left for Europe, leaving the USA.

They traveled to Greece and France too,

Taking in all the scenery as all the tourists do.

Now they are settled at home
in California State,

Both in a condo, and life is great!

Now they will be adding something new,

Mr. Stork is bringing a bundle of two.

Two little girls will arrive on a spring day,

Making Lindsey and Bryan a mom
and dad in a creative way.

May God's blessings rest on this family of four,

And health and happiness be
theirs forever more.

On a sad note, Barbara's husband, Paul, died in January of 2016. When we last saw him while we were all visiting Sis in Indiana, we noticed that Paul, generally full of pep and energy, seemed very tired and lethargic. While we were playing cards, he just wanted to lie on the couch and sleep. He was soon diagnosed with lung cancer and died a few months later.

Among the highlights of 2016 was a visit in March by Wes's cousin Blaun and her husband Joe, from South Carolina. My niece Barbara also visited, and my grandniece Pam and her husband, Ken, from Michigan came for two days. My sixtieth (can you believe it?) high school reunion was held in August in Mishawaka. It was special, as our friends Tim and Linda Doll, from Texas, attended the reunion.

2016: The family celebrating at Sis' 100th birthday party.

We celebrated Sis's one hundredth birthday early while we were in Indiana. Barbara and I hosted an open house for Sis at St. Paul's retirement home, where she lived. About one hundred people came, including many out-of-state relatives. Kim, Michelle, Ron, and Jan were there to celebrate with us. It was wonderful! Sis didn't want to buy a new dress, but Kim and I went to Dillard's and bought one for her. She looked beautiful at the open house and was in good health. She even gave a speech to everyone. Sis wrote this poem about Wes in 2016:

Wes
by Winifred Rea
October 15, 2016

Wes was born in the North Carolina State

In May, and it was beautiful and great.

He had a younger brother too

And they both found a lot to do.

Soon Wes went off to college
to get his degree

For success to happiness he wanted to be.

He ended up in Indianapolis,
a great place to be,

His job was marketing for the fraternity TKE.

But he found the weather too cold with snow.

He said it was time to look for
another place to go.

He went to Arizona, a state that's warm.

It has flowers, beautiful scenery,
and lots of charm.

He joined the force of AT&T;

He loved his job as many could see.

Then Martha came to his church one day,

Martha A. Pierce

They got together and had
many pleasant days.

Now they've been married
for thirty-eight years,

They've had an interesting life
and many friends dear.

They've always kept God first
in all that they do.

He's kept their marriage strong
and troubles few.

May God bless them always
in everything they do.

CHAPTER 28

The Birth of Our Twin Great-Grandbabies (2017)

In January I flew to Indiana to visit Sis, who was in the hospital again and not expected to live. Barbara flew in from Florida, where she had a small park model to stay in for the winter months. Sis once again surprised everyone when she improved and was released from the hospital to St. Paul's nursing home. We knew she would never go back to her room in assisted living, so Barbara and I cleared out her room. We took a small amount of her things to her room in the nursing section, which she shared with another lady. Barbara and I gave away Sis's furnishings in her room. We had just moved her from independent living to assisted living a year or two before. That's hard work for people our age! Barbara stayed with Sis, and I needed to return home to care for Wes. Since both Barbara and I had flown into Indianapolis and rented a car, I drove by myself to Indianapolis to catch the flight to Arizona. About halfway to Indianapolis, it started snowing. Soon it was a whiteout, and I had trouble seeing. I was concerned about arriving in

Indianapolis, as I might not be able to see signs directing me to the airport. However, when I got closer to Indianapolis, I found it hadn't snowed at all. Once again God was taking care of me.

Sis graduated to heaven on February 28 at the age of one hundred and four months. Wes and I both flew back to Indiana for the funeral. Wes was honored to give the eulogy for Sis. We held the funeral and reception at St. Paul's. She had led a wonderful life and was now in heaven with her Lord and Savior. Her grandson Doug sang her favorite song, "Because He Lives." Sis's picture now hangs on the wall at St. Paul's with all of the other residents who lived to be one hundred years old.

May 2017: Blakely and Charley; nine weeks

The biggest and best news this year was the birth of our twin great-granddaughters. They were born on March 10, 2017, to our granddaughter Lindsey and her husband, Bryan, in Santa Ana, California. Charley Rinke Binninger entered this world at 2:14 p.m., weighing six pounds, two ounces. Blakely Brynn Binninger followed one minute later at 2:15 p.m., weighing in at six pounds, eleven ounces. Big babies for twins! We were privileged to see them three times during the year and hold them and feed them. In November we all met in Sedona for several days and enjoyed the babies and family. Bryan's family was there also.

July 2017: Blakely and Charley at the beach; four months old

Twenty seventeen was a very different year for us! There were multiple doctor appointments (sixty-plus), assorted medical tests (six), physical therapy (thirty sessions), and surgery for me—a partial knee replacement on my right knee. The surgery and recovery went pretty well. I had in-house physical therapy for six weeks. Wes was diagnosed with neuropathy and neurogenic orthostatic hypotension (low blood pressure). He also had the beginnings of dementia. We still remained positive and had hope for the future. Jesus was still on the throne and in charge of our lives!

This was the year, starting in September, that I was asked by Pastor Bill Meiter to be an IN-JOY director again, along with Gayle Molenaar. We worked most of the summer, planning the fall meetings. Since I had the knee surgery on August 25, I missed the first three meetings of IN-JOY in September. I thought I'd be down for a week or so and be back to normal.

Wrong! I was down for at least three weeks. Wes became involved in the prayer ministry at church. He and a few others prayed together with Pastor Bill on Sunday mornings before the first service.

CHAPTER 29

A Life Changing
Year (2018)

Wow! What a year 2018 turned out to be! Not to be a downer, but just the facts: between the two of us, we had fifty-six doctor appointments, four hospital stays, two surgeries, eight weeks of rehab at La Estancia Rehab Center, two months in long-term care, nine in-home nurse visits, and nine in-home therapy appointments. We were thankful for good medical insurance!

Charley and Blakely enjoying birthday cake.

The twins celebrated their first birthdays on March 10 with a party for the Arizona friends and relatives at Kim and Mike's house in Peoria. Then they celebrated again in California for friends and relatives there.

We also had good things happen: both of us turned eighty years old, IN-JOY celebrated twenty years since Wes and I started it in 1998, and Wes and I celebrated our fortieth anniversary on December 23. We tried twice to have a 20/40/80 party, but we had to cancel both of them due to health reasons.

Our first 20/40/80 (twenty years of IN-JOY, forty years of marriage, and eighty years of life) was supposed to be on April 28, 2018. We asked Chuck Nickell from IN-JOY to make us a video, and we supplied him with a countless number of pictures. We made arrangements with a caterer to serve appetizers and drinks. Friends were asked to do the guest book, and the entertainment had been established. The only thing I had yet to do was to set up a seating chart.

On Monday, April 23, I became very sick. My stomach hurt so badly, and nothing I took eased the pain. I started vomiting. Wes fixed soup for me, but it wouldn't stay down. I had never felt so sick in my life! On Tuesday I asked Wes if he could drive me to the emergency room on Chandler Boulevard, about a mile away. (By this time, Wes was not driving much at all.) He did, and I checked into the ER. They did an MRI, and it showed I had an obstruction in the small intestine, and it was blocking everything I ate. I would have to be admitted to the hospital. I didn't want Wes to drive to the hospital, so I suggested that he go home and get some rest. Chandler Regional Hospital was called and a room reserved for me. In the meantime I developed A-fib; now it also became a heart issue, and I needed a room in the heart unit of the hospital. It took until eight o'clock that evening before I was finally transported to the hospital in an ambulance.

I was really sick! I was hooked up to at least eleven IVs. A tube was put down my throat to drain everything from my stomach. I couldn't eat or drink anything, and my mouth became very dry. I was allowed to suck on ice chips but couldn't swallow them or the melted water. I asked for chewing gum, and the nurse actually bought me two packages. The nurses were all so nice at the hospital.

As Wes couldn't be left alone, Kim came and stayed with him at our house. Pastor Bill and Maryellen came to visit me the next day to talk about the upcoming party in three days. We decided we'd better postpone it. I told Kim where the list of people was located, and she brought it to me. I gave the list to Maryellen. There were 217 people who needed to be notified. Maryellen and others called or emailed all of the ones from the church, and Kim contacted the others. Barbara and her daughter Pam had come from Michigan for the party, so they helped with anything that needed to be done. Barbara's son Mike and family from El Paso also came. Only two people who couldn't be notified showed up at the church that Saturday for the party.

In the meantime I had surgery on Saturday, the very day the party was supposed to take place. Dr. Leeds did the laparoscopic surgery. Afterward the tube in my throat was taken out. What a nice feeling that was! After a couple of days, I started throwing up again. So—back in went the tube. The nurse tried to insert it, but it hurt me so badly that she wouldn't try anymore. I was wheeled to a room where they guided the tube down my throat while watching the procedure on a scanning machine. It hurt, but not nearly as badly. I was then moved to ICU.

On Wednesday, May 2, I had a second surgery. This time the doctor did it by incision. She discovered many perforations on my intestine and needed to cut out part of it and staple the intestine back together. I woke up during surgery to a very bright light, and I felt paralyzed. I also had a huge wooden block (that's what it felt like) in my mouth, which I suppose was the ventilator. I think the doctor should have warned me about what to expect. I wanted to tell someone after the surgery, but I couldn't talk. My arms were tied down also. I tried to motion to Kim with my hand that I wanted paper to write on, but the nurse said, "Oh, she's agitated. We'll give her a sedative." When I woke up, Kim was gone, and Ron had arrived. He kept asking me questions, and then he realized I could only answer yes or no. I stayed in the ICU for several days.

When I tried to get out of bed to walk to the chair, I got dizzy, light-headed, and had trouble breathing. So, in order to sit in the chair, I was put in a sling that was hooked up to a huge pulley in the ceiling. It transported me over to the chair. After this was done several times, I told them I would rather walk to the chair. I had a very large room in the ICU with a big window and a nice view. On Sunday the tube was taken out of my throat. Yeah! I could now eat and drink liquids, gelatin, and juice. I had trouble sleeping in the hospital, so I watched television during the night. (I probably slept too much during the day.) When I did sleep, I dreamed a very disturbing dream. I was in a deep hole, and I couldn't get out. I would get near the top of the hole and then fall back down. I had this dream over and over. One time I finally got out of the hole, but I found myself in the attic of an unfinished house. And I couldn't get out of there. I don't know what these dreams meant, but sometimes I was glad I wasn't sleeping at night, as I didn't want to dream. I know I came close to death several times. I was so weak I couldn't move in the bed without help. I was also close to having pneumonia, so I was given daily breathing treatments.

On Tuesday, May 8, I moved out of ICU and back into a regular room. My A-fib had come and gone a couple of times, but they were still monitoring it. I had some visitors. I graduated to eating pudding, applesauce, and iced tea. After three more days, I was able to eat an English muffin, scrambled eggs, and yogurt. Food didn't taste good to me, though, so I didn't actually eat very much.

On Friday, May 11, a transport came and took me to La Estancia Nursing and Rehabilitation Center in Ahwatukee, Room 230. I chose that place because it was about a mile from home. It was quite a large room, with a hospital bed, dresser, bookshelves, a wardrobe, a round dining table with chairs, a TV (of course), and private bathroom. I was there for nineteen days.

While I was there, the doctors said I had diabetes, which I had not been diagnosed with before entering the hospital. They gave me an insulin shot every day and checked my blood sugar. I had physical therapy and occupational therapy five days a week. I was talking with Holly, one of the therapists, and she asked me where I was from. I told her, "Mishawaka." She couldn't believe it, as that was where she was born and lived until she was five years old. She went back often to visit her grandparents. She actually lived on the same road where my brother Jack and family lived. It's a small world!

At first, all of the meals were brought to my room. The food was always cold, because I was at the end of the hallway and the last one to be served. I was told if I went to the dining room to eat, the food would be hotter. So I made my way to the dining room for all three meals when I felt well enough. I met several nice people there. I also met some Christian ladies, and we said grace together before eating.

While I was in therapy, the therapist asked me to try to walk. Up until this time, I had been in a wheelchair. I couldn't even take one step without feeling I might fall! I was amazed! I just assumed I could walk, but my legs were still too weak. Getting strong enough to walk again became my goal. I also had trouble eating. Food just wouldn't go down, and sometimes I would throw up again. I also started having heartburn whenever I ate anything. They tested my ability to swallow, and that tested normal.

I had a lot of company, and Kim or someone else brought Wes about every other day. Ronn Howell from church started staying with Wes at night. He brought Wes up to see me one evening after dinner at Cracker Barrel. They had stopped at McDonald's and brought hot fudge sundaes for the three of us. I didn't seem to have any trouble getting the ice cream down! I was happy to learn that La Estancia had a beauty shop. I hadn't been able to get my hair done for months, so it was nice getting it shampooed and styled for a change. It was amazing how much better that made me feel!

May 25 was Wes's eightieth birthday. I was hoping to be at home by then so I could do something special for him. However, I wasn't discharged until May 30. Kim came to get me and helped me pack up everything. It was amazing how much "stuff" I had accumulated in that short time.

After I arrived at home, members from our Sunday school class and IN-JOY brought in food two or three times a week. The therapist also came three times a week, and the home nurse came twice a week. I had to learn to give myself insulin shots two times a day and check my blood sugar. In time I went to my primary care doctor, and she checked my blood sugar and said I did *not* have diabetes. I was taken off of the shots, thank goodness!

Both Wes and I had several doctor appointments to go to, but neither of us could drive. Various people from IN-JOY drove us to the doctor or lab. We were so appreciative of everyone who helped us!

Wes and I had planned an eight-day IN-JOY Alaskan cruise for July. We didn't know if we would make it or not. Wes really wanted to go, so we decided to try. There were twenty-four in our group, and they were all willing to help us, even though we were the leaders of the group! We had originally planned to take Norm and Nora Hammer and drive our van to the airport and leave it. Gayle Molenaar found out about that and said she would take us all to the airport, even though it was in the middle of the night. It's a good thing she did, because as soon as she dropped us off at the airport, Wes said he couldn't walk. I immediately got him a wheelchair, and he was pushed to the gate, with me tagging along. Peggy Wheatley took charge of the group and did a great job. Originally Wes and I weren't sitting together on the plane, and we each had middle seats. Peggy talked with someone, and the airline found an aisle seat for Wes with me right beside him. Wes couldn't even walk onto the plane. They transferred him to a very narrow wheelchair that ran on a track, which put him directly into his seat. I had never seen that done before. During the flight, Wes had to go to the bathroom. The man sitting across the aisle heard him, helped him get up, and practically carried him back to the restroom. He even waited for him and helped him back to his seat! God had put angels everywhere for us!

I rented electric carts for both of us to be used on the ship. They were a godsend! At night they were supposed to be charged, and the nearest plug was on the other side of our king-size bed in the room. We drove the two carts into the room and charged them. The next morning Wes tried to back them out of the room, and he couldn't get them around the bed. We must have spent an hour trying to get them out. We finally talked with our steward, and he called someone who was able to maneuver them out. After that our steward took them each night and charged them in another area, returning them in the morning in time for us to go to breakfast.

Everyone in our group was so helpful. A lot of people back home were praying that we'd make it okay. Barbara Schaper took our picture at dinner one evening and posted it on Facebook. We received a lot of responses from people saying they were glad to see we had made it and were doing okay.

Wes and I decided to stay on the ship instead of trying to do any day trips. We did go out one time to have clam chowder at a restaurant Wes had read about in the AAA magazine. That wore us both out! On the flight home, people from our group helped us with our luggage and carry-ons. We were happy to arrive home.

Wes was beginning to have more and more health problems. He was having hallucinations and delusions and was able to do less and less for himself. I was feeling very unhappy with our lives, and I was beginning to wonder how we were going to continue to live like we were. I checked out home care with several institutions, as Wes told me he would prefer staying at home instead of going to a care home. Wes had long-term care insurance, but it wasn't enough to cover someone at home for 24/7. But God was still in control and had a plan for our lives.

Shortly after the cruise, we went to our Flagstaff cabin. Kim came over to our Phoenix house, helped us pack and get things in the van, and drove us to Flagstaff. Mike drove their car, and Kim went home with him after the weekend was over. Wes and I spent a few weeks in Flagstaff, enjoying the cooler weather. One Sunday I drove into town to get gas, and while I was gone, Wes fell. He didn't break anything, but his legs and hips were hurting. We had planned to leave the next morning, October 1, for home, and I was trying to pack up everything. I put the light crates and boxes in the van, but I knew I would need help with the cooler and heavier items. Our neighbor Brad came over to tell us good-bye. He asked if there was anything he could do to help, and I asked him if he could carry the heavy things to the van the next day, which he did. We started out for Phoenix the next morning, and I was concerned about how I was going to get everything into the house. When I pulled into our driveway, our neighbor Brian had just pulled into his driveway. I asked if it would be possible for him to help me with the items that I couldn't lift. He came right over and brought *everything* into the house. All I had to do was put it all away! God is so good! He always puts someone into our lives when we need help!

Wes was still having trouble walking. In the middle of the night, he needed to get up and use the restroom. He couldn't walk at all, and he hurt so badly. He asked me to call 911. The paramedics came and transported him to Chandler Regional Hospital. I got dressed and drove to the hospital. He was admitted to the hospital for tests and was there for three days. He was diagnosed with spinal stenosis, which was causing the pain in his leg and hip. After that, on October 4, he was sent to La Estancia Nursing and Rehab Center, where I used to be.

Wes was given therapy and stayed there until November 30, part of that time in the nursing unit. While Wes was at La Estancia, I often had lunch with him and recognized some of the other residents from the time I was there. During lunch I often played the piano for them. Wes had long-term care insurance with John Hancock, and I started the process to see if his stay would be covered. It was!

I visited Ruth Coutts (longtime member of IN-JOY), who was in Hawthorn Court at Ahwatukee, about two miles from our house. It was for people with memory problems, and Wes's dementia was getting progressively worse. I talked with the executive director at Hawthorn Court, and they had one room available. I looked at it and was given a tour of the facility. I also visited Ruth, who said she liked it there. I took Wes to look at it on Thanksgiving when I had him at home for dinner. Kim and Lindsey went with us. Wes took one look at the room and said, "Well, this is a no-brainer." We signed the papers right away, and we moved Wes into Hawthorn Court on December 1, 2018. Ron bought a dresser, end table, and a small round table with four chairs from Craigslist and delivered and set them up. Ron and Jan had a TV they weren't using, so he brought it also. Wes loved the place from the beginning. At La Estancia, in the nursing area, he shared his room and bath with another man. The room was so small that there wasn't even enough room for a chair for me to sit on when I visited him. This new place was another answer from God!

CHAPTER 30

The 20/40/80 Party (2019)

Would you believe we had planned another 20/40/80 party for November 2? I had sent out new invitations, and 193 responded that they would attend. This time Wes was recuperating at La Estancia from his hospital stay, so we decided to cancel once again. Pastor Bill didn't think we should try for a third time. Maryellen suggested that we have it on Tuesday morning, along with an IN-JOY meeting. The more Wes and I thought about it, we decided that would be a good alternative.

Gayle, director of IN-JOY, had the date of February 5, 2019, with a musical group coming for only half of the meeting. She said we could have the second half for our celebration. Once again I sent out new invitations. As the time got closer, the musical group had to cancel, which gave us the entire meeting time. There were 209 people who attended our party, including 175 from IN-Joy. One hundred ninety-three stayed for lunch, which we furnished.

We started out in style, as Don Finch, from IN-JOY, had made arrangements for a 1949 Packard limousine, driven by owner Mike Post, to pick us up at Hawthorn Court and

2019: Martha, Wes, Mike, and Sarah Post in front of the limo

take us to church and back. The staff at Hawthorn Court took pictures of us with the Packard. We were greeted at church by people who had come early. We even had the red carpet rolled out for us to walk on! The Packard was parked in the middle of the church plaza for people to see it.

Ernestine Hatt and Sharol Cisney were in charge of the guest book, and Del Tipton and Barbara Schaper were photographers. Peggy Wheatley cut the cakes. Pastor Bill Meiter was our emcee, and he did a terrific job! I had asked Arnold Karraker to play the trumpet. He played "Star Dust" and "I'll Fly Away." Greg Schaefer played "It Is Well with My Soul" on the violin. Merry Karraker gave the devotions, and Jim Carpenter led in singing "Joyful, Joyful, We Adore Thee," which was our original theme song for IN-JOY. Near the end we sang "Victory in Jesus." I introduced our family and friends who had come from out of state or who were other than the 175 IN-Joy members: Joan Hill from California, Kim and family, Ron and Jan, people from our Sunday school class, and several from Grace Community Church. We had three large cakes: the first one said "Happy Twentieth Anniversary, IN-JOY," the second one said, "Happy Fortieth Anniversary, Wes and Martha," and the third one said "Happy Eightieth Birthday, Wes and Martha." A good friend of ours who couldn't come surprised us and paid for the cakes.

Martha and Wes at our 20/40/80 party

Pastor Bill took the microphone and asked people to tell stories about us. There were many funny stories told. Prior to the party, I kept reminding Wes he should think about what he was going to say to everyone, but he never did. He just ad-libbed and actually did a great job. I finally took the microphone away from him so I could speak! We invited everyone to stay for lunch, which was Wes's and Pastor Bill's favorite: Swedish meatballs, prepared by Debbie Swanson. Then the cakes were cut and served. Throughout the meeting, the video Chuck Nickell had worked many hours putting together for us was shown on the front screen.

What a wonderful celebration to enjoy with all our family and friends. Maryellen Hawkinson did an outstanding job helping me put it together. I never could have done it without her! Gayle Molenaar and I burned the midnight oil, brainstorming what should be done and said. She also played the piano for the congregational singing. The various committees of IN-JOY also helped set things up and clean up. We finally made it! I guess the saying "the third time's a charm" really is true!

After the celebration was over, Wes and I were exhausted! The limo took us back to Hawthorn Court, and I drove home from there. Ron and Jan came by, and we talked about the party. At first they hadn't planned on coming to our party, as Ron thought it was mainly just for our friends. I think he heard the disappointment in my voice, as a few days later he told me they were planning to come. He said he learned several things about me that he didn't know.

CHAPTER 31

Life Goes On (2019)

Things soon got back to a normal pace. In March I went to California with Kim and Mike to celebrate the twins' second birthday. The next week Lindsey, Bryan, and the twins came to Phoenix to celebrate with the Arizona family. Wes was able to attend that party and enjoyed seeing the twins.

We put our Flagstaff cabin up for sale in April of 2019. Kim, Mike, and I drove up to Flagstaff over two weekends and got rid of everything. We took many loads to Goodwill in Flagstaff. Within the first week, we received an offer, which we accepted. One of our neighbors and his brother were the potential buyers, and they wanted the property for their parents. After a couple weeks, the brother backed out, leaving our neighbor no option but to cancel. We soon had another offer. After the inspection was done, we discovered we needed to have a new septic system put in to the tune of $25,000! We asked the buyer if he would go halves with us, but he declined. So—back to the drawing board! It took forever to get all of the permits and plans for the new septic system. We actually took the cabin off the market for a month. The summer was over, and the best time to sell property in Flagstaff was at an end. We received a lower offer and decided to accept it.

We closed on the property in February of 2020. It was sad to sell it, as we really enjoyed the summers at the cabin.

2019: Casey Bagley and Michelle

Michelle turned thirty in 2019. Wes and I both attended her surprise birthday party, which she told Kim she wanted! Michelle and Casey were still dating. Michelle became very involved with acting in various plays at the One Step Beyond Program, which she attended Monday through Friday. She had a part in *Winnie the Pooh* and did a terrific job.

Wes was still in a wheelchair and was happy at Hawthorn Court. Once a month, about twelve of us caregivers met at Hawthorn Court to discuss our loved ones and any problems that we've had. It felt good to talk it over with others who were going through the same situations or had done so in the past. It was good to know we weren't alone.

Whenever someone new comes to live at Hawthorn Court, a sign is posted on their door, welcoming that person and posting their name. As I was leaving after visiting Wes, I saw the sign welcoming Joyce Nyquist. We knew her as a member of ACC and IN-JOY. I quickly returned to Wes's room to tell him. She hadn't moved in yet but would soon. When she arrived, Wes was there to greet her.

We soon learned about another man who would be arriving soon whose name was also Wes. We found out that his full name was John Wesley Holden. My Wes would be called Wes #1 and the new resident would be Wes #2. We were both anxious to meet him. When he first arrived, we met Wes #2 and his wife, Suzi. We all hit it off immediately and ate lunch or dinner together in the dining room many times. Wes #2 had some serious health issues in addition to dementia. A couple months after he arrived at Hawthorn Court, he was taken to the hospital, where he passed away. I found out about his death at our next caregivers' meeting on Saturday, and I was shocked! I called Suzi right away and attended Wes's memorial service and reception at Green Acres Mortuary in Scottsdale. I still keep in touch with Suzi, as we all just seemed to bond together. Another man who sat at my Wes's table was Jack Schroeder. He didn't talk very much, but he liked to eat dessert. We had to watch him, as he would often reach over and steal Wes's cookie or whatever was served that day for dessert. Jack died a few months later, and I still have contact with his wife, Edie. Everyone becomes like a family there, as we all have so much in common.

CHAPTER 32
The Year of COVID-19 (2020)

I've progressed now to the current year. Wes was at Hawthorn Court for thirteen months as of January 2020. The staff was wonderful there, and many of them have been at Hawthorn Court for several years. There was a feature article about the Hawthorn staff, "Longevity of Staff Makes the Hearts Grow Fonder," in the magazine *Healthy Cells*, which is circulated in many doctors' offices in the Valley. At the time the article was written, there were ten staff members who had worked at the facility for ten to eighteen years. In addition, there were eleven employees who had been there for three to five years. With many assisted living communities in Arizona, staff longevity is important when choosing a place for a loved one to live.

In this same magazine, a few months later, was an article about Wes and me. The executive director interviewed us and asked if she could write an article about us for the magazine. There was a picture of us in front of the Packard limo, being escorted to our 20/40/80 party in 2019. The article told how we met, about starting IN-JOY Seniors, and described some of the trips we've taken. It also mentioned how we chose Hawthorn Court for Wes's new home.

All of the residents in Hawthorn Court have some degree of memory problem. Music has always been important and soothing for dementia patients. The activities director at Hawthorn Court lined up a different individual or group to sing at least three times a week. On Monday morning two young singers, Peter and Melissa, sang well-known songs for the residents. It was amazing to watch the people as they sang along and knew every word! Many of the spouses and family members came on Monday morning to hear them, including me. They quite often sang Wes's favorite song, "Edelweiss," from *The Sound of Music.* My favorite song they sang was "The Prayer." They both have wonderful, well-trained voices. They have sung at IN-JOY twice and are also scheduled for April 2021.

I was able to have lunch or dinner quite often with Wes in the dining room, prior to the pandemic lockdown, by paying a small fee for the food. Rich Johnson, a member of our church, was admitted to Hawthorn Court in the spring of 2020. His wife, Ilene, joined him a lot for the meals, so the four of us quite often sat together. One time at dinner, Pastor Bill Meiter surprised us and came to visit Wes. He joined us at the dinner table, and we introduced him to an elderly Black lady who was sitting with us. She kept saying, "You're not a pastor! I don't believe you." Bill asked her why she didn't believe it, and she told him he was too cute to be a pastor. We all just burst out laughing. Bill loved it!

Once a week the activities director often made arrangements for a small group to eat lunch at a nearby restaurant. She generally asked me if I wanted to go along, and I did when

I could. We ate at On the Border Mexican Grill, Panda Garden, and Z'tejas southwestern grill. It was a nice deviation from the regular food.

I had some health issues in 2020. For nearly five months, from December of 2019 until May of 2020, I had a type of vertigo every day, all day long. Fortunately I wasn't dizzy while lying or sitting, so I was able to drive. However, when I stood up, I was very dizzy and light-headed. I started using a walker, which gave me security from the possibility of falling. I still visited Wes on a daily basis and continued taking him to doctor and dental appointments as needed. Several friends often met me at Hawthorn Court and helped me take him to the doctor. Ruth Steele, Roger Scott, Norm Hammer, and Tom Waldron were so helpful in that area. Bob and Dar Trzepkowski, my neighbors across the street, started helping me also. Bob offered to get my mail every day and bring it to me, and he also put out the trash and recyclable barrels every week.

The doctors tried all kinds of things to find out what was causing my dizziness. I had physical therapy, had my ears and eyes tested, had an MRA, CT scan, MRI, and my meds were checked and some of them changed. I went to a neurologist, and he ran various tests, ruling out anything like a previous stroke or brain tumor. All of a sudden, I woke up one morning in May, and I was no longer dizzy or light-headed! Praise the Lord! It was a real answer to prayer!

After getting over the dizziness, I started feeling shaky all over. It was on the inside of my body and not visible on the outside. My primary care doctor diagnosed it as anxiety and stress and prescribed a new medication, which has helped. She also told me to exercise more! I've been trying to ride the exercise bike every day for at least thirty minutes. (Sometimes I remember, and sometimes I don't.)

The last time I was able to visit Wes inside Hawthorn Court was March 11. After that the doors were closed for any physical visitation. This was very difficult for Wes, especially at first. I then visited him "through the front window," and we talked on the cell phone with each other. When it was 115 degrees outside, it was very hot having to sit outside while talking. Wes was on the inside with the air-conditioning blowing on him, and he was cold.

I also talked with him on his own cell phone in his room. He lost the first cell phone, and I purchased another one for him. Many times it was either turned off or needed charging, as I had trouble reaching him. He had difficulty calling or answering the phone, as he couldn't remember how to use it.

Wes had fallen several times in the past year. I was always afraid to answer a call that came from Hawthorn Court, as it was often from the nurse, telling me that he had fallen. Fortunately he didn't break any bones, but he usually scraped up his forehead and the top of his head. At one time he had a huge gash on the top of his head. When it was about to be healed, he fell again, breaking it open. He was supposed to use his wheelchair when he wasn't in bed, but he tried to walk to the bathroom without the chair. That's when he fell. During one week, he fell three times.

August 21, 2020, Senior Citizens' Day, was celebrated at Hawthorn Court. Each resident was asked to say something. Wes's quote was, "Be kind to your friends. Be kind to your enemies. Be kind to yourself."

A funny thing happened in August. The month of August 2020 at Hawthorn Court was Hawaiian month, with a luau to be held on Friday, August 28. I told Wes I was going to bring him one of his Hawaiian shirts so he could wear it for the luau. Since I still couldn't go inside, I gave the shirt (after I washed it and carefully ironed it) to the receptionist to take to Wes's room. I didn't think any more about it until I was attending a dementia meeting on August 26 at church with Ilene Johnson, Rich's wife. She mentioned to me that she had just visited Rich that morning, and he was wearing a new Hawaiian shirt. She asked him where he got the shirt, and he said it was hanging in his closet, so he put it on. Friday evening I was looking at the luau pictures that were posted on Facebook by Hawthorn Court, and Rich was wearing Wes's shirt! I talked with one of the caregivers, who went to Rich's room, found the shirt, and put it in Wes's hamper, also telling Rich the shirt belonged to Wes. About a week later, Rich was wearing Wes's shirt again! Evidently, when another caregiver washed the shirt, she had seen Rich wearing it earlier, thought it belonged to Rich, and put it back in his closet.

The residents and staff at Hawthorn Court were tested for the coronavirus every week. In November, I received a call that Wes tested positive but was asymptomatic. Even though he was asymptomatic, he still had to be quarantined for ten days. Lindsey, Bryan, the twins, Kim, Mike, Michelle, and I visited him one afternoon near Thanksgiving through the window. I'll include the picture that Lindsey took, even though it's not very clear.

A few weeks after he was out of quarantine, Wes started running a fever. For over a week, he started becoming weaker and weaker. He was so weak that he could no longer go to the window or talk to me on the phone. His caregiver called me daily to give me updates. On December 26, I insisted that

Blakeley and Charley looking at their Papa through the window.

he be taken to the emergency room. I followed the ambulance to Mercy Gilbert Hospital in Gilbert, where he was admitted with the virus, pneumonia, and a UTI. He was in critical condition and going downhill fast. I was unable to visit with him, but I was in twice-a-day contact with his nurse. He only opened his eyes once in a while but was otherwise unresponsive. He couldn't eat, drink, or swallow. On December 31, he was transferred to a hospice facility where I could visit him. I visited him for two hours that day. He never opened his eyes, but when I talked to him, he breathed a little heavier, and his cheeks turned rosy. On January 1, I was with him from 11 a.m. until 5:30 p.m. when he took his last breath. About five minutes before he died, he opened his eyes, which I feel was a sign that he knew I was there. I am so thankful that I was able to talk to him, sing hymns for him, read Bible verses to him, and tell him good-bye. I was looking forward to being able to visit him in person when the virus subsided, but I didn't want visiting him to be this way. I know that he's in heaven with his Lord and Savior, his family, and friends, which is very comforting. He no longer has myelofibrosis, Parkinson's disease, dementia, or neuropathy. His pain is gone and he's whole again. Praise the Lord! We had a wonderful marriage together, and I will miss him.

I'm doing okay. Because I was with him, I have had to quarantine for ten days in case I get the virus. I'm staying busy doing all the things that need to be done when someone passes away. My family, friends, and neighbors are making sure that if I need anything, they are there for me.

CHAPTER 33

Hospitality With Educational Opportunities (EO)

Working Hospitality in Israel: 1995, 1996, and 1997

1995: Martha working at the hotel in Jerusalem.

I've already talked a little bit about our volunteer job in Israel. We worked in January and February for three different years. Two of the years, we were stationed at the Holiday Inn, Crowne Plaza. In 1996 we worked at the Renaissance Hotel. We lived in the hotel where the passengers stayed. We were given a large room by the hotel, since we were there for two months. We were at our desk in the hotel lobby early in the morning and prior to the passengers returning from their day trips in case someone had a question or needed help.

We had a large bulletin board where we put information for each group: meal time, luggage out, departure time, and so on. Each group had a different color assigned to it, and that color was posted on the front window of their bus. At times we might have had thirteen buses in at the same time.

When a bus first arrived, one of us went on the bus, greeted them, and gave them instructions. We were given a list of names and where they were from. On one occasion we greeted the group from Grace Community Church in Tempe. That was exciting! When the groups were in the hotel, we stayed at our desk in the lobby until 9:00 p.m. to answer any questions. If someone got sick or injured and had to go to the hospital, we called the insurance company and opened a claim (if they had taken the travel insurance). When a group was leaving the hotel, we checked off each piece of luggage to make sure they were all there.

We always felt pretty safe while working in Israel. One thing that was emphasized was to stay off the local buses. This was reinforced one day when we heard a loud explosion. One of the public buses had just been bombed. All of the passengers were killed. A few days later, another bus was blown up.

When we later put together our trips for IN-JOY, we insisted that people take the travel insurance. We had seen too many people fall and injure themselves. One passenger fell and broke her hip; another fell and fractured her shoulder; a lady fell getting off the bus and fractured her elbow; someone else broke a leg. Many of these people had to be flown back home, sometimes with a medical escort.

We had a large Catholic group in the hotel, and their priest was traveling with them. Someone from the hotel called us in the middle of the night, stating that one of the men, Andy, was trying to jump out of the fourth-story window. He was an anesthesiologist, and just prior to going on this trip, he had made a mistake, and the patient died. He was afraid he was going to be arrested or sued. Wes and I talked and prayed with Andy. We decided to wake up the bus captain and ask him to help. I called him, and he thought the call was his wake-up call. He got up, showered, and was getting dressed when we finally knocked on his door. He immediately got the priest, who then went to Andy's room and calmed him down. After that we did not leave Andy alone. Someone stayed with him constantly. We learned later that Andy did commit suicide when he got back home.

Another time a new bus had just arrived. An elderly lady named Gertrude got off the bus and tried to give Wes a handful of dollar bills. Wes told her he could not take money from her. She said she wanted to give it to the poor people in Israel, and now she was ready to go back home. We explained that she needed to stay with her group and couldn't go home. She tried to call a taxi from her room to take her back to Arkansas. We called her cousin, whom she had listed on her medical form as emergency contact. He did not even know she had gone to Israel! Gertrude and her roommate were friends, not related, and they were not from the same church as the group on the bus. She was a problem for the entire trip, and we assigned someone on the bus to help her when they were out on day trips.

Then there was the case of the missing piece of luggage! A man who had returned to the United States did not receive his luggage. Someone from the airport looked all over for it, and we looked at the hotel, but no luck. Wes went to the airport one day and decided to look for himself. He found it in the lost and found. The main problem was that the passenger had switched buses when he was touring, and the color of the luggage tag didn't get changed with him. Such a simple thing, but it made a big difference!

*1996: Martha behind a camel with the city
of Jerusalem in the background.*

Fahim, one of our Muslim waiters in the dining room, invited Wes and me to his home for dinner one evening at the close of Ramadan. He picked us up at the hotel and took us to his home. We couldn't eat until the moon was in a certain position and someone gave the all clear on TV. We really had a feast! Fahim's little girl was learning English by reading children's books. She spoke a few words to us in English.

We were able to visit many places while in Israel. We often rode with one of the groups on their day trips. Wes and I visited Shepherds' Field, the Tomb of Lazarus, walked the Via Dolorosa, walked the Ramparts, and went to the Garden of Gethsemane and the Mount of Olives. On our own we went to various museums. Our favorite place to go was the Old City in Jerusalem. We took the shuttle there and just roamed the various quarters. We met Murphy, a Muslim, who owned a shop in the Old City. He invited us to lunch one day, and we thought we would be going to a restaurant. He pulled out three stools in the back of his shop to sit on, two stools and a board for the table, and newspaper for the tablecloth, and he served chicken, rice, vegetables, pita bread, and soda. He also ate with us and was still able to wait on customers in his shop. The food was remarkably good.

One of the things we did the most on our job was to handle complaints and solve problems, such things as "The room is too small," "My luggage didn't show up," "I lost my passport," and "I'm sick—I need a doctor." One day a lady was bitten on her arm by a camel, and the camel wouldn't let go. The guide hit the camel on the head until he finally released her. The lady was taken to the hospital. The guide said the camel was put in "prison" to make sure he didn't have rabies.

The Jewish people have some different rules, and we tried to explain them to our groups. For instance, they do not mix meat and dairy products. Therefore the hotel had one dining room where meat was served, and another where dairy products could be eaten. We could order a cheese pizza in the dairy restaurant, but with no meat on it. In the meat dining room, we could not have butter with our meal, or milk to drink. One group brought a birthday cake to the meat restaurant. They couldn't serve it, as it had whipped cream on it.

On Shabbat (Sabbath), one of the four elevators was called the "Shabbat elevator," as it automatically stopped on each of the twenty-one floors of the hotel without riders having to push a button. We warned our groups not to get on that elevator if it was Shabbat—they would certainly be late to wherever they were going! Many Jewish people stayed at the hotel on the weekends so they didn't have to do any work.

George and Wilma Weber were our supervisors, and they worked at another hotel. Their hotel was much larger, and we often walked to their hotel and helped out. There were four hotels being used in Jerusalem, each one with a hospitality couple. Once a week the four couples got together for a meeting and lunch, and we discussed problems. Some of the things were unbelievable, and we dubbed them the "Jerusalem syndrome." It seemed as if some people did very strange things once they arrived in the Holy Land.

In 1997, when we left Israel, we knew it would be our last time to work there. The staff at the Holiday Inn called us into the office and gave us a going-away gift and thanked us for being so easy to work with.

Working Hospitality in Greece: 1995, 1996 and 1997—"The Journeys of Paul"

Since Wes and I had previously been to Greece a couple times, we were asked to work in hospitality in Greece. The concept there was completely different than it was in Israel, as we had to split up. While one of us stayed in Athens with the groups there, the other one flew or drove to Thessaloniki to meet the groups flying in from the United States. The next week we switched. We were always together in Athens for three days. You will notice that I used "Thessaloniki" instead of Thessalonica, as in the Bible. We learned to use the Greek spelling of the cities rather than the English spelling.

After visiting Thessaloniki, the groups went to Philippi, where Paul and Silas were once in jail; then to Kalambaka to visit one or two of the Meteora monasteries, which were built on very high rocks or cliffs. In 1991 they celebrated six hundred years of existence. These monasteries are unbelievable as to how they were built. Six of them are still in use today and are open to tourists. The Monastery of the Holy Trinity had a rope ladder and a net that were originally used to go up and down from the monastery. In 1925 a staircase with 140 steps was chiseled in the rock in order to reach the building. (We did not use the rope ladder!)

The first year we worked in Greece, the local travel company was Blue Bell, and we stayed at the Royal Olympic Hotel. Andreas was our "boss." We noticed that sometimes his name was Andreas and sometimes just Andrea, without the *s*. We asked him which one was correct, and he said in Greece, when you are talking directly to a man, you say his name without the *s*, Andrea. When you are talking about him, you say his name with the *s*, Andreas. Interesting! We did not know that. Wes was eventually given the Greek name of Visilious or Visili, as there was no equivalent of the name Wes in Greek. While at the Royal Olympic Hotel, we met Demetris Keratsas, who owned a jewelry store in the hotel. We became very good friends and referred many of our passengers who wanted to buy Greek jewelry to him.

We were always treated like royalty in the hotels when we were on the road. We were often given a suite, and flowers and wine or fruit always greeted us in the room. It would have been nicer if both of us could have been together, though, as we were generally occupying the room alone. While it was my turn to work in Athens, I received a call from Wes, who was at the airport on his way to Thessaloniki. He had been bumped from the flight! I had mistakenly given him my airline ticket for the following week. He was able to work it out and got on the next plane.

1995: Martha and Wes with Greek ruins in background.

During our first year, Blue Bell offered a sound and light show at the Acropolis at night, which was pretty spectacular. The group was also offered a folklore night in the Plaka at a taverna, which included folk dances and bouzouki music.

Nikos (Nick), one of the bus drivers, told Yannis (John), one of our guides, to ask us if we would go out for dinner one evening with him and his family. He couldn't ask us himself as he didn't speak English. We said we would be honored to go. Nikos and his wife, Tina, and daughter, Teta, took us to a Greek taverna. We had small dishes of octopus, squid, cod, mussels, shrimp, Greek salad, fried cheese, pancakes, and tzatziki, which we all shared. Teta was the only one who spoke English, so she translated all evening. Greeks eat very late, generally around ten o'clock. We arrived at our hotel at about one.

We had a lecturer in Athens whose name was Pericles (Perry) Alexander. His heritage was Greek, but he was an

American citizen. He lectured three times a week to the groups. He was such a good (and funny) speaker that I generally stayed and listened each time. He pastored at St. Andrew's Church in Athens, which we attended when we were in town. Alma, one of the ladies in his congregation, became a friend of mine. Perry gave me a little warning, though, as he thought she was an illegal immigrant from Albania. She told me she wanted to come to America and live with us, which I discouraged. Then she called me one day and said she wanted to commit suicide. I talked with her for quite a long time, telling her how much God loved her. I called Perry immediately afterward, and he said he would also talk with her.

We had some interesting things happen in Greece. One man kept getting a nosebleed, and it would not stop. He was on Wes's bus in the north. He had gone to several of the small public hospitals, and when he was released, his nose would bleed again. He finally took a taxi from fifty miles north to one of the large, private hospitals in Athens. I met him at the hospital to make sure everything was okay. They were able to help him at this hospital, and he was released to go back to the hotel.

The Greek free public hospitals were very different from what we're used to. They did not feed the patient or change the sheets on the bed. A family member or friend had to do those jobs. We did not know this until Perry Alexander told us.

One time when we met the flight in Thessaloniki coming in from New York, there were six people missing. They finally arrived at the hotel at 3:00 a.m. They told us they had missed their flight at JFK and were put on a flight to Frankfort, then to Budapest, and finally flew into Thessaloniki on a Russian plane. Then their bags were lost. The luggage was finally found and was delivered a few days later in Athens.

The second and third years we worked in Greece, the local travel company was Cruise Club. They discontinued flying to Thessaloniki. Instead, all passengers flew directly into Athens from the United States, spent a couple of days in Athens, and then were bused to Thessaloniki. During this trip north, we stopped several times for restroom breaks and lunch. In many of the villages, the toilets were just holes in the floor. One of our passengers had a wooden leg, and she had to take the leg off in order to use the facility. Many places did not have toilet paper, either. I would generally go into the restroom first and report back to the group whether it was a three-star, four-star, or five-star restroom. Five stars meant 1) a regular toilet, 2) a seat on the toilet, 3) toilet paper, 4) paper towels, and 5) soap. More often than not, it was not a five-star restroom!

On the return trip from Thessaloniki and Kalambaka, the group stayed overnight in Delphi. Wes met a store owner there whose name was Demetris. He invited Wes to his home for octopus spaghetti. He told Wes to have me come for the same menu the next time I was in Delphi with my group. As I knew I could not eat octopus spaghetti, I never went to his store.

When we were in Athens, our groups were assigned to two different hotels: the Divani Caravel and the Divani Acropolis Palace. Depending on which hotel was being used that week, Wes and I had to keep moving from one to the other. We put things in storage so we didn't have to move everything, as we had four large suitcases between us. Fortunately there was a shuttle that went back and forth between the two hotels and also went downtown.

We not only had all of our expenses paid, but we earned travel credits for trips with EO. We asked Kim, Mike, and Lindsey if they would like to come to Greece using some of our credits. Of course they jumped at the chance! The guides and hotel staff all knew they were coming with one of the groups. They were treated like royalty! The hotel gave them a suite, and the travel company gave them all of the options free (three-day cruise and folklore night). One of the guides gave Lindsey a Greek doll. You may recall that our granddaughter Michelle has Down syndrome. Wes and I met a vendor when we were at the Monastery of Varlaam. Her twenty-year-old daughter, Maria, who has Down syndrome, was with her. We introduced her to Kim and Mike and showed her Michelle's picture. That evening Maria and her mother came to our hotel and brought cookies. They didn't speak English, but our guide translated for us. It was Maria's name day, when all of the females named Maria celebrate by sharing sweets with others.

Wes and I were invited to go on a three-day cruise, which was offered as a group option. We visited the Greek islands of Mykonos, Rhodes, and Patmos, and the Turkish city of Kusadasi. From Kusadasi we took a thirty-minute bus ride to Ephesus, the best reconstructed ruins in the world. This is where the disciple John visited three times and where he was buried. We saw the Temple of Diana, one of the seven wonders of the ancient world. We had devotions at the stadium, which holds fourteen thousand people. From there we went to the island of Patmos, where we visited the grotto where John saw the vision and wrote the Book of Revelation.

Working Hospitality in Austria: 2000

We could no longer work in Israel or Greece, since we had started IN-JOY in 1998. However, we were asked if we could work in Austria during the summer months of 2000, and we readily agreed.

We were stationed in Kufstein, Austria. The groups that came from the United States were coming for the Passion play in Oberammergau, Germany. We were given a one-bedroom apartment about six blocks away from one of three different hotels we were responsible for. The main one was the Hotel Thaler, where we ate and spent most of our time.

The local travel company was Rainbow Travel Company. They had hired and trained college students to be the guides and bus drivers. During the first part of the season, before they had become experienced, there were quite a few problems. Martin, one of the new guides, just didn't talk on the bus. Everyone complained that they didn't learn a thing that day! We talked with our supervisor, and Martin didn't come back the second day. The bus driver on a different bus got lost for one and a half hours. He also drove under a viaduct that was too low for the bus. The top of the bus was really scraped up. Toward the end of the tours, the guides and drivers did much better and were quite enjoyable.

We fell in love with Austria and the people. We were there two months and learned so much. We learned that the restaurants don't give "doggie bags." We ate at the Auracher restaurant one evening. I ordered lasagna, and it was a very large portion and also very good. I asked for a doggie bag, and Maria (Ria), the waitress and owner, wrapped foil around the plate and brought it to me. She said to bring back the plate next time. We asked if they served ice cream, and she said no. She soon came back with two ice cream cones for us from the ice cream parlor across the street. We found out later that she owned two restaurants *and* the ice cream parlor. We became pretty good friends with her and ate at her restaurant quite often.

We also found out we could not buy peanut butter at the grocery stores. We finally found out the German words for peanut butter, but no store carried it. When we went grocery shopping for the first time, we didn't know that we needed to take our own grocery bags. We hurriedly bought some at the checkout counter. We also had to bag our own groceries.

One evening we were waiting at the Hotel Thaler for a group to arrive from the United States. They were late, and no one seemed to know where they were. The groups would generally fly into Munich, Germany, and then were bused to our location in Kufstein. The regular employees at the reception desk had gone home for the night, and the night watchman was there to answer the phone. The phone rang at 1:00 a.m., and as he did not speak English, he quickly brought the phone to me. It was the bus captain from the missing group, calling from Goose Bay, Labrador! He explained to us that their flight had had a medical emergency with one of our passengers, and the nearest place to land was in Goose Bay. They planned to arrive the next day. Everyone did arrive except the lady who'd had the emergency and her roommate. They came a few days later.

The options that passengers could go to were a Tyrolean evening and music from *The Sound of Music*. We enjoyed them both so much that we attended every time with the groups.

While we were in Austria, we rented a car and drove to the small country of Lichtenstein, which is just west of Austria. We also attended the Passion play in Oberammergau, Germany. It lasted from 9:30 a.m. until noon. Then there was a three-hour break for lunch (and shopping). It started up again and ran from 3:00 until 6:15. It was all in German, but we were all familiar with the story, so the language didn't matter.

We visited Vienna one afternoon and rode the huge "grand Ferris wheel." It was a little disappointing, as it stopped so often that we hardly felt like we were moving.

Another couple we knew from hospitality in Israel came to relieve us. We moved out of our apartment, and they moved in. We had told them that Greeks don't use shower curtains, so they brought their own and hung it. Smart! We were always mopping up water off the bathroom floor. They also brought their own peanut butter!

We thoroughly enjoyed working in hospitality for Educational Opportunities, and it was a wonderful experience for us.

CHAPTER 34

Travel Adventures

In this chapter, I'm only going to talk about the out-of-state trips that Wes and I have taken since we got married in 1978. I hadn't done much traveling before, but I became more adventuresome after I married Wes. Some of the trips I've already shared with you, so I'll just talk about the major ones that were more spectacular. The trips won't necessarily be in date order, as I will lump together all of the Greek trips, Alaska trips, and Branson trips.

Here's a recap of the major trips that we've taken:

1977: Greece (Susan Harris and I)

1979: Greece, Portugal, Denmark, Switzerland, and Norway (Wes and I)

1984: Bahamas (Wes and I); England, Belgium, France, Germany, Switzerland, and Amsterdam (XYZ)

1987: Nashville, Annapolis, Washington, DC (Wes and I)

1990: Los Angeles, San Francisco, San Diego (Wes and I)

1991: New Orleans (Wes and I)

1992: Greece; New England (where we killed the moose)

1993: Northwest trip (XYZ); New Zealand and Australia (Wes and I)

1994: Israel and Egypt (GCC); Alaska Highway (Wes and I)

1995: Worked in Israel and Greece

1996: Worked in Israel, Jordan, and Greece; Branson (IN-JOY)

1997: Worked in Israel and Greece

1998: Ecuador (Wes and I); Hawaii (XYZ)

1999: Ecuador (Wes and I); Israel and Jordan (IN-JOY)

2000: Ecuador (Wes and I); worked in Austria; Germany, Prague, and Italy (IN-JOY)

2001: Palm Springs, California (Wes and I); Greece (IN-JOY)

2002: Palm Springs, California; Canyon de Chelly; Alaska cruise; Branson (all IN-JOY)

2003: Kartchner Caverns, Bisbee, and Douglas; northern Arizona; Branson (all IN-JOY); Hawaii (Wes and I, Ron and Jan)

2004: Austria and Germany (Wes and I and the Van Ausdles)

2005: Panama Canal cruise; Kartchner Caverns and Tucson; Branson (all IN-JOY)

2006: New York City (with choir); Alaska cruise (IN-JOY)

2007: Israel (IN-JOY); Russian riverboat cruise (Wes and I)

2008: New England (IN-JOY)

2009: Branson; Greece and Turkey cruise (all IN-JOY)

2010: New Brunswick (Wes and I); Germany, Austria, Italy, and Prague (IN-JOY)

2011: Texas (Wes and I); Washington, DC (Wes and I and Van Ausdles)

2012: Russian riverboat cruise (IN-JOY); New Brunswick (twelve of us)

2013: Hawaii (IN-JOY)

2014: South American cruise (IN-JOY)

2015: Canada/New England cruise (IN-JOY)

2016: Branson (IN-JOY); Hawaii (Wes and I and the Cisneys)

2017: Memphis and Nashville (IN-JOY)

2018: Alaska Inside Passage cruise (IN-JOY)

Greece: 1992, 2001 and 2009

In 1992 Wes and I went to Greece with XYZ from Grace Community Church from April 16 until May 2. Helen and Arnie File were the leaders. There were thirty-four people on the trip. We flew from Phoenix to JFK in New York, but we were delayed there due to a fire on one of the nearby planes, which shut down the airport for two hours. We then flew to Paris, changed planes, and then went on to Athens. Since I don't sleep on the plane, I was pretty tired, along with everyone else, by the time we arrived.

The next morning we had a tour of the city of Athens. The next day, Sunday, was our Easter Sunday. Wes and I had often attended St. Paul's Anglican Church where the service was in English. We walked the group there and enjoyed communion. The church was packed, with standing room only. In the afternoon we were bused to Cape Sounion on the Aegean Sea. It was beautiful. Two days later we drove north to tour the monasteries. The women had to wear skirts in order to enter the monasteries. They were built on top of cliffs, and the scenery from the top was spectacular.

During the next few days, we visited Delphi and Olympia. We arrived in Sparta in time to celebrate Orthodox Good Friday in one of the large Greek Orthodox churches. At the end of the service, everyone lit a candle, and we walked with the Greek parishioners in a procession to the town square.

In the meantime, a lot of our group were getting sick. It seemed as if the flu bug was running rampant throughout our group. One by one, someone new got sick. Sometimes the bus had to stop for them. The guide told us not to drink anything but bottled water, in case the local water was a problem. We were all taking lots of Pepto-Bismol!

During our trip many of the hotels and restaurants served lamb. Several of the single ladies did not like lamb. Since Wes loved lamb, he was given two or three portions. He ate every bit of it!

Greeks love to strike! During our stay in Greece, there was a garbage strike going on. We saw garbage piled up all over. What a shame, especially for tourists to witness that. One thing we kept noticing while we were driving through the countryside was many of the homes looked as if they were unfinished. They had rebar sticking up on the top of the houses.

The guide told us one reason was that they didn't have to pay taxes on an unfinished house, and the other reason was that when a child grows up and marries, the new family generally lives with their parents. All they had to do was to add another floor.

After we returned to Athens, we boarded a ship at the Port of Piraeus and went on a five-day trip to Mykonos, Santorini, Rhodes, Crete, and Ephesus. In Rhodes Wes and I rode a donkey to the Acropolis of Lindos. At the end of the cruise, the waiters paraded around the dining room carrying flaming baked Alaska dessert. It was a nice way to end our trip.

In 2001 Wes and I took a group of twenty-six to Greece under the umbrella of IN-JOY. Prior to the trip, we made arrangements for the group to experience some Greek food at the Greektown Restaurant in Phoenix. I love the names of some of the Greek foods. We tried spanakopita (spinach pie); pastitsio (Greek lasagna); dolmades (grape leaves stuffed with meat and rice); saganaki (flaming cheese); octopus; and baklava for dessert.

We left Phoenix on March 15 and returned on April 5. We stayed at the Hilton hotel in Athens when we weren't traveling to the north. The first night we took a group to our friend Demitris's jewelry shop. On the way back, we rode the new Metro. We were riding up on the escalator, which was much faster than ours, and we were at the top before I realized it. I took a tumble getting off and hit my back on the corner of the wall. I was really hurting and should have gone to the hospital, but I said I would be okay. That night I asked the front desk for some ice in a plastic bag, and I slept with it on my back all night. I woke up the next morning in a puddle of cold water in my bed. After that I bought frozen peas and slept on those. My back hurt for most of the trip.

Since we didn't have enough in our group for a full bus, we were paired with a group of twenty Lutherans from California traveling with their pastor, Thom Johnson. Along with him were his wife, two sisters, and nephew, Evan. This is significant, as I will explain later. Our guide was Yiannis (John), whom we had requested, as we knew him when we worked in hospitality. Wes was named the bus captain, and we were the orange bus, also at our request. (Wes always wore an orange cap so people could see him when he was leading the group.) I generally brought up the rear.

We toured all of the usual places in Athens, including the Acropolis and the Changing of the Guard at Syntagma Square. The next day we drove to Thessaloniki for two days and then went on to see the Meteora monasteries. Evan did not want to tour the monasteries, and he yelled at his uncle Thom and took a swing at him. Our guide told him he didn't have to go with us and told him how to walk to the hotel, which Evan did. The next day we visited Delphi. We completely lost Evan there, as he was supposed to meet the bus at a certain location and a certain time. He didn't show, so Wes, Thom, and Yiannis went looking for him. They finally filed a missing-person report with the police. We all prayed while we were waiting. We waited three hours, and then our guide felt we needed to drive on to Athens. Evan's mother and her sister stayed in Delphi. The next day we learned that Evan had taken a baseball bat and used it to break several front windows of cars parked in the area. Thom, his uncle, told us Evan had Tourette's syndrome and ADD but was on medication. We wondered if the nine-hour time change had something to do with the fact that his medication times would have all been off. Evan's father was a doctor, and he finally flew to Greece from California, brought Evan medicine, and flew with him back home. What an experience!

In 2009 we took another group of twenty-seven people to Greece from March 16 to March 30 on "Paul's Second and Third Missionary Journey," which was a cruise. We all signed up for a pretour that took us to the ancient ruins of Delphi. We learned on the drive there that the agriculture products in the area were cotton, rice, fruit, wheat, citrus, and olives. The Germans occupied Greece in World War II, and it took until the 1950s for Greece to recover. We saw beautiful flowers and trees. The white-flowered trees were almond trees, and the pink-flowered trees were called Judas trees.

From there we drove to Kalambaka to tour the famous Byzantine monasteries, perched precariously on summits of soaring, sheer-sided rocks. We wanted our group to see these spectacular edifices. We stayed that night at the Meteora Hotel, which had a beautiful view of the monasteries. The following day, after visiting a shop where icons are made, we drove to Athens and spent the night at a hotel with other groups going on the cruise. We had to put our bags out by midnight that night. The next morning at five, our phone rang. It was one of the ladies in our group. She had packed all of her clothes and had nothing to wear except her nightgown! Wes called the hospitality desk, and we were told that all of the suitcases were still in the hotel lobby; none had yet been taken to the ship. Wes went to the lobby and took the suitcase to her room. We were certainly glad the bags were still there! We still had another day of touring before boarding the ship.

Our first stop that day was the Corinth Canal. Dena Brinkman, one of the ladies from our church, was originally from Greece, and she had a cousin living in the Corinth area. We met the cousin there and gave her supplies from Arizona that she could not buy in Greece, things like Cheerios, instant coffee, cookies, and Splenda. We had our pictures taken with her before driving to Ancient Corinth. Then another cousin of Dena's met us and brought us food—cheese pie and pasta flora, which were delicious. We drove to Athens, where we toured the Parthenon, Propylaea, and the Erechtheum at the Acropolis. We viewed Mars Hill, where Paul preached the Gospel to the intellectual Athenians. We were taken to the Olympic Stadium, where the modern Olympics began and where the games were played in 2004.

From there we drove to the port where we went through security and boarded the *Cristal Ship*. We all went to bed exhausted! The ship sailed to Thessaloniki, where we disembarked the next morning and met our guide and bus for a city tour. We drove up on a narrow, winding road to ancient Thessaloniki, called the Ramparts, where we scraped the side of another bus coming down. It didn't do too much damage to either bus, but it was very frightening!

We drove back to the ship and went to dinner. It was Greek night, or Blue and White Night (the colors of Greece). We celebrated Murchie Hatt's birthday with a cake and sang "Happy Birthday" to him.

The next morning the ship docked at Kavala, one of Greece's most picturesque ports, and we were taken to Lydia's stream, where Paul preached his first sermon in Europe to women who had gathered at the river. Among them was Lydia, a cloth merchant, who became the first Christian to be baptized on European soil. This is where Wes baptized three ladies from our group. He thought he was finished when two Catholic nuns from another group asked if Wes would baptize them. What an honor! Wes was overwhelmed! We later sang "How Great Thou Art" in a church nearby. We were taken to the ancient ruins of Philippi, where Paul and Silas had been in jail. We returned to the ship and attended a Sunday afternoon church service. That evening we sailed for Turkey.

We docked in Istanbul, Turkey, the following morning and met our guide and driver. Istanbul is located in both Europe and Asia. We took off our shoes and walked into the famous Blue Mosque and had to carry the shoes with us in a plastic bag. In the afternoon we went to the Grand Bazaar, which is five miles long. We were all pretty tired of walking and returned to the ship exhausted!

We sailed to Pergamum, Sardis, Thyatira, and Smyrna, four of the seven churches of Revelation. The following day we sailed to Kusadasi and were bused to Ephesus, where the apostle Paul stayed for two and a half years on his third missionary journey. Jesus's mother, Mary, was thought to have lived in Ephesus for part of her life, and there is a church there called the Church of Mary. There were a lot more ruins excavated since we were last in Ephesus. We had a group picture taken in front on the library ruins. Some people sat on the ancient public toilets and had their pictures taken. There were fifteen cement seats side by side. A communion service in the ancient stadium was the highlight of the day.

The next day we were taken by tenders to the island of Patmos, where the exiled apostle John wrote the Book of Revelation in the Grotto of the Apocalypse. Wes and I had been there several times, but it was still an emotional visit.

Tourism is the main income of Patmos. We drove by the island's oldest chapel, built in the fifth century. It is still active today.

We disembarked the ship the next morning and were met by Christiana, a guide that we knew from hospitality. She and the bus driver took us to Cape Sounion to view the temple ruins. On the return to Athens, which was a beautiful drive, we stopped for lunch at Milos Windmill restaurant, where we ate homemade food, sat on tables outside, and had a spectacular view of the mountains in the distance. It was a nice, sunny day.

We checked into the Divani Palace Acropolis hotel in Athens. Several of our people were getting sick. I asked the front desk at the hotel to call their hotel doctor. He visited two of our group, gave them a shot in their hand, and told them they would feel better within two hours. And they did! Others in the group did not want to see the doctor, and they were still sick the next day.

Nine of us took the Metro on Sunday to St. Andrew's International Church, where Wes and I attended when we were previously in Greece. We saw many of the people we had met on our earlier trips.

That evening we all packed our suitcases. The next morning we checked out of the hotel and said good-bye to Greece. It was another wonderful trip.

New Zealand and Australia: 1993

One of Wes's and my most memorable trips was to New Zealand and Australia for five weeks in 1993. It started out super nice, as we had first-class tickets on the flight to Honolulu,

Hawaii (thanks to frequent flyer miles). Since we had a ten-hour layover, we rented a car and drove around the island. Wes had never had any desire to visit Hawaii, so I couldn't get him to plan a trip there. This was an eye-opener for him, and he really enjoyed Hawaii. Our flight to Auckland, New Zealand, was also first class on Continental Airlines. It was a long flight to Auckland; thank goodness we could put our seats back and practically lie flat. We both slept well. Since we crossed the International Date Line, we lost a day. There was a twenty-hour difference in time between Phoenix and Auckland. Geoff and Cathy Ralls, who had earlier purchased our Packard, were there to meet us, and they took us on a tour of the area.

We were actually in New Zealand to help start the Packard Club and go on tour. We visited a museum where one of the individuals himself owned twenty-three Packard cars. One night we stayed at a private farmhouse owned by the McDonalds (appropriate—Old MacDonald had a farm). A few days later, we attended a Packard rally. Wes was able to drive our old pink 1956 Packard. He was thrilled!

We really enjoyed New Zealand. We visited both the South Island and the North Island. We enjoyed their culture. We were quite often served a dessert called pavlova, which is made of baked egg whites with whipped cream and fruit (generally kiwi) on top. I made it several times after we arrived home.

We stayed a few days with Geoff and Cathy and then stayed with a pastor friend named Harry Morgan and his wife, Pam. We had met them on our trip in 1984 to Germany and the Passion play. Harry asked Wes to preach a sermon the next Sunday to his congregation. Wes said, "But I'm not a preacher." Harry said they were expecting him to preach, so he'd better put something together. Wes got his Bible and put together a three-point sermon. Most of the congregation at St. Andrew's Presbyterian Church were Cook Island people. After the service they served a luncheon for the four of us. We sat at a table on the platform while they sang and watched us eat. They wouldn't eat until we were finished.

We said good-bye to New Zealand and flew to Sydney, Australia. While in Australia we rode a camel, saw kangaroos, koalas, wombats, emus, wallabies, Tasmanian devils, dingoes (wild dogs), kookaburras, and lots and lots of flies! While we were in the outback (desert), we climbed Uluru, also called Ayers Rock (a one-thousand-foot-high red rock), where we wore fly nets over our faces to keep from eating the flies! We also snorkeled in the Great Barrier Reef and saw beautiful coral and tropical fish.

Even though they speak English in New Zealand and Australia, some of their words are different. Here are some of the new words we learned and what they mean: metal road (gravel road), jumper (sweater), sealed roads (paved roads), push bike (bicycle), nappies or napkins (diapers), serviette (napkin), wind screen (windshield), naked light (fire), lolly (candy), sleepers (railroad ties), chilly bin (cooler), verge (shoulder), and tomato sauce (ketchup).

Driving the Alaska Highway: 1994

Wes had always wanted to drive to Alaska, and this was the year! I wasn't very excited about it, but it was actually one of the best vacations we've ever taken. We visited several friends along the way: Bill and Dee Van Egmond (now Cornelison) in Manhattan, Montana (near Bozeman), and Jim and Marge

Garrison in Hungry Horse, Montana. We drove through Banff National Park; visited Moraine Lake, where Wes fell into the water trying to take a picture; and toured the Fairmont Chateau Lake Louise. At Jasper National Park, we rode on a snow coach to the Columbia Icefield, where we walked on a glacier and about froze! We also drove in the Northwest Territory, British Columbia, and the Yukon. We were looking for a motel in Muncho Lake, British Columbia, and found this sign on the front door of the motel: "If we're closed when you arrive, find an empty room (drapes open and door unlocked). Pay in the morning."

We drove on the Alaska Highway from its beginning at Dawson Creek, British Columbia, to its ending at Fairbanks, Alaska. We had three blowouts but no other problems. Our daughter, Kim, and her husband, Mike, flew to Anchorage, and we all toured Alaska together for a week. We drove on a dirt road for many miles and hours to go to the Arctic Circle. After all that driving, there was just a large billboard saying, "You've arrived at the Arctic Circle." We had our pictures taken in front of the sign and turned around and went back to Fairbanks, where we had rented a cabin at Birch Lake.

One of the highlights of our trip was a ride on a five-person Cessna plane out of Talkeetna, landing on Ruth Glacier. We walked in deep snow, sinking in sometimes up to a foot or more. We also enjoyed the Iditarod sled dog facility, where we rode on a wagon pulled by eleven huskies. They had sixty-seven dogs and sixteen puppies. Kim and I each held and petted a puppy. Kim wanted to take hers home. They were beautiful dogs and cuddly puppies. We soon said good-bye to Kim and Mike and continued our trip.

We really enjoyed Whitehorse and Dawson City in the Yukon Territory. We attended Whitehorse Nazarene Church one Sunday morning and met George and Maggie Johnson. They invited us for lunch at their home after the service. Maggie said she would thaw a roast and put it in the oven. As we had plans to visit a museum that afternoon, we took a rain check, knowing it would take several hours for lunch to be ready! We did visit them after we left Alaska and drove through Whitehorse on the way home.

By the time we returned home, we had driven 13,825 miles!

Three-Day Alaska Cruise and Nine-Day Land Tour (IN-JOY Trips): 2002 and 2006

Both of these Alaska trips were with Holland America Cruise Line and were very similar, with the exception of a three-day pretour in 2002 to Seattle and Vancouver. In Seattle we went to the famous Pike's Market, where they throw fish. We rode the monorail to the Space Needle and took the elevator to the observation deck to take pictures of the city. We ate at the SkyCity revolving restaurant on top for dinner. We were then bused and ferried to Vancouver, British Columbia, with a stop at Butchart Gardens. We had just a small group of eight on this trip. We boarded the Holland American ship in Vancouver.

Just prior to going on the 2002 cruise, there were two fires raging in Arizona: the Rodeo fire near Heber and Overgaard, and the Chediski fire, just west of the Rodeo fire. Fifty-two hundred people had been evacuated. A total of ninety thousand acres had burned, and fifty buildings burned down. A week later we checked the news, and we learned the fire had consumed 350 homes, and thirty thousand people were evacuated.

On the 2006 Alaskan adventure cruise, we flew directly from Phoenix to Vancouver and boarded the ship there. Here again we only had a small group with us: Mike and Gene Schoonmaker, and Jim and Karen Enos, for a total of six individuals.

The three-day cruise consisted of sailing to Juneau and Skagway. While we were in Juneau, we went on the Taste of Juneau tour, where we learned there are thirty-one thousand permanent residents in the city. We visited a salmon hatchery, Mendenhall Glacier, and toured Glacier Gardens, where we were served Russian tea and cakes. For lunch we ate at the Red Dog Saloon. That evening we went to a salmon bake on Salmon Creek at the old Chilkoot mine.

We disembarked from the ship in Skagway and went on a six-hour Yukon Jeep tour to Carcross, Yukon. We saw mother bears, bear cubs, and sheep. The next day we had a city tour of Skagway, which included the Gold Rush Cemetery. We ate lunch at the Red Onion Saloon. Skagway means "Home of North Wind."

The next morning the six of us left Skagway and boarded a vintage parlor car on the White Pass and Yukon Route Railroad. We followed in the footsteps of the gold rushers as we traveled the Trail of '98, through beautiful mountains and countryside. After stopping for Canadian customs, we boarded a bus that stopped at Emerald Lake for a photo stop and then went on to Whitehorse, Yukon, for the night. We then saw the Frantic Follies Vaudeville Revue.

On to Dawson City, Yukon, the following morning, over the Klondike Highway, with a stop at Moose Creek. (I love the names of these places!) Dawson City, a gold-rush boom town, looks much the same as it did in 1898, with dirt streets, hitching posts, and saloons with swinging doors.

After arriving in Dawson City, we ate dinner at Klondike Kate's. Wes drank the "Sourtoe Cocktail" both in 2002 and 2006 and received certificates for it. If you're not familiar with what this is, a real toe was put into a glass of whiskey (or choice of drink), and Wes had to drink the whiskey and at least let the toe touch his lips. Then everyone cheered. No one else in our group did it!

The Sourtoe Cocktail is connected to a legend that dates back to the 1920s about two bootlegging brothers who placed one of their amputated frostbitten toes in moonshine as a "memen-toe." In 1973 the preserved toe was discovered, put into drinks for people brave enough to drink it, and the Sourtoe Cocktail Club was born. The original toe lasted for seven years, and they are now on their tenth toe. The toe has been dehydrated and preserved in salt. There is a saying that someone who lost his toe said: "Don't wear open-toed sandals while mowing the lawn." This set of rules goes with the drinking of the cocktail: "You can drink it fast, you can drink it slow—but the lips have gotta touch the toe."

That evening we all attended the Diamond Tooth Gertie's show at the saloon. The following day Wes and I ate at the Drunken Goat Greek restaurant for lunch.

We left Dawson City and cruised down the "River of Gold" aboard the *Yukon Queen II* for four and a half hours to Eagle, Alaska, where we participated in a mock trial at the Eagle courthouse. If I remember right, Wes was the villain, and I testified against him!

One of my favorite places to visit was Chicken, Alaska, population thirty-seven. There's not much there—just a few old wooden buildings and a huge metal chicken named Egger, which overlooks the Chicken Gold Camp. This metal chicken was created by high school students with recycled lockers. The town of Chicken was a nice place to stop for ice cream and a rest stop. The original name was supposed to be Ptarmigan, which means chicken. However, it was too hard for everyone to spell, thus the name Chicken. We spent that night at Tok, Alaska, where we toured Gold Dredge 8 and panned for gold. It was originally part of the Klondike Gold Rush.

From there we rode on the motor coach to Fairbanks, where we ate at the Red Lantern Saloon and spent the night at Westmark Inn. (All of the Westmark Inns were owned by Holland America.) We learned all about the construction of the Alaska Highway and the Alaska Pipeline at Delta Junction. The next day we went by train to Denali National Park on the McKinley Explorer train, observing moose along the way.

In Denali National Park, we boarded a school bus and were taken on an eight-hour ride to see wild animals. We saw nine caribou, eight ptarmigans, two bears, twenty Dall sheep, one squirrel, three magpies, one wolf, one marmot, one hawk, two rabbits, and one porcupine. It was quite a trip! On the 2002 trip, Wes and I rode horses in Denali Park.

From Denali Park we boarded the train again and rode to Anchorage. Wes purchased a gold-quartz ring at the Alaska Mint in Anchorage for $700. We did quite a lot of shopping at some nice souvenir shops and ate dinner that evening at the Snow Goose Restaurant. After spending the night at Westmark Inn, we flew home the next morning.

Trips to Hawaii: 1998, 2002, 2003, and 2013

From April 23 to May 2, 1998, Wes and I put together a seven-day cruise with Jim and Vera Marco of Camelback Odyssey Travel for XYZ at Grace Community Church. It was a very popular trip, with fifty-nine people on the cruise and fifteen on a two-day pretrip in Honolulu. We visited the Polynesian Cultural Center and toured the USS *Arizona* Memorial and Pearl Harbor, plus enjoyed a city tour of Honolulu. After spending the night at a luxurious hotel, we ate breakfast at Cheeseburgers in Paradise, where we enjoyed eating macadamia-nut pancakes.

In addition to many friends from XYZ as passengers, we also had family members go: Kim, Mike, Lindsey, and Michelle Rinke; Sis and her friend Treva Ramsey; Barbara and Jim Armstead; and Kim's friend Cheryl and her daughter Lindsay. Our granddaughter, Lindsey, was twelve years old, her friend Lindsay was fourteen, and our granddaughter Michelle was nine. They all enjoyed learning how to line dance. Michelle was (and is still) a neat freak, and she enjoyed walking from her cabin to ours and "straightening up" our messy room.

After boarding the S.S. *Independence* with American Hawaii Cruises in Honolulu, our first port was the island of Kauai, known as the Garden Island. Wes and I went on a four-wheel drive vehicle and drove to Koke'e State Park, Na Pali-Kona Forest Reserve, and saw Waimea Canyon, which is called the Grand Canyon of the Pacific.

The ship sailed to Kahului, Maui, the next day. While there, we visited the Haleakala Crater, which is ten thousand feet high and the highest inactive volcano on Maui. We also went to Iao Valley and rode a tram to the Maui Tropical Plantation, where we were shown how sugarcane and pineapple grow. We enjoyed a Hawaiian luau that evening.

Our next stop was the city of Hilo, which is on the eastern coast of the island of Hawaii. Hilo is considered the wettest city in the country. We went on a tour of the city and two volcanoes. We rode on a bus to Nani Mau Gardens and to Hawaii Volcanoes National Park. Kilauea volcano was still erupting while we were there and has for many years. At one time in the past, eight miles of the highway were covered with lava.

We returned to the ship and sailed to Kona on the other side of the Big Island of Hawaii, where we toured two churches, then drove to Puuhonua o Honaunau, a national historic park once known as a place of refuge for ancient Hawaiian lawbreakers. Since this was our last stop on the cruise, Wes and I purchased twenty-four anthurium flowers to take back to Arizona for decorating the IN-JOY tables.

We disembarked from the ship in Honolulu after a wonderful cruise. We flew home with a stop in San Francisco, arriving home in Phoenix at midnight on Saturday, May 2. Our first meeting of IN-JOY was on Tuesday, May 5.

In November 2002 Wes and I had free accommodations at the Kauai Coast Resort at the Beachboy in Kapa'a, on the island of Kauai. We had listened to a time-share presentation in 2001 and were given this trip. We also purchased additional time-share points. We flew from Los Angeles directly to the city of Lihue, Kauai, a five-hour flight. We rented a car and drove ten miles to the resort in Kapa'a. The resort was quite nice, right on the water. We had a one-bedroom suite with living room, bath, kitchen, and a partial view of the ocean.

The first day we took a helicopter ride over the entire island. The helicopter held six people, and Wes and I were in the front. One of the most beautiful views was flying over Waimea Canyon. We had on earphones in order to hear everything the pilot was telling us. The next day we went on a movie tour. We were taken to places where various movies were filmed: *Jurassic Park*, *Pagan Love Song*, *Blue Hawaii*, *The Beachcombers*, *South Pacific*, *Fantasy Island*, and *Raiders of the Lost Ark*, which included the rope that Harrison Ford used to escape from the natives. Anyone in our group who felt brave enough to do it was invited to swing on the rope, which Wes did! (I did not!) On that same trip, we saw wild boars and peacocks.

The following evening we went to the Kilohana Plantation estate for a luau. Prior to the luau we took a carriage ride around the grounds and saw beautiful flowers and trees. One of the horses was named Kim. We watched the imu ceremony, which entailed taking a roasted pig out of the ground. At least six layers of burlap were taken off of the pig. After the buffet of beef, mahi-mahi, chicken, pork, salad, pineapple, and more, we watched the hula dancers.

Groceries were very expensive in Hawaii. Milk ran six or seven dollars a gallon. We found the best places to buy food. Produce was cheapest at the local farmers' markets, and we discovered some of the smaller markets sold items in smaller quantities. We had taken a lot of food with us, like spices and canned goods. Our condo was fully equipped with dishes, silverware, cooking utensils, and pans.

An interesting thing we learned while we were there was about the Hawaiian alphabet, which consists of only the following twelve letters: H K L M N P W A E I O U. Each one of the letters in a word is always pronounced separately.

I love the unique Hawaiian words and names. We ate some very different food at the local restaurants: saimin (fresh-made noodles); manapua (steamed, shredded-pork-filled bun); and lilikoi chiffon pie, made with passion fruit juice.

There was so much to see and do on the island of Kauai: the Guava Kai Plantation, Kilauea Lighthouse, Wailua River, and the Opaeka'a Falls, which were beautiful. I'll talk about some of the rest of the places on the next trip.

Our next Hawaiian trip was in November of 2003. We used our time-share points at the same location on the same island of Kauai. This time we invited my son, Ron, and his wife, Jan, to stay with us. They slept on the pullout bed in the living room; it was not very comfortable, but at least it was free! They rented their own vehicle so they could go and do whatever they wanted.

On this trip we were in Hawaii for two weeks. We repeated some of the things we had done in 2002, but we saw and did a lot more this time. We went to Kipu Falls, drove on a dirt road back to Ninini Point and found an old nonworking lighthouse, went to Wailua Falls, walked on the Glass Beach, and attended a luau at the Coconut Beach Resort next to our resort. We enjoyed the movie tour so much in 2002 that we went on it again. This one took us to some different movie locations. One was the Coco Palms Resort hotel, where Elvis Presley starred in *Blue Hawaii*. The hotel opened in 1953 and closed in 1985. It was in the process of being refurbished while we were there. Other movie and television locations were for *Gilligan's Island* and *South Pacific*, which was filmed at Hanalei Bay and Bali Hai. Peter, Paul, and Mary wrote and sang "Puff the Magic Dragon" in this location. When we got back on the bus, we all sang "There Is Nothing Like a Dame," from *South Pacific*, and "Puff the Magic Dragon." It was a very nice tour.

One afternoon all four of us drove to Port Allen and boarded a catamaran called *Lucky Lady*. The water was pretty rough, and Jan got seasick. She went below and went to sleep. The boat stopped for those who wanted to snorkel, which Ron did. Wes and I stayed above and watched the turtles and spinner dolphins. The dolphins jumped out of the water and spun around in front of us.

We ate at Bubba's Burgers one day for lunch. We had "sloppers and fringes," which was chili over a burger and french fries/onion rings. We visited Fern Grotto in Wailua State Park, where there were many sword ferns (called kupu kupu) and hanging moss. Since 1962, ten thousand weddings have been performed at the grotto. The "Hawaiian Wedding Song" was sung while we stood in front of the grotto.

In the evenings we enjoyed playing dominoes and cards with Ron and Jan. Ron won most of the time, which isn't unusual. One evening Wes won all three games. Ron did most of the cooking, as he's a very good cook. We had delicious thick steaks one evening, cooked on the grill. Ron later grilled Portuguese sausages, which were also very good.

We flew home on Thanksgiving Day, through Honolulu and Los Angeles. It was a wonderful, relaxing trip, and we enjoyed having Ron and Jan with us.

In April of 2013, we led eighteen people on a nine-day Hawaiian cruise on Norwegian Cruise Line. Karen and Ken Goetz, from ACC, brought four others in their family, including Ken's mother, Anita Gauerke, from IN-JOY. We all flew into Honolulu and stayed at the Waikiki Beach Resort. Burger King was nearby, and it was one of the cheaper places to eat. We kept running into others from our group eating breakfast at Burger King or getting a quick ice cream sundae.

Before boarding the ship, we had a tour of Honolulu. We saw the Punch Bowl and were shown where movies and TV shows were filmed: *From Here to Eternity*, *Magnum P.I.*, *Pirates of the Caribbean*, *Fantasy Island*, and *Gilligan's Island*. Our guide told us "aloha" means "to give power" and is used to say hello, good-bye, and I love you. We went to the Polynesian Cultural Center, where we watched the canoe pageant and the show "Breath of Life." Both were very good.

The following day we boarded the *Pride of America* and sailed to Kahului, Maui. We ate breakfast with Jim and Barbara Schaper and dinner that evening with Jan and Del Main, all friends from IN-JOY. Then we all went to the Polynesian show with dancing from various islands.

On the Big Island (Hawaii), we docked at Hilo and went on a tour. The Big Island has forty-five thousand people. They receive 130 inches of rainfall per year, and a record thirty-one inches of rain fell in one day. There are five volcanoes on the island and eleven different climates. We entered Hawaii Volcanoes National Park, where the active Kilauea volcano is. The US Marines have a plaque dedicated to them from 1942 to 1945 for introducing Spam to the island. The people in Hawaii love Spam—they eat sixteen million cans a year!

After the ship docked at Nawiliwili Harbor on the island of Kauai, we went on another movie tour. We had been on two tours on previous trips, but each one was a little bit different. On this tour we were taken to the areas where *Castaway Cowboy*, *Dragonfly*, *Voodoo Island*, *Donovan's Reef*, *Soul Surfer*, *Descendants*, *McHale's Navy*, *Wackiest Ship in the Army*, and a Coca-Cola commercial were filmed. Over a hundred films were made on the island of Kauai, and five hundred documentaries, foreign films, and commercials were produced.

We learned there are sixty-five thousand full-time residents in Kauai, and one million visitors that come each year.

Kauai was our last stop, and we sailed back to Honolulu on the island of Oahu. As usual, we had to put our big suitcases outside our cabin door by midnight. The next morning, while eating breakfast, I tipped my plate over and spilled coconut pancake syrup all over my lap. Since my clean clothes were not available, I rushed to our cabin and tried to wash off the syrup. Thank goodness I had on black capris, and the wetness didn't show too much!

After we disembarked from the ship, we were driven to Pearl Harbor where we visited the USS *Arizona*.. We also toured the USS *Missouri*, where Japan signed the surrender on September 2, 1945. Our last stop for the day was at the Dole Plantation, where we saw how pineapple grows and looked at beautiful flowers. We ate some soft pineapple ice cream, which was really good (and expensive)!

Our trip was over, and we were taken to the airport. As we had quite a lot of time before our flight, we ordered a pizza at one of the airport restaurants. Wes ordered a large beer, and it was huge! After drinking every bit of it, he slept all the way home on the plane and never moved. Jim Schaper said he thought he was dead! It was a good flight, and we were glad once again to be home.

Israel Trips: 1994, 1999, and 2007

In March of 1994, Wes and I traveled to Israel with fifty others from Grace Community Church, which was our first time to the Holy Land. We flew El Al Airlines from JFK to Israel. Security on El Al was very strict. Everyone was questioned separately for several minutes. Wes and I were chosen as the first ones to be interviewed, and we were questioned for twenty minutes! It took three hours for all of us to get through security.

When we arrived in Israel, we were picked up by our guide, Avner Rum, and the driver on the brown bus. One of our first stops was Bethlehem, which is five miles from Jerusalem. Bethlehem is an Arab city. We saw lots of Israeli soldiers with guns, which we weren't accustomed to seeing. As we were walking from the bus to the Church of the Nativity, the police set off some tear gas. We started running into the church, as our eyes and throats were burning. We found out later there had been some previous problems in the area. One of our passengers had his wallet stolen by a peddler, losing $300. After that we pinned our fanny packs closed, as the peddlers were experts in unzipping the fanny packs without our knowledge.

Throughout the trip we visited the usual: the Chapel of the Ascension, where Jesus ascended into heaven; the Garden of Gethsemane; the Garden Tomb; the Wailing Wall; and the fourteen Stations of the Cross. One day we drove south to the Dead Sea, where we dropped four thousand feet, the lowest point on earth. On the way we saw sheep, goats, and Bedouins in their tents. We visited Masada, which was originally Herod the Great's fortress. There was originally a ten-year supply of food and water within the fortress, but it was never used by Herod. It was eventually used by Jewish fanatics to escape from the Romans. The Roman army built a ramp and charged it. All of the Jews committed suicide, with the exception of two women.

Wes and some of the others floated in the Dead Sea, after which we went to Qumran, where the Dead Sea Scrolls were found. Another day we were taken to St. Mark's Church in the Old City, where the Upper Room may have been. The priest sang the Lord's Prayer for us in Aramaic.

While we were in Jericho, we saw the watchtower, which was nine thousand years old and considered to be the oldest building in the world. While waiting in line at the restroom nearby, I asked the others where they were from. One woman said she was from Mishawaka, Indiana. I asked her if she graduated from Mishawaka High School, and if so, what year? She graduated in 1950, when my sister Nancy graduated. She knew Nancy and asked if she had ever made it to China as a missionary. I told her that the doors had closed to China but she had gone to Korea instead. It's a small world!

Other places we visited were Armageddon and Nazareth. We rode a boat on the Sea of Galilee and sang "How Great Thou Art" at the Church of the Beatitudes. Seven people from our group were baptized in the Jordan River.

We said good-bye to the group going home, and twenty-three of us rode a bus to Egypt, through the town of Rafah. At the Israeli border, we picked up a new guide and a new bus. Due to some past problems in this area, we traveled in a convoy of seven buses with an armed soldier on each bus. We traveled 240 miles to Cairo, the capital of Egypt, with a population of seventeen million. Traffic looked as if it were always rush hour. We were told not to drink the water in Egypt and not to eat fresh fruit, as it would have been washed with water. The hard part to remember was not using the local water to brush our teeth.

We saw the Step Pyramids, the Giza Pyramid, went to the Sound and Light Show, rode a camel, and sailed the Nile River. On Palm Sunday we had a church service on the beach of the Mediterranean Sea.

This was the trip where Wes and I met George and Wilma Weber from Educational Opportunities hospitality.

In November of 1999, we led twenty-five people from IN-JOY to the Holy Land, flying into Amman, Jordan. What we saw and did was very similar to the 1994 trip, just in a different order. On this trip we returned to Jordan, where we visited Mount Nebo, Jerash, and Petra. When we arrived at Petra, we walked back into the ruins. On the return Wes and I rode horses the last mile, as we were very tired. My horse's name was Indiana Jones, and Wes's horse's name was Suzanna.

Some of our group flew home from Amman, and eight of us flew to Cairo, Egypt (unlike the last trip, when we bused there in a convoy). We visited the pyramids and then took an overnight train to Luxor. We had a small sleeping compartment with bunk beds. We received a wake-up call at 4:30 a.m. and arrived in Luxor at 5:30 a.m. Our guide's name was Abdullah, and he was dressed in a white robe and turban. We visited the ruins of Luxor Temple, went to the Sound and Light Show at Karnak Temple, and were bused to the Valley of the Queens and the Valley of the Kings. We then flew back to Cairo, where we were taken to see Anwar Sadat's tomb.

We flew that evening back to Amman, Jordan, where we stayed in the royal suite at the Le Meridian Amman hotel. The following morning we flew home after another wonderful trip.

In March 2007 forty-five of us went just to Israel. This was an all-church trip with Pastor Jeff and Kathy Meyer and Pastor Bill and Jodi Meiter. Our guide's name was Hilel, and he was an excellent guide and spoke very good English. This time we began our journey in Tiberias. There were fifteen people in our group who were baptized in the Jordan River. At the city of Cana, Wes and I renewed our wedding vows, along with our friends the Hatts, Mains, Scotts, and Van Ausdles. Del Main sang the Lord's Prayer after the ceremony.

In addition to visiting the places mentioned earlier, we also visited the Church of the Primacy, where Jesus fed the five thousand. We also went to Shepherds' Field in Bethlehem. Our guide, Hillel, couldn't go into Bethlehem since he was a Jew. We dropped him off at a park bench just prior to entering Bethlehem, an Arab city. We picked him up on our way back, happy to see that he was okay. We saw where David wrote the Twenty-Third Psalm, and we also visited St. Anne's Church, the Pool of Bethesda, and the Pool of Siloam in the Old City of Jerusalem. We visited the Holocaust Museum (Yad Vashem), where carob trees were planted on the grounds. There was a new tree planted in memory of Corrie ten Boom, as her original tree died the day she died.

After an eleven-hour flight home through JFK, we were all exhausted but happy to be home.

Austria and Germany with Larry and Lynn Van Ausdle: September 15-18, 2004

Wes and I tried to put together a trip to Germany and Austria with a company other than EO. We couldn't get enough people to go, so we canceled the trip. Our friends Larry and Lynn Van Ausdle asked why the four of us couldn't go on our own. We decided to do that, and we made arrangements to stay at the Hotel Thaler in Kufstein, Austria, where we used to work.

When we checked into the hotel, some of the same people were still working there. Marta, in charge of the dining room, made up a special table for four, with flowers and name tags. Only one problem: our names were correct, but Larry and Lynn's names were now "Larry and Lynn Van Rens." We went to the front desk and asked them to correct it. The next day it was still wrong, so we gave up. We jokingly called them Mr. and Mrs. Van Rens for quite a while.

We visited many places. I already mentioned the festival of the cows, which we thoroughly enjoyed. Another highlight was a trip to Salzburg, where *The Sound of Music* was filmed. We saw the fountain where the kids played and the cemetery where the Von Trapp family hid. We went on a bus trip to Berchtesgaden in Germany's Bavaria region. From there we were taken to the Eagle's Nest, or Kehlstein House, which was Hitler's hideout. We found out that thirty-five hundred people helped build the Eagle's Nest. One day we visited Dachau, Germany, one of the concentration camps. That was a sobering visit. We ate at a nearby restaurant afterward. Lynn was hungry for meatloaf, which she thought she had ordered. What they brought her was ham!

We checked out of our hotel and drove to Garmisch-Partenkirchen in Germany. We checked into the Post Hotel and then drove to Linderhof to tour the castle of Mad King Ludwig II. The next day, we drove to Oberammergau and toured the theater where the Passion play was held. We were taken backstage and saw the costumes and props for the twenty-two hundred people in the play. It runs for six months every ten years. When we returned to the hotel, I asked if I could play the old piano in the lobby. I played several songs, including "Jesus Loves the Little Children." Christiana, the hotel clerk, said she knew that song and promptly started singing "She'll be Comin' 'Round the Mountain When She

Comes." We didn't tell her that was not the song I was playing. I then played "Silent Night," and she sang it for us in German. It was beautiful. Lynn didn't particularly like cats, but the hotel cat jumped up on her lap and slept there for a while. Lynn called the cat "HC" for Hotel Cat. It was truly a magical evening!

We drove back to Kufstein, Austria, and checked back into the Hotel Thaler. The next day we toured the Riedel glass factory and watched the workers make glass bowls and wineglasses. Earlier we had taken the elevator to the top of the Festung Kufstein (fortress). There is an organ at the bottom of the fortress that is played every day at noon. We walked down 191 steps instead of taking the elevator.

It was time to say good-bye to Austria and Germany and drive to Munich for our flight back to Arizona. It was a wonderful trip!

Panama Canal Cruise: February 19 to March 5, 2005

This was by far our biggest IN-JOY trip as far as the number of people who went. We had fifty-two people on this cruise. We had so many that we had to split up into two groups for the airline flights. Wes and I were part of the larger group of thirty people who flew to Fort Lauderdale, Florida, in the afternoon, and a large bus was supposed to pick us up. The company got it mixed up and sent the smaller bus, which had a small luggage compartment. We had to put luggage in the aisles, and some of us had to sit on the luggage. Wes stood in the aisle for the ride to the hotel. Our bus driver couldn't speak English, and he got lost taking us to the hotel for the night. He then took a shortcut through a Walgreens drive-through, scraping the top of the bus. In addition to that, he knocked down a stop sign trying to get out of the parking lot! (I think it was his first time driving a bus.)

After boarding the *Legend of the Seas* ship, our first stop was Oranjestad, Aruba, where there are seven women to one man. We learned something interesting from our guide: the jewelers were generally from India, Italians owned most of the cafes, Americans owned the resorts, and the Chinese and Japanese owned the supermarkets. After a day at sea, we cruised through the Panama Canal, the world's largest shortcut, which we watched from our balcony. The canal's shoreline was filled with lush rain forests, exotic wildlife, and quaint villages. Our next stop was Puntarenas, Costa Rica, which is the gateway to San Jose, the capital of Costa Rica. We traveled on the Pan-American Highway to tour historic San Jose. We stopped at Grasshopper Bay, where they had samples of chips and dips and fried grasshoppers. Wes tried them all, including the grasshoppers!

Huatulco, a small fishing village, situated at the foothills of the Sierra Madre and the Pacific coastline, was our next stop. There are over twenty miles of unspoiled beaches in this area. After sailing through the night, we docked the following morning in Acapulco, which boasts one of the most beautiful bays in the world. We watched five cliff divers plummet fifty feet into the ocean at sixty miles per hour. Our last port was Cabo San Lucas, which is located on the southernmost tip of Baja California. We took a scenic drive to see the majestic rock arches called Los Arcos.

It was so much fun constantly running into someone from our group on the ship. We had such a great time together. When the ship was not in port, we held devotions in one of the meeting rooms on the ship. The word got around to some of the others on the ship, and they asked if they could come also. A lady mistakenly came into our meeting room while looking for the bridge class, and she decided to stay. A group of graduates from the Naval Academy also joined us. We had different people give the devotions each time, and some of them told stories how they became a Christian. We also told some funny stories and laughed a lot! Jack Dear told about his cat who had died while they were on vacation. When he and Phyllis got home, they found the dead cat in the freezer! Arloa Siers said she could top that story. She had her cat cremated and the ashes put into a coffee can. When she moved, the people helping her put the coffee can in the kitchen cupboard. One morning, she made coffee and drank the dead cat's ashes! Ooh! How awful!

This cruise was the first time Wes and I had booked a veranda, since we wanted to be able to see the canal better. However, it spoiled us, as we wanted a balcony for every future cruise we booked. When the ship was at sea, Anita Wennmacher from our group climbed the rock wall twice. One morning she also took part in the talent show, where she danced and sang "Tea for Two." She also talked Truman Nall into playing several songs on his harmonica in the talent show.

This cruise was our first time with Royal Caribbean, and we were very impressed. The food was wonderful, and the entertainment was great! We had a very congenial group, and everyone got along well.

Russian Riverboat Cruise: 2007 and 2012

In 2007 Wes and I joined another group from a Lutheran church in California. We had met Thom Johnson, the pastor, on one of our Greek trips. We enjoyed the cruise down the Volga River so much that we planned and booked the same trip for our IN-JOY group in 2012. Since the two trips were basically the same, I'll talk more about the IN-JOY trip.

The one thing I'll talk about from the first trip was our lecturer, who was a professor at Moscow University. She was an excellent and interesting speaker. She told us that the people of Russia have always thought of the United States as their friend, not an enemy. They were never afraid of us like we were of them! At one of the lectures, she spoke on the various reforms that have happened in Russia since the dissolution of the Soviet Union on December 26, 1991. The Soviet flag flew over the Kremlin in Moscow for the last time on Christmas Day 1991. Mikhail Gorbachev led the new government thinking known as glasnost. It included political openness, elimination of the secret police, and an end to the banning of certain books for the public. Newspapers could begin printing even controversial news. Perestroika was the name given to the economic restructuring of the country. Prior to 1991 there were very few newspapers or magazines available. Few items essential for everyday life were available in stores. Many workers were not paid in cash but by goods. After 1991 there were forty thousand newspapers and twenty channels on TV, including cable TV and internet. In 1993 there was very high inflation, and unemployment doubled. The Russian government took control again in Soviet-style management. Companies were again taken over by the state.

We were all spellbound and could hardly wait for the next lecture! Unfortunately, the professor was not the lecturer on the 2012 cruise when we took IN-JOY.

Our 2012 IN-JOY Russian riverboat trip was a thirteen-day cruise. There were fourteen of us on the trip, along with other groups from various English-speaking countries. ACC's music director, Greg Schaefer, and his wife, Brenda, as well as Pastor Bill Meiter's mother, Grete Meiter, were part of our group. Also in our group were the Hallecks, Schapers, Peggy Wheatley, and several friends and relatives.

We started our trip in Moscow, where we enjoyed a city tour. Our guide took us on the Metro, where each train station had pictures and ornate statues. We then went to Red Square and saw Lenin's tomb and the Kremlin. The ship sailed, and we arrived at the town of Uglich, where we went on a walking tour and visited several beautiful churches, including the magnificent Church of Dmitry on the Blood, dedicated to Ivan the Terrible's son. We visited a Russian home and were served cookies and tea.

Yaroslavl was our stop the next day, which was my favorite city. We were taken to the governor's house, where the guide asked us a question. Whoever answered it correctly could sit in the governor's chair at his desk. (The governor was in St. Petersburg for the day.) Wes answered the question correctly as to which two rivers flowed into the city—the Volga River and the Kotorosi River. So Wes was the governor of Yaroslavl for five minutes! We then went into the ballroom, where a combo was playing. Three couples danced and then asked certain people in our group to dance with them. Greg and Brenda were chosen, and they danced beautifully.

Our next stop was the river town of Goritsy, a peaceful farming town and typical Russian village. We visited St. Cyril's Monastery on the White Lake, then sailed for the island of Kizhi. This island is home to some of the most amazing wooden architecture in Russia. In 1764 the local people built the Church of the Intercession, which included twenty-two domes, without the use of a single nail. Svirstroy was our next stop, with a population of only a thousand. We were told that this unspoiled Russian village was the best place to purchase souvenirs. Since we had free time here, we all went shopping!

Our last stop was St. Petersburg. We rode to Peterhof gardens and viewed the 144 fountains and two hundred statues. We also toured the summer palace, which was blown up and burned by the Germans in 1941 and later rebuilt. The next day we took the hydrofoil to the Hermitage Museum, the former palace of the czars, which houses the royal art collection with over three million works of art. It is one of the largest art museums in the world. The following day the group went to Catherine Palace in Pushkin.

Our group really enjoyed this trip, and I think we all learned a lot about the Russian people. The waitresses and guides on the ship were all college students who were majoring in English, so we understood them quite well. (And they could practice their English on us.) It was a long flight home, as we changed planes at JFK and Charlotte, North Carolina. It felt good to be home!

Autumn Majesty in New England Land Tour: 2008

From October 8 to October 15, we were tour hosts for twenty-five people from IN-JOY. We planned the trip for October in order to see the beautiful fall colors in New England. We hit it just perfectly, as the colors, especially in New Hampshire, were at their peak. Our guide was Roxanne, and she was excellent.

We flew from Phoenix to Boston, where we spent the night and had a sightseeing tour of the city of Boston the following morning. We visited the Old South Meeting House, Old North Church, Beacon Hill, and the USS *Constitution*. We drove by Fenway Park and Harvard University. We stopped at the famed Faneuil Hall marketplace before departing for Vermont, known as "the Green Mountain State."

While driving from Boston to Burlington, Vermont, we stopped at Adams Farm, one of Vermont's picturesque working farms that has opened its doors to visitors. We enjoyed a wonderful farm experience while learning about maple syrup, hand-spun woolens, garden products, and farm animals. Wes even milked a goat while we were there. We were served a huge meal at the farm.

In Burlington we visited the Vermont Teddy Bear Factory and took a dinner cruise on Lake Champlain. On Sunday we all attended a church service at the historical First Congregational Church. The next morning we visited the Shelburne Museum, which showcases a complex of thirty-seven historic buildings with huge collections of art, paintings, and folk sculptures. As we were leaving Burlington, we toured the Cold Hollow Cider Mill, where we were served free cider and donuts. Then on to Ben and Jerry's Ice Cream for free samples there. (Of course, the free samples weren't quite enough, so we had to have more.) We stopped at the Von Trapp Lodge in Stowe, Vermont. While traveling through the countryside of Vermont and New Hampshire, the fall colors were outstanding! For miles and miles, we viewed the red, gold, and orange trees.

In New Hampshire we had a full day of sightseeing in the scenic White Mountains, which included a gondola ride. We had a group picture taken in front of the Albany Bridge, built in 1858.

The next day we drove into Maine, where we visited the L. L. Bean Outlet. Nearly 90 percent of the state of Maine is forest, with three thousand lakes and four thousand islands. We noticed that in all of the New England states we visited, the residents went all out decorating their homes for Halloween. We drove by the Bushes' summer home in Kennebunkport, and we went to a lobster bake, where we put on lobster bibs and really dug into the delicious lobster meal. In Portland we had a city tour and a brief stop at the famous Portland Head Light, where we had another group picture taken.

After a hearty seaside breakfast in Ogunquit, Maine, we drove to Boston and caught the flight home. Another great trip!

Germany, Austria, and Prague: 2010

In 2010 Wes and I took thirty-three IN-JOY seniors on a nine-day European adventure called the Alpine Wonders. We flew from Phoenix (twenty-one of us) to Philadelphia, where we met Gene Schoonmaker from Florida, Donna Grimm from Pittsburgh, eight ladies from San Francisco area, and one person from Milwaukee. After an eight-hour flight, we were picked up in Munich, Germany, by our guide, Willi Flicker, and the orange bus. Yes, once again, we were the orange bus, thanks to Wes's request. (He likes orange.)

We were taken on a tour of the Dachau concentration camp, which was very sobering. At noon we rode to the Marienplatz in downtown Munich to watch and listen to the chiming of forty-three different bells on the Rathaus-Glockenspiel clock. On two levels of the clock, there are reenactments of two different stories with thirty-two life-sized figures. The top half of the Glockenspiel tells the story of the marriage of the local duke Wilhelm V. In honor of the happy couple, there was a joust with life-sized knights on horseback that represented Bavaria (southern Germany) and Lothringen. The Bavarian knight won every time!

The bottom half tells the second story: According to myth, 1517 was a year of plague in Munich. The coopers were said to have danced through the streets to bring vitality and to ease the fears of the residents. The entire show lasted fifteen minutes. At the end of the show, a small golden rooster at the top of the Glockenspiel chirped three times, marking the end of the performance.

On the two-hour bus trip to our hotel in Steinach, Austria, our guide, Willi, let us all sleep. We checked into Hotel Wilder Mann, which was 350 years old. After a good night's rest, we visited Innsbruck, the capital of Austria's Tyrol region. We enjoyed the quaint medieval streets of Old Town and had a beautiful view of the ski jump area from the 1964 and 1976 Winter Olympics in Innsbruck.

We had an early day the next morning, as we had a two-hour drive to Oberammergau, Germany, to see the Passion play. We wore many layers of clothing, as it was cold, foggy, and rainy that day. The theater was an open-air theater that holds five thousand people. The town has beautiful houses with paintings and flower boxes on most of them. We had free time before settling into our seats at 2:30. The play was in German, and although we were given a translation book in English, we all knew the story of the passion of Jesus. After breaking for dinner at five, we returned for the second half from 8:00 p.m. until 11:00 p.m. We arrived back at our hotel at 2:00 a.m., very tired!

In case you don't know much about this musical drama, I'll give you a brief explanation. By the summer of 1633, nearly a hundred people in the small village of Oberammergau had died from the Black Plague, which was sweeping through Europe. The villagers pleaded with God, pledging to perform a reenactment of the passion of Jesus if God would save the town. The deaths stopped, and since that day, the villagers have stepped on stage once every ten years. Only natives or those who have lived in the town for at least twenty years can audition. The first play was performed in 1634 in the church's choir loft. They soon outgrew the loft, and the play was moved to the churchyard and then to a nearby field, where, in 1930, the modern theater was built. The theater has an open stage and natural backdrop of blue sky and mountains. It was a rainy day while we were there, but we noticed it did not rain during the performance; the rain came during the dinner break and then stopped when the play resumed.

Castles and churches were the subjects of our next day's trip. We visited the beautiful Ettal Abbey, a Benedictine monastery in Bavaria, and the picture-perfect Pilgrimage Church of Weis, also known as the church in the Meadow. We toured the magnificent castle of Linderhof, the royal palace of Mad King Ludwig.

Salzburg is one of my favorite cities in Austria. Wes and I had been there many times, but I never grew tired of it. Its population was 140,000, according to our guide, and it was the birthplace of Mozart and where *The Sound of Music* was filmed. We walked through Mirabell Gardens, full of beautiful flowers. We then drove to Kufstein, where Wes and I had stayed in 2000 for two months. We showed some of the group the hotels where we worked and found Maria (Ria) at the Kufsteiner Markt, which she and her husband owned. We had our picture taken with her. I also purchased two scarves and two rings from her shop. All the ladies on the trip were looking for these small scarves and rings, which we first found at the gift shop at Linderhof Palace. I bought a total of eight of them throughout the trip.

We visited another castle—Neuschwanstein Castle, which inspired the castle in Walt Disney's Magic Kingdom. We had a forty-five-minute tour of the inside of the castle, which wasn't very impressive. That evening we said good-bye to our guide,

Willi, and bus driver, Hansas, plus nine people who were not going on the extension to Vienna and Prague. Willi was such a wonderful guide; everyone just loved him!

Robert was our new bus driver, and Mary was our new guide. We had a bathroom stop in the morning, and the store had the scarves that everyone was looking for. Willi had spoiled us, and Mary would not let one of our passengers, who wasn't feeling well, stay on the bus while we were out touring. Mary made her get off and sit on a park bench. Wes was not very happy with Mary. We drove to Vienna, Austria, where we spent the night.

The next day we drove to Prague in the Czech Republic. We enjoyed a walking tour in Prague's Old Town. We walked over the famous Charles Bridge and toured Prague Palace. We stayed two nights in Prague at the Courtyard by Marriott, which was a very nice, modern hotel.

After visiting a few more places in the city, we drove to Nuremberg, Germany, where we toured the Documentation museum and spent the night. The next day, at our morning coffee stop, we found more scarves. We explored the medieval Old Town in Heidelberg, where we had lunch. Wes and I ordered something very different for lunch: it was called flammkuchen, (German pizza), which consisted of a cherry tomato, pesto, ham, and marinated arugula leaves on a flat bread, served on a wooden paddle. It was quite good. Then we walked over the Heidelberg Bridge, which is the oldest bridge in Germany, built in 1242. It was bombed in WWII and rebuilt in 1947.

We traveled to Worms, Germany, and went into the Worms Lutheran Church, where Martin Luther refused to back down from his criticism of the church. From Worms we were taken to Frankfurt, Germany, where we spent the night before flying home the next morning.

South American Cruise: 2014

In March we took a small group of thirteen people on a twenty-six-day South American cruise, visiting Argentina, Uruguay, and Chile (flying into Buenos Aires, Argentina, with a return from Santiago, Chile). The highlight of the trip was a pretour of Iguazu Falls (in Argentina) in a high-speed Zodiac watercraft. We all were completely drenched but loved every minute of it. Other highlights included a special tango dinner dance in Buenos Aires (a city of some fifteen million inhabitants) and walking among a few of the 1.2 million Magellanic penguins in the nature reserve in Puerto Madryn, Argentina. We also had a visit to the "end of the world" in Ushuaia, which is said to be the most southerly town in the world. It was gorgeous among the snow-covered Andes mountains at the southern tip of Argentina. We cruised through the Straits of Magellan and the Chilean fjords and around Cape Horn.

On our return trip home, at the Santiago Airport, we had a three-hour wait before we could check in. Since the airport had no chairs available to sit on, we went to the airport restaurant to eat a snack and have a place to sit. I ordered a banana split, and it was enough for four people! By this time everyone else had already ordered something, so I was *forced* to eat it all by myself! It was a wonderful trip, and we all had a great time and a good flight home!

Memphis and Nashville, Tennessee: 2017

In May Peggy Wheatley and I led a group of thirty-nine from IN-JOY to Memphis and Nashville, Tennessee. We visited many places in a week: Graceland, Memphis Queen dinner cruise, Loretta Lynn's Ranch museum, historic Ryman Auditorium, RCA Studio B and the Country Music Hall of Fame, Belle Meade Plantation, Opryland, and the Grand Ole Opry Show. We ate lots of BBQ beef and pulled pork, so much that I actually grew tired of it.

My previous boss from Denver, Les Stallings, and his wife, Carol, lived in the Nashville area. I made arrangements for them to come and have dinner and attend the program at Ryman Auditorium with the group. I hadn't seen them for several years.

At Studio B our group recorded one of Elvis Presley's songs, "Good Luck Charm." The "IN-JOY Elvis Choir" then sang it at the kickoff meeting for IN-JOY.

Many people said this was one of the best trips they had ever taken.

Various Branson Trips: 1999, 2002,
2005, 2009, 2012, and 2016

One of the favorite places that members of IN-JOY loved to visit was Branson, as you can tell by the number of times we were there. Branson Country Tours has always put our trips together and has done a wonderful job. The first four times we visited Branson, we flew into Kansas City or Tulsa and were bused to Branson. On those trips we only stayed five days, from Monday to Friday, and generally attended ten shows, as well as visited the Precious Moments Chapel in Carthage, Missouri, on our way to Branson. When Allegiant Airline started flying nonstop from Mesa Gateway Airport to Springfield, Missouri, we booked the group's round-trip flight on Allegiant. Due to their schedule of flying only on certain days each week, our next trips in 2009 and 2012 were seven days in length, with fifteen shows planned.

During the 2002 trip, which was in November, we woke up one morning to six inches of snow. Our hotel's parking lot was recessed, and the bus driver wasn't sure he was going to be able to get the bus out of the icy parking lot. He did, though, and we were able to go to the morning show. Many of the other groups didn't make it that morning. Branson gets very little snow.

We had fifty-four people on the November 2016 trip. In fact, at one time, we had a waiting list of twenty-five people. The bus was a fifty-five-passenger vehicle, so we had to limit the number of people going. Unfortunately, the microphone on the bus did not work. Therefore we could not do daily devotions, and it was very difficult to make announcements. We finally had someone stand in the middle of the bus and relay what was being said to the back of the bus. It was very frustrating! The nice thing about Branson is that all of the shows are clean, with no suggestive jokes or bad language. The shows always honor veterans and are very patriotic. The military songs are played, and the veterans are asked to stand when their military song is sung or played.

Some of our favorite shows were Shoji Tabuchi, the Duttons, Pierce Arrow, Sight and Sound Theater presentations (Moses, Joseph, Noah, etc.), Sons of the Pioneers,

Yakov Smirnoff, Oak Ridge Boys, and Texas Tenors. Others that we saw were the Andy Williams Show, Dino Kartsonakis, Wayne Newton, and the Bobby Vinton show, where he sang his signature song, "Roses Are Red." One of the most moving shows that we only saw at Christmastime was the Radio City Rockettes. At the end of their show, the manger scene was displayed, and someone read "One Solitary Life." Wes's favorite Christmas song was "O Holy Night." In 2016 Wes was unable to go to Branson with us due to his health, and "his" song was sung twelve or more times at the various shows. Everyone looked at me each time it was sung or played.

The ladies on the trips loved to shop! We generally gave a prize to whoever spent the most money. Peggy Wheatley usually won the prize, although one year Ellen Bradley won, as she had purchased a beautiful rhinestone cowboy hat.

On several of the earlier trips, we toured the Precious Moments Chapel in Carthage, Missouri. Precious Moments figurines were created by Samuel Butcher thirty-five years ago. The chapel had colorful murals on the walls and ceilings inspired by the Precious Moments figurines. We also visited Wedding Island, where many couples were married. We also had tickets for the Fountains of Angels show, which was a water and fountain show.

Peggy and I planned a trip to Branson in April of 2020, but we couldn't get enough people to sign up. We then changed the date to November of 2020, and the coronavirus pandemic hit. We also canceled that trip.

CHAPTER 35
Endicott Family Genealogy

I've always been fascinated with my father's side of the family, and I was proud of the Endicott name.

The name Endicott appears in ancient records in various spellings: Ynndecote, Yendicott, Endecote, Endecott, and others. True surnames or family names, as we know them, are less than a thousand years old. Generally the surnames denoted the place of residence. The name Endecott meant "an end cottage." I have a book called *Some Descendants of John Endecott, Governor of Mass. Bay Colony*, that says this about the Endicotts: "A sturdy self-reliant, progressive race, with physical stamina, perseverance and resourcefulness, the Endicotts have won success in all lines of human endeavor." Wow! What a legacy to follow!

English records from 1327 show the name Johannes de Yndecote of Devonshire; the records of 1448 list John Yendecote of Devonshire.

On June 20, 1628, Captain John Endicott sailed from Weymouth, England, on the *Abigail* with fifty to sixty others. After a voyage of two months and sixteen days, they landed at Naumkeag (now Salem), Massachusetts, on September 6, 1628. John Endicott was one of the six patentees to whom a royal charter was granted under the name of the Governor and Company of Massachusetts Bay in New England. He came to Naumkeag as governor. Naumkeag, meaning "place of eels," was soon changed to Salem, which is a Hebrew word for "peace."

The real purpose of the Massachusetts Bay Colony may have been to form a religious commonwealth where the Gospel could be enjoyed in "primitive purity." There was unrest in the Church of England, which prompted many to migrate to America.

There are very few records regarding John Endicott's early life in England. He married Anna Gower in London prior to them coming to Massachusetts Colony. She was in poor health and died in 1629, her first winter in America. They had no children. The winter of 1628–29 was very severe. There was much suffering and sickness, and many deaths. Houses were few and badly built. There was a food shortage, and supplies from England had failed to show up. There were no doctors, so Governor Endicott requested one from the Plymouth settlement, which filled their needs. In the next two years, he was responsible for the building of roads and houses and was influential in establishing a stable government.

John Endicott was described as a man with sincere affection, honesty, frankness, fearlessness, and generosity. He may be known as the father of Massachusetts more than any other man in history. He was devout in his faith and a man of action, with a lifelong obedience to God. Another commentary said he was bold and energetic, a sincere and zealous Puritan, rigid in his principles and severe in the execution of the laws of the colony. John Endicott served as governor of the colony four different times for a total of fourteen years. In 1645 he was in command of the colonial army and led a bloody and useless expedition against Block Island and the Pequot Indians.

John married Elizabeth Gibson on August 18, 1630. They had two sons: John Jr., who died in 1667 with no children, and Zerubbabel, who married and fathered ten children. When John Endicott died in 1665, Zerubbabel inherited his father's vast estate and wealth.

Following is the list of the ten generations between Governor John Endicott and me:

1. John Endicott (1588–1665); governor of Massachusetts Bay Colony; born in Chagford, Devonshire, England.
2. Zerubbabel Endicott (1635–1684); physician; born and lived in Salem, Massachusetts; married Mary Smith 1654.
3. Joseph Endicott (1672–1747); farmer; born in Massachusetts; moved to New Jersey in 1698; married Hannah.
4. Joseph Endicott Jr. (1711–1749); farmer; born in New Jersey; married Ann Gillam 1736.
5. Thomas Endicott Sr. (1737–1831); farmer and carpenter; born in New Jersey; moved to Virginia, North Carolina, Kentucky, and Indiana in 1818; married Sarah Welsh 1759.
6. John Endicott (1791–1840); farmer; born in North Carolina, moved to Kentucky and Indiana in 1834; married Ann Saddler.
7a. Jesse Endicott (1817–1854); bookkeeper; born in Kentucky; married Mary Stephens 1839; moved to Indiana; parents of John Thomas Endicott.

7b. Sarah Ann Endicott (1819–1902); born in KY; married Bazalel Marsh in Indiana 1845; parents of Ann Fenton Marsh.

8. John Thomas Endicott (1842–1919); born in Indiana; married Ann Fenton Marsh 1865; died in Illinois. Ann Fenton Marsh (1846--1930); born in Indiana; married John Thomas Endicott 1865.

9. Harley LeRoy Endicott (1892–1950); born in Champaign, Illinois; married Vena Ethel Lewis 1915; moved to Indiana.

10. Martha Ann Endicott (1938); born in Mishawaka, Indiana; moved to Arizona; married Bill Kelsey 1956; Murry Ginis 1972; Jon Wesley Pierce 1978;

An interesting thing: John Endicott #6 had two children: Jesse #7a and Sarah Ann #7b; Jesse's son, John Thomas Endicott #8, married Sarah Endicott Marsh's daughter, Ann Fenton Marsh #8, which makes them first cousins! Maybe back then it was okay for first cousins to marry.

I mentioned in chapter 2 that my dad was the youngest of ten children. The next picture shows six of Dad's siblings who were still living in about 1912.

Circa 1912: Dad's parents and siblings in Champaign, Illinois: Seated, left to right: John Thomas and Ann Fenton Endicott (grandpa and grandma); John Marcus, Standing, left to right: Mark, Dad, Sarah, Marion, and Josephine.

I only knew Dad's oldest brother, Uncle Mark, and his family. Uncle Mark was born in 1869 and died in 1953. Uncle Mark held office for thirty-four years in the court system in Champaign, Illinois. He retired at the age of eighty as police magistrate, but the voters put him back in office as justice of the peace the same year. He was affectionately known as "the judge." He died at the age of eighty-four, a little less than a year after he closed out his public career. He and his wife, Aunt Bell, were the parents of six children, two of which died in infancy. Uncle Mark and Aunt Bell owned a small grocery story, run by one of their sons. Barbara and I loved to visit the store and pick out candy.

Circa 1938: Uncle Mark:s family in Champaign, Illinois

Another of Dad's brothers was Uncle Marion. I never knew him but heard a lot about him. He was kind of a rebel in the family. He married and moved to San Fernando Valley in California before I was born. My brother Lewie looked for him for years after Lewie and his family moved to California. After Lewie died, I took on the job of trying to find Uncle Marion. Whenever Wes and I were in California, I looked in the local phone directory for any Endicotts, and then I called them. We had heard that Uncle Marion and his wife had a son whose name was Charles. One time I called a Charles Endicott in the Los Angeles area, but it wasn't my cousin. Another time I called Charles Endicott in Sun Lakes, Arizona, and I was informed that he had moved from California to Sun Lakes, and I had already called him in California.

2007: Averil and Chuck Endicott

Wes and I were visiting our granddaughter Lindsey in Costa Mesa, staying at a nearby motel. Shortly before we left to drive home, I found a Charles Endicott who lived in Fountain Valley. I called the number listed; a woman answered, and I explained who I was. I asked her if Marion Endicott was by chance a relative of theirs. There was silence for a minute or two, and she said, "Yes, Marion was my husband's father, but he's no longer living." I was so excited I could hardly contain myself! I told her our family had been looking for Marion for years. She explained to me that her husband, Chuck, didn't have much to do with his father or the Endicott family, as his dad and mom had divorced, and Chuck was closer to his mother. Only in the later years of Marion's life, when he needed help, did Chuck have contact with him. Uncle Marion had died in 1965 and was buried at Forest Lawn in Hollywood Hills. I told her I would put together some Endicott pictures and information and bring them the next time we were in town. We met Charles and Averil a month or so later at a nearby Coco's Bakery and Restaurant for lunch. Charles, or Chuck, was at that time eighty years old and looked a lot like my brother Lewie. We met several times after that. They have since moved to Golden Valley, Arizona, which is near Kingman. I wish we could have visited them before Wes became sick. Chuck was born in 1927, so he's now ninety-three years old at the time of this writing.

Another of Dad's siblings was (Mary) Josephine Endicott, who married Ernest Hanson. She was fifteen years older than my dad. Shortly after their son, John, was born, Josephine died. Ernest remarried and owned a farm near Champaign, which I remember visiting on our way to Champaign. John Hanson and his wife, Opal, had two children, Chuck and Lou. Chuck and his parents, John and Opal, came to many of our Endicott reunions in Michigan and at Potawatomi Park in South Bend. John and Opal are no longer living. Chuck also came to Sis's one hundredth birthday celebration and became the official photographer.

CHAPTER 36

Lewis Family Genealogy

I don't know as much about my mother's (Lewis) ancestors. Four brothers, Stephen, William, Henry, and John Lewis, came to America from Wales. Our family comes from Stephen. Following are five generations until my birth:

1. Stephen D. Lewis (1786–1856); born in Washington County, Pennsylvania; married Mary Vermillion (1788–1856).
2. Joseph Powers Lewis (1811–1889); farmer; born in Kentucky; married Mancy Summers (second wife).
3. Charles Albert Lewis (1857–1930); born in Indiana; married Martha Francis Johnston (1860–1923).
4. Vena Ethel Lewis (1895–1949); born in Nebraska; married Harley LeRoy Endicott 1915; moved to Illinois and Indiana.
5. Martha Ann Endicott (1938); see Endicott genealogy for information.

1946: The Lewis and Endicott families in Champaign, Illinois: Front row left to right: Mom, Nancy behind Lewis and Martha, Uncle Clyde; Second row: Alene holding Diana, Aunt Mabel, Aunt Elsie; Third row: Eulalia, Vena, Lewie ; Back row: Jimmy and Wayne.

My mother was the youngest of four children born to Charles and Martha Lewis. Their first baby, Delores Alma Lewis, died when she was three or four months old. By the time Mom was born in 1895, she already had two older brothers: Clyde and Orla, both born in Nebraska in 1887 and 1892, respectively.

Mom was born in a covered wagon near Lincoln, Nebraska, upon the family's return to Champaign, Illinois. Uncle Clyde was employed at the University of Illinois in Urbana, in the electrical department. He invented the first electric scoreboard for the football field at the university. Uncle Clyde and his wife, Mabel, had two daughters. Eulalia married Harold Copeland and had one son, Jimmy. When Jimmy was in the military, he was stationed in Germany, where he met and married Gerda. For years they lived in Manhattan, Kansas, where Jimmy taught at the university. Jimmy and Gerda had one son, James Harold Copeland, who married Susan. They in turn had a son and daughter, who all live in Kansas as far as I know.

Uncle Clyde's other daughter, Vena (named after my mother), married Wayne Jones and had one son, Lewis. Lewis was just one year younger than Barbara and I, so we enjoyed being with him when we visited Champaign. Lewis married Phyllis Keene but had no children. He died from diabetes at the age of twenty-nine. That line ended with the death of Vena in 1991 at the age of eighty. Vena was a wonderful lady. She was close in age to Sis, so they got together when we visited Champaign.

Uncle Orla married Elsie Gault, and they also had two children. Richard was the oldest. He never married and died at the age of thirty-eight in a freak accident. He was working underneath his car when the jack slipped, causing the car to drop down and crush him. Uncle Orla's second child, Maxine, was born in 1927. Uncle Orla was a Gospel artist and minister and pastored several churches. They lived in Minneapolis, Minnesota, when I first knew them. When I was eight years old, Mom and I rode on the New York Central train to attend Maxine and Ken Seymour's wedding in 1946. We had a sleeper car, and the porter told me to put my shoes on the floor outside the berth, and he would polish them. Mom and I were sleeping in the same berth, and shortly after we went to bed, a man "knocked" on our curtain and told us we were in his berth! I thought we were going to be kicked out, but another berth was found for the man. Whew! I thought he was going to climb in with us!

Maxine and Ken had two sons, Douglas and Scott Seymour. Douglas Seymour married Karen, and they had five children: Michael, Christopher, Timothy, Colleen, and Kevin. Michael, the oldest child, married Rebecca and, last that I knew, had one child. I have never seen any of these children. They were all born in California, after Maxine and Ken moved to California from Minnesota.

My uncles and aunts, along with my first cousins Eulalia, Vena, Richard, and Maxine, have all passed away. My first cousins were all much older than I, ranging from eleven to twenty-seven years older.

I've always tried to keep track of my extended family, but I've lost track of some of the latest generation.

CHAPTER 37

History and Meaning of Mishawaka

Many of you may be wondering about the name of my city, Mishawaka, Indiana. It is a Potawatomi Indian word meaning "big rapids" or "swift water." There's a romantic legend about the name that we all grew up hearing. Princess Mishawaka was the daughter of Shawnee chief Elkhart. There was a romance between the princess and a white fur trapper called Deadshot. Her Potawatomi Indian suitor, Chief Greywolf, abducted the princess and started a war with the Shawnees. Prior to Chief Greywolf being killed, he stabbed and wounded Princess Mishawaka. This all supposedly happened in the area now known as Mishawaka. The city of Elkhart is ten miles to the east of Mishawaka.

A letter written by George Merrifield, a local resident of early Mishawaka, says the following: "Mishawaka is situated on both sides of the St. Joseph River, about eighty miles from its mouth. It is ninety miles east of Chicago and one hundred and fifty-seven miles west of Toledo. The river is one of the most beautiful rivers in our country."

Here is a snapshot of the history of Mishawaka. I think it's fascinating to learn how a city began. I'm also including some information about Mishawaka's twin city, South Bend, and the Studebaker Corporation. South Bend was located on the south bend of St. Joseph River. Both Mishawaka and South Bend are in St. Joseph County.

1679: First white man, LaSalle, arrived in the area.

1800: Indian wars involved the Shawnees, Potawatomi, and Ottawa tribes.

1820: Due to a smallpox epidemic, the Indians all left the area. When they wanted to return, the US Army forced 850 Potawatomi Indians to walk nine hundred miles to Kansas, known as the Trail of Death.

1832: Deposits of bog iron were found in the area; one hundred men came from Detroit to work. They opened a tavern, boardinghouse, and a company store. They named the company St. Joseph Iron Works.

1833: St. Joseph Iron Works became incorporated as a village.

1834: The first post office was opened. The postmaster suggested the name of Mishawaka.

1835: The town of Mishawaka incorporated, the first town to do so. A few months later, the town of South Bend, Mishawaka's twin city, also incorporated.

1836: The first bridge was built over the St. Joseph River. Prior to this, canoes were used to cross.

1836: Indiana City was developed on the north side of St. Joseph River.

1838: The Indiana General Assembly combined all four villages (Indiana City, St. Joseph Iron Works, Mishawaka, and Battell Village) under the name of Mishawaka.

1839: The first school building was built.

1840: First Christian Church (my first church) met temporarily until the church building was built in 1850.

1842: The University of Notre Dame was founded in South Bend.

1848: A covered bridge was built and painted bright red. People said it was spooky at night, so the city paid a man three dollars a month to light candles inside the bridge and keep them burning all night.

1851: The first passenger train traveled through Mishawaka with thirty-five passengers. (There are as many as one hundred trains passing through Mishawaka to this day.)

1852: The Studebaker brothers, Henry and Clement, started the Studebaker Wagon Works in nearby South Bend.

1859: The Great Mishawaka/South Bend railroad disaster took place at midnight after the collapse of the railway bridge into the river. Of the 150 passengers, sixty died immediately, fifty to sixty were wounded or unhurt, and the rest were found later, drowned in the river. The church bells rang in the middle of the night to alert the townspeople about the disaster. Many went out to help.

1872: The Great Mishawaka Fire destroyed 90 percent of the downtown business district. Forty-nine buildings in a three-block area were completely destroyed. Within one year everything was rebuilt.

1878: The Dodge brothers formed the Magic Jack Company, which later evolved into the Dodge Manufacturing Company, one of the largest makers of power transmissions in the world.

1878: The all-knit woolen boot created by Adolphus Eberhart and Martin Beiger led to the growth of the Mishawaka Woolen Company, which later became Ball-Band.

1880: The telephone came to Mishawaka, with four miles of telephone wire strung to South Bend.

1882: Moonlight river excursions became popular after the launching of a pleasure cruiser that held eight hundred to a thousand passengers and sailed on the St. Joseph River between Mishawaka and South Bend for a cost of twenty-five cents.

1890: The first electric streetcars or trolleys ran between Mishawaka and South Bend.

1899: The town of Mishawaka voted to incorporate into a city.

1899: The first horseless carriage, called the Winton, was brought to Mishawaka by the Eberharts.

1899: First National Bank of Mishawaka (where Sis and I later worked) was chartered in January 1899; Martin Beiger was its first president.

1902: Studebaker Corporation began producing and selling its first automobile.

1903: Martin and Susan Beiger started construction on their four-level limestone home, similar to the Vanderbilt cottage known as The Breakers in Newport, Rhode Island. Martin Beiger died during the first year of construction. He was Mishawaka's first self-made millionaire. His wife, Susan, lived in the home from 1908 until 1927, when she fell down the grand staircase, broke her hip, and died from complications. It was later put on the National Registry of Historic Places and is now a unique bed and breakfast and banquet facility known as the Beiger Mansion.

1908: The South Shore Railroad, an electric train, was completed between South Bend and Chicago.

1910: St. Joseph Hospital (where I was born) was built with forty beds; additions came in 1918 and 1948.

1915: Immanuel Baptist Church (my second church home) moved to its current location.

1917: Beiger School (my grade school) was built on the east side and named after the late Martin Beiger.

1928: Bonnie Doon's Ice Cream Parlor was founded as the first drive-in with carhop service in the city.

1931: Tribe-O-Rea, a family-owned pharmacy, was opened on the north side of Mishawaka by William and Kenneth Rea. Kenneth's son, Kenny Rea (Sis's second husband), took over and soon moved the store to the east side of Mishawaka. Kenny's son, Phil, became the owner after Kenny retired.

1932: Mishawaka's centennial was celebrated with a historical pageant of the early life of Princess Mishawaka, with a cast of two hundred. A student from MHS was crowned Princess Mishawka.

1952: The city's first wastewater treatment plant began operations, treating sewage before it returned to the river. Prior to this, the untreated sewage was dumped into the river; therefore no one could swim in the river because of the pollution.

1952: The first TV channel, WSBT-TV, began in South Bend.

1954: On October 1, Studebaker Corporation and the Packard Motor Car Company of Detroit merged.

1963: The Studebaker Corporation ended production of the Studebaker/Packard automobile.

1979: University Park Mall opened on Grape Road (which was once farmland when I was living there).

1982: The Studebaker National Museum opened in South Bend in the former Studebaker dealership.

1997: The Ball-Band (Uniroyal) closed, and buildings were later torn down.

2015: The South Bend Cubs, a Class A affiliate of the Chicago Cubs, played their first home game. For the previous seventeen years, they were the Silver Hawks, affiliated with the Arizona Diamondbacks.

FYI: Since I moved away from Mishawaka in December of 1959, many restaurants and fast-food establishments have opened on Grape Road. Traffic on this road is terrible now. Unless we're going to a place on Grape Road, we try to use another route.

I'm very proud to be from Mishawaka. There was very little crime in the city. The population of Mishawaka when I left in 1959 was 33,000, and South Bend was 150,000. In 2020 the population of Mishawaka is 50,339, and South Bend's population is 102,028.

CHAPTER 38

Odds and Ends

I recently purchased a book called *My Life, My Way*, in which was suggested some things to talk about when writing an autobiography. Some of the information that it suggested just didn't seem to fit in any particular spot in the book. I will talk about the "odds and ends" now.

Health Issues

I started having intermittent migraine headaches when I was in my thirties. By the time I turned forty, they became more frequent and gradually developed into a chronic daily headache. I went to various headache doctors for over thirty years, taking many different preventative and pain medication (depakote, propranolol, nortriptyline, Inderal, Topamax, Fiorinal, and fioricet). I finally quit taking any of the preventative medicine (with the doctor's permission), and the headaches disappeared. I was sixty-five years old at the time.

In my forties I was diagnosed with hypoglycemia, which is low blood sugar. I have to eat immediately when I get up in the morning, or I feel nauseated, weak, and shaky. I also need to eat a snack about every two hours. I generally eat a granola bar.

When I was forty-two years old, I had a food allergy test done. The results showed I was allergic to chocolate, wheat, and dairy products. That didn't leave me much to eat! At that time there weren't very many things I could substitute for the wheat and dairy. Shortly after the diagnosis, we moved to Denver. I was able to find nondairy ice cream, milk, and cheese. I substituted rice flour for wheat flour and carob for chocolate. Ten years later I had the allergy test repeated, and it showed I wasn't allergic to any food items. I started eating chocolate immediately and am now trying to make up for all the years I eliminated chocolate from my diet!

I started wearing glasses when I was twelve years old. I began wearing hard contacts when I turned twenty-one and wore them until I retired at age fifty-four. I purchased hearing aids in 2000, and they have basically been in my dresser drawer ever since!

I once mixed up our dog Peanuts's daily pill and my headache pill. Almost immediately, Peanuts collapsed and couldn't stay upright. I called the vet, and he said she would be okay in a few hours after the pill wore off. When I went to work that day, I told my fellow workers what I had done. I told them if I started barking, they would know why. One of them responded with, "Just don't pee on the carpet!"

I remember my first commercial plane ride, which was to Chicago, then on to South Bend, Indiana, in 1968 when I was thirty years old. I was scared to death. Kim and Ron were with me and had flown once before. Ron had always been very adventuresome. He knew exactly what to do, like asking the stewardess for a deck of cards, pilot's wings, free soda, and peanuts. What made me feel better was to picture the plane cradled in the hands of Jesus, holding us up. I still picture that in my mind to this day.

Favorites:

- My favorite clothing stores: Dillard's, Penney's, and BonWorth.
- My favorite grocery stores: Fry's, Safeway, and Bashas.
- My favorite hobbies: playing the piano at home for my own enjoyment, working on genealogy, and reading.
- My favorite restaurants: Carrabba's, Panda Express, and Texas Roadhouse.
- My favorite restaurants in the past: Monti's (now closed), Reatta Pass, and Steak 'n Shake (in Mishawaka).
- My favorite magazines: *Guideposts* and *Reader's Digest*.
- My favorite authors: Joel Rosenberg, Brock and Brodie Thoene, and Karen Kingston.
- My favorite books: Anything written by the above authors.
- My favorite TV programs in the past: *Father Knows Best*, *My Three Sons*, and *JAG*.
- My current favorite TV programs: *Wheel of Fortune*, *Jeopardy*, and *NCIS*.
- My favorite movie: *The Sound of Music*.
- My favorite hymns: "Day by Day," "Because He Lives," and "How Great Thou Art."
- My favorite Christian songs: "I Bowed on My Knees and Cried Holy," "The Lighthouse," and "Ancient Words."

- My favorite Christmas song: "Still, Still, Still."
- My favorite songs from the 1950s: "Unchained Melody," Melody of Love," and "Earth Angel."
- My favorite countries outside the United States to visit: Austria, Israel, and Greece.
- My favorite places within the United States to visit: Sedona; Mishawaka; the island of Kawaii; and San Diego and Costa Mesa, California.
- My favorite desserts: pistachio ice cream, mayonnaise cake, and pumpkin pie with whipped cream.
- My favorite drinks: cherry cola, sweet tea, and water with lemon.
- My favorite foods: steak, spaghetti, and Mexican food.
- My favorite candies: Snickers bars and turtles.
- My favorite nut: cashews.
- My favorite games: Skip-Bo and Mexican Train dominoes.
- My favorite childhood games: canasta and Clue.
- My favorite time of the year: fall.
- My favorite color: blue (also pink, lavender, purple, and turquoise).
- My favorite puzzles: Sudoku, celebrity cipher, hidden message word-finds, and Jumble.
- I collect: music boxes, dolls, and flags and Christmas ornaments from countries we've visited.

Not-So-Favorites:

- I do not like coffee. When I worked, I drank half a cup of coffee during my coffee break, loaded with creamer and sugar. Since I retired in 1992, I have not had any coffee.

- I don't like the smell of beer, much less the taste.
- I don't prefer brussels sprouts, broccoli, cauliflower, asparagus, stewed tomatoes, or eggplant.

Other Odds and Ends

I have visited six continents, thirty-five countries, eleven provinces in Canada, and forty-nine states. (I have not been to North Dakota.)

Description of myself: At age eighty-two, I don't have much gray hair (just a little on the sides) and have very few wrinkles (good family genes!). I'm a little overweight, which I said I would never let happen. I seldom lose my temper. I'm quite sensitive. If someone says something that hurts my feelings, I generally become very quiet.

In 1980 I left the following note for Vicki, a neighbor girl who was going to take care of our dog, Thor, while both Wes and I were going out of town. I had left earlier than Wes, so this is the note I wrote to Vicki: "Wes will leave Tuesday morning. Please come over Tuesday and Wednesday when you get home from school and let him out. Feed him Tuesday and Wednesday at 5:00 or 6:00 p.m. Let him out again before you go to bed and let him back inside. Come over Wednesday morning before you go to school and let him outside to go to the bathroom and then back in." Before Wes left, he read the note and started laughing! He called to tell me that I had left out the name "Thor." I ran across this note recently, as Wes had kept it all these years.

Approximately twenty years ago, Kim, Ron, Michelle, and Lindsey gave me a small tin box with a lid that said "Just a little something to say thanks for all you do." The box was filled with memories they had written on small pieces of paper. Here are some of their comments:

From Kim:

"I remember when you put some clothes in the oven to dry and scorched them."

"I remember going to the Stockyards office of the bank and thinking how neat it was to look in your desk for candy."

"I remember when you hung all the laundry on the clothesline."

"I remember how I loved to listen to you and Barbara talk about school and old times when we went back to Indiana."

"I remember calling you at work because Ron and I were fighting and you would say, 'I'm with a customer. I can't talk right now!'"

"I remember going with you to the Camel Square office on the weekend, and our dog, Peanuts, peed on the beautiful gold carpet."

"I remember seeing your face at the door of the hospital delivery room when I gave birth to Michelle and feeling that I didn't have to be brave about the situation anymore because you were there."

From Ron:

"I remember when I found a pack of cigarettes and you let me smoke one."

"When Kim and I had to wash dishes side by side. At the time we didn't like it, but it helped build strong bonds."

"I remember when we had 1-2-3 Jell-O."

"I remember Coke floats with the plastic bubble full of ice cream."

"I remember when you spilled the *huge* coffee maker in my truck!"

"Mom, you always made us feel like everything was all right and safe."

"I remember eating pizza or Mexican food every Friday for dinner because you worked late at the bank." (All four of us, in earlier times, could eat Mexican food at Pepino's Patio in Scottsdale for a total of five dollars.)

From Lindsey (who was a teenager at the time):

"Letting me crawl through the doggie door."

"Always coming to take care of me when I was very sick."

"Letting me decorate the top of the Christmas tree while standing on a stool."

"Giving me flowers after the drama club play *Grease*."

"Buying a lot of Girl Scout cookies so I could win the stuffed animal." (We must have ordered twenty boxes of cookies from Lindsey; the next year, Michelle was a Brownie and was selling cookies. She met us with her order sheet as we were getting out of our car, ready to take our cookie order.)

From Michelle:

"I remember always decorating the Christmas tree the day after Thanksgiving." (This is still a tradition.)

"I remember flowers at my dance recital and plays."

Sports:

I'm a pretty big sports fan. When Murry and I were dating, he took me to many Roadrunner hockey games, which I knew nothing about. I enjoyed hockey and learned most of the terminology and rules. The Roadrunners played at Veterans Memorial Coliseum, a.k.a. "the Madhouse on McDowell." During the 1973 and 1974 seasons, they won the championship trophy, the Patrick Cup. The last Roadrunners game was in April 1977. After Wes and I were married, we attended the Coyotes hockey games. Hockey is the only sport I knew more about than Wes did. We also took IN-JOY to several Coyotes games.

I also like baseball, which was Wes's favorite sport. The Arizona Diamondbacks are my favorite team. Football is enjoyable too. I root for the Arizona Cardinals and Arizona State University. Since Lindsey played in many basketball games in high school and college, I enjoyed watching basketball at that time. It doesn't interest me very much now.

Some of My Idiosyncrasies:

Whenever I go up or down steps, I count the steps.

When I slice bananas for cereal, I count the slices.

I put everything in alphabetical order: spices, files, recipes, music, Christmas card list, and computer information.

I have a file box with all of my passwords on three-by-five index cards, filed in alphabetical order by the website name.

I have another file box with index cards with instructions on how to do specific things on the computer.

I order many things from catalogs. Some things are good, and others are not worth keeping.

I enjoy cleaning and organizing drawers and closets when I have time.

I eat the same thing for breakfast every morning: a toasted English muffin with blackberry preserves and occasionally a bowl of Frosted Mini-Wheats with blueberries or sliced bananas.

I eat basically the same thing each day for lunch: half a ham sandwich with peanut butter, mayo, and lettuce.

I read magazines from the back to the front. I never knew why until Sis told me that she did the same thing because Mom did also.

I write lists for everything: to-do lists, grocery lists, future projects, jobs to do in the future, things to do for IN-JOY.

I have a typed medical sheet that shows medications, past surgeries, serious illnesses, immunizations, tests done, family medical history, doctors' names and phone numbers, active diseases and date of diagnosis, and pharmacy name and location. When I have a doctor appointment, I give this updated form to the nurse, and it gives them all the information they need.

I don't think I will ever run out of projects or things to do during my lifetime. I have thirty-five shoeboxes of pictures, one box for each year from 1988 to 2013, that need to have something done with them.

Summary

I have enjoyed writing this book. It has been fun looking up information, dates, and details in my daily diaries, photo albums, annual Christmas or New Year's letters, and discussing events with friends and relatives. I've also learned a lot about how to self-publish a book, as I knew absolutely nothing about it prior to this. I have received help either verbally or from referring to the books of several friends who have written and published books: Dee Cornelison, Tom Waldron, Kitty Chappel, Pat Wellman, and Sylvia Pierce-Little-Sweat, Wes's cousin. Sylvia is an English professor at Wingate University in Wingate, North Carolina, and she gave me some valuable and helpful information, since she's written several books.

Some of the chapters were difficult to write and brought back some sad memories. The chapters on my divorce from Bill and the effect it had on Kim and Ron were hard to relive. The fact that I fell in love with someone else while still married to Bill went against every fiber in my Christian belief and witness. I know God has forgiven me, but it is sometimes hard to forgive myself.

As I finish writing the book, the coronavirus pandemic is still causing much uncertainty. On June 28 the daily new

Arizona cases were an all-time high of 3,850. One of the lowest days was September 8, with eighty-one new cases and only two deaths. The daily figures are rising again, with 11,658 new cases and 197 deaths in Arizona as of January 8, 2021. Most of the schools had reopened, including the universities. However, because of the spike, some are closing again. Two vaccines have recently been approved and are starting to be given to the population in various stages. I hope and pray this will be the beginning of the end to the virus.

The year 2020 has been a tumultuous year in other ways also. The United States has had protests and riots; states in the Southeast have had a record number of hurricanes; California has had many fires; and Arizona has had record-breaking summer heat, in addition to wildfires. Colorado had two very large fires during the summer months.

The protests and riots started on May 25, 2020, when George Floyd, a forty-six-year-old Black man, died in police custody in Minneapolis, Minnesota. A video showed four police officers trying to arrest Floyd, who was handcuffed and pinned to the ground by one officer's knee. The main officer was fired and charged with second-degree murder. The other three officers were fired and later charged with aiding and abetting the first officer. The next few days, an estimated half a million people joined in protests in over 550 towns and cities throughout the country. The protests in many cities turned into riots, looting, and burning buildings and police cars. Many monuments and historical statues were torn down. It is considered the largest movement in the nation's history, with fifteen to twenty-six million protesters participating in over two thousand cities in all fifty states. Black Lives Matter was a predominant movement. The people wanted police reform and justice, and many wanted to defund the police. Arizona had five weeks of protests. Portland had over three months of continuous daily demonstrations.

As of mid-October, there have been over eight thousand wildfires in California in 2020. Many are contained, but some are still burning. Smoky skies are now blue again. The blazes scorched more than four million acres this year. California had been very dry and hot during the summer months. There were also several fires in Arizona. The Horse Fire in Crown King was finally contained, and evacuated residents returned to their homes.

For the first time in history, the names of major storms and hurricanes used up all of the letters in our alphabet and had to start with the Greek alphabet. Many homes and businesses have been destroyed. Another hurricane recently hit New Orleans.

Arizona has broken many heat records this year. The most days at or above 100 degrees within a calendar year was tied on October 13 and broken on October 15, a record set in 1989 at 143 days.

Barbara and I are now the matriarchs of the family. Sis used to be the matriarch before she died. I hope we can still keep in touch with our extended families. When Barbara and I are gone or no longer able to do it, I hope someone else will step up to the plate and continue to contact and keep track of our family members.

Our pastor's recent sermon emphasized that we as Christians need to focus on God's kingdom, which is eternal. We should not look to the kingdom of this world, which is temporary.

I pray that America has a revival, and we all look to God for our strength and salvation.

About the Author

Martha Ann (Endicott) Pierce was born in Mishawaka, Indiana, and graduated from Mishawaka High School in 1956 as salutatorian of her class of four hundred graduates. She moved to Arizona in 1959. She has two grown children, three grandchildren, and twin great-grandchildren. Her career was in banking, and she retired from Bank of America in 1992 as assistant vice president and branch manager. She was president of the Soroptimist Club of Mesa in 1978 and was chosen to be in the 1978–79 edition of *Who's Who in the West*. After retirement Martha and her husband, Wes, worked in Greece and Israel in hospitality for Educational Opportunities, a Christian travel company. In 1998 Martha and Wes founded the IN-JOY Senior Ministry at Arizona Community Church in Tempe, Arizona, where they held weekly meetings and lunches and planned and led trips and events. After eight years they retired as directors but continued planning and leading the trips and events. During the last twenty-two years, Wes and Martha have led IN-JOY on thirty-seven trips, including ten cruises, and 135 local events (plays, concerts, museums, mystery trips, and caroling at nursing homes). She is currently on the board of directors of AZBAR (Arizona Bank of America Retirees) and is now the assistant director of IN-JOY. Martha plays the piano and likes to read and work puzzles. IN-JOY keeps her busy, as she does the finances, keeps attendance, processes new members, and assists the director. Her husband, Wes, was in an assisted living facility near their home for two years, prior to passing into his heavenly home on January 1, 2021.